The Governors of Georgia, 1754–1995

Revised and expanded

The Governors of Georgia, 1754–1995

Revised and expanded

James F. Cook

MERCER UNIVERSITY PRESS

Macon, Georgia

ISBN 0-86554-480-8

The Governors of Georgia, 1754–1995
by James F. Cook

Copyright © 1995
Mercer University Press, Macon GA 31210-3960

Library of Congress Cataloging-in-Publication Data

Cook, James F.
    The Governors of Georgia, 1754–1995 / by James F. Cook
        x + 89 photographs + 342pp. 6x9"
    Includes bibliographic references and index.
    ISBN 086554-480-8
    1. Governors—Georgia—Biography.
    2. Georgia—Politics and government—1754–1995.
        I. Title.
        [Full CIP on file with the Library of Congress.]

Contents

Illustrations

The following photos were provided courtesy of the *Atlanta Journal-Constitution* (numbers correspond to *figure* number): 48, 50, 52, 54, 55, 56, 57, 58, 59, 62, 63, 64, 65, 66, 68, 69, 72, 73, 74, 77, 79, 80, 81, 82. The following by the author: 85, 87. The following by the Carl Edward Sanders Collection, Law Library, University of Georgia Libraries: 76. The following by the Georgia Department of Archives and History: 1, 4, 5, 6, 8, 9, 10, 11, 14, 15, 16, 17, 19, 21, 23, 24, 25, 26, 27, 29, 30, 31, 32, 33, 35, 36, 37, 38, 39, 40, 41, 43, 44, 45, 46, 49, 51, 53, 61, 71, 75, 78. The following by the Hargrett Rare Book and Manuscript Library, University of Georgia Libraries: 2, 3, 7, 12, 13, 18, 20, 22, 28, 34, 42, 47, 60, 70. The following by the Office of the Governor of Georgia: 83, 84, 86, 88. The following by the Richard B. Russell Memorial Library, University of Georgia Libraries: 67. The following by the State Highway Department: 89.

Introduction

In studying the governors of Georgia, one quickly encounters a paradox. Southerners, with their renowned interest in politics and respect for tradition, should, it seems, have a particularly high regard for their governors, but insofar as Georgia is concerned that is not the case. Indeed, for reasons that are not altogether clear, many of Georgia's chief executives have become forgotten figures. Aside from contemporary political leaders, such as Jimmy Carter, Herman Talmadge, Richard Russell, Lester Maddox, and Zell Miller, the most outstanding feature of Georgia governors, taken as a whole, may be their obscurity. Only the student specializing in Georgia history is likely to remember Herschel V. Johnson, John Milledge, Joseph E. Brown, or James Jackson, though all served prominently on the state level for many years and held national office too. And even scholars have difficulty remembering Richard Howley, Jared Irwin, Peter Early, Joseph Terrell, Clifford Walker, and several others who guided Georgia's government. In many instances Georgia's governors have been so neglected that it is now impossible to paint a satisfactory picture of their lives because the details needed for a complete biography have been lost to posterity.

Yet, the seventy-six men included in these pages deserve recognition, if for no other reason than serving as the chief executive of the state, the highest honor a state can bestow. Additionally, most of them exerted influence on the state level for many years as legislators or judges, and several filled important offices on the national level. Sixteen of Georgia's governors also served as United States senators, and Richard Russell became president pro tempore of the Senate; seventeen of the governors served in the United States House of Representatives, though none since Tom Hardwick in 1914. Several governors held cabinet positions. John Forsyth served as secretary of state (and minister to Spain), Hoke Smith was secretary of interior, George W. Crawford was secretary of war, and Howell Cobb served as secretary of treasury (and speaker of the house). During the Civil War, Alexander Stephens served as vice president of the Confederacy, and in 1976 Jimmy Carter was elected president of the United States.

The vast majority of Georgia's governors also achieved success in a variety of nonpolitical endeavors. Henry Ellis, an explorer and scientist, became a member of the Royal Society; John Clark and George Mathews gained fame as Indian fighters; many others, including James Jackson, Howell Cobb, Thomas Ruger, and John B. Gordon, rendered outstanding military service. Several governors made literary contributions; especially noteworthy are the writings of Joseph M. Brown, William J. Northen, Allen Candler, Clifford Walker, Alexander Stephens, Ellis Arnall, and Jimmy Carter. Three governors—Lyman Hall, Nathan Brownson, and L. G. Hardman—were physicians. The most popular profession, however, has been law, as nearly two-thirds of Georgia's governors either studied or practiced law. Practically all of the governors were men of means, many having extensive farming and business interests. Rarely did a governor fail to provide leadership, either on the state or local level, to religious, civic, cultural, charitable, or educational activities. Among the seventy-six men who have directed Georgia's government are several extraordinary leaders and a few miserable failures, but on the whole they have been ambitious and able individuals, successful in a variety of endeavors, who dedicated at least a portion of their careers to public service.

Thus far all of Georgia's governors have been white men, and, as far as can be determined, all but David Emanuel were Protestants (and there is some doubt about whether he actually was Jewish). Of the twenty who served as governor of Georgia in the eighteenth century, nine were born in Europe. In the nineteenth century many of Georgia's governors were natives of Virginia, the Carolinas, and New York, but in the twentieth century all but three were born in Georgia. With exceptions, such as Richard Russell who never married and Herman Talmadge who had two divorces, practically all of the governors have enjoyed happy and stable marriages. Before serving as governor, most had extensive political experience, usually several terms in the legislature. Despite the recent gains of the Republican party, all of Georgia's governors since Reconstruction have been Democrats.

For the most part, Georgia governors have been well educated. With the exception of Lester Maddox, all of the governors since Hoke Smith have earned college degrees. In the nineteenth century Princeton was the choice of five governors, while in the twentieth century the University of Georgia has predominated, educating fourteen of the twenty-three governors. At age thirty, George Walton probably was the youngest to serve as a governor of Georgia, but thirteen others in the eighteenth and nineteenth centuries were under forty when they became the state's chief executive. The youngest to launch a gubernatorial career in the twentieth century was Richard Russell at the age of thirty-three. He was followed closely by Herman Talmadge and Ellis Arnall, both thirty-five when elected, and Carl Sanders, thirty-seven. The oldest Georgia governors were Alexander Stephens and L. G. Hardman, both seventy when elected, and Hardman gained reelection at age seventy-two. The average age of Georgia governors at the time of their election has been forty-seven. In the modern era Georgia's governors have been long-lived, as only three of the governors who served after the Civil War have died before reaching the age of seventy.

Some confusion exists concerning the number of governors Georgia has had. State publications ordinarily include William Stephens, Henry Parker, and Patrick Graham as the first three governors, making the total seventy-nine. Many books also refer to James Oglethorpe as governor. I have not included these four men because none of them actually had the title "governor." Oglethorpe was a trustee, the only one who came to Georgia, while Stephens, Parker, and Graham had the title "President of the Colony of Georgia." Also, during the Revolutionary War, when normal elective procedures were disrupted and political power shifted with the fortunes of war, half a dozen individuals surfaced briefly with some claim to executive authority. None of them technically held the title "governor." Since their legitimacy was questioned, their terms short, and their authority practically *nil*, I have omitted them. For a complete listing of the state's chief executives, see *A History of Georgia* by Kenneth Coleman, Appendix A.

While focusing on the major achievements of each governor's administration, I have also included brief references to his family, personal traits, and subsequent political and/or professional career. I have also attempted to cover, albeit sketchily, the major themes and developments of Georgia's political history. My purpose is to present brief biographical sketches that may be read in a single setting or used as a convenient reference.

Since the publication of *Governors of Georgia* in 1979, much valuable research has been done on Georgia politics. Excellent new biographies have appeared on Henry Ellis, Rufus Bullock, Alexander Stephens, John B. Gordon, Richard Russell, Ellis Arnall, and Jimmy Carter, plus my own work on Carl Sanders. Herman Talmadge published his memoirs, and Jimmy Carter wrote several books, including *Turning Point*, which described his first political campaign. Revealing oral interviews of governors and other leaders were included in the Georgia Government

Documentation Project at Georgia State University. After reprinting all of *Governors of Georgia* from John Reynolds to Richard Russell, *Georgia Journal* published helpful new essays on the modern governors by noted scholars. My chapters "Ellis Arnall," "Carl Sanders," and "George Busbee" were published in slightly different forms in *Georgia Journal* volumes 12, 13, 14, respectively. (More detailed coverage of the governors from Arnall to Busbee was provided in *Georgia Governors in an Age of Change*, edited by Harold Henderson and Gary Roberts.) Especially helpful in compiling this book were the biographical sketches in *Dictionary of Georgia Biography* edited by Kenneth Coleman and Stephen Gurr.

In writing this book I have received assistance from many sources. The library staffs of Floyd College, the University of Georgia, and the Georgia Department of Archives and History were invariably helpful. Tom Weatherly of the Office of the Governor provided pertinent documents and photographs. I am especially grateful to my colleagues Fred Green and Bill Mugleston and to Raymond Cook of Valdosta for proofreading the entire manuscript and making many helpful suggestions. I am also indebted to Mercer University Press for undertaking this project and to my editors, Scott Nash and Jon Peede. A special word of thanks goes to my wife Ida for her patience and understanding. To all these individuals who made this book possible I express my sincerest gratitude.

March 1995
James Cook

John Reynolds
1754–1757

"He never came down from the quarter-deck"

On 29 October 1754, Captain John Reynolds arrived in Savannah to take over the reins of government as Georgia's first royal governor. Though ill-suited by training and temperament for the tasks ahead, he was welcomed with great rejoicing by the people of Savannah, for the change in government brought hope to a dispirited people.

The grand and idealistic vision of the altruistic trustees who founded Georgia had long since faded in the realities of the American frontier. The expectation that Georgia would become a thriving haven for the "deserving poor" of England, would shore up the defenses of the British colonies against the Spanish menace in Florida, and would be a rich producer of silk, wine, and other products needed to strengthen the British economy simply had not materialized. After a decade of frustrations, most of the trustees, including James Oglethorpe, had lost their enthusiasm for Georgia and had turned their attentions elsewhere. Authorized to govern Georgia for twenty-one years, the trustees yielded their charter two years before it expired.

The colony Reynolds encountered was in a deplorable condition. Only the continued support of Parliament had kept it going, for the numerous economic restrictions imposed by the good-intentioned but impractical trustees in England had retarded economic development and discouraged settlement. When Reynolds arrived, the population totalled little more than 3,000 men, women, and children. The inhabitants were scattered over a 300-mile region stretching from Augusta, an Indian trading outpost on the Savannah River 150 miles from the Atlantic, to Frederica, an abandoned fort established by Oglethorpe on St. Simons Island at the mouth of the Altamaha River. The only sizable settlement in the colony was Savannah, a desolate town of perhaps 150 wooden houses, which served as the colony's main port and capital.

A week after he arrived in the colony, Governor Reynolds was meeting with his Council in the old Council House when a member called attention to the "ruinous condition" of their meeting place and noted that it was "in great danger of falling." The gentleman had hardly finished speaking when the building collapsed with a roar. Its fall was symbolic of the prematurely decayed condition of King George's youngest and weakest mainland colony in America.

As the royal governor, Reynolds had extensive powers as his official title—Captain-General and Governor in Chief of His Majesty's Province of Georgia, and Vice-Admiral of the same—would indicate. He could convene or adjourn the Assembly, suggest legislation, veto bills, pardon prisoners, set up courts, command the militia, erect forts, declare martial law, commission privateers, try maritime cases, appoint numerous officials, grant land, have custody of the Great Seal, and see that God was worshipped properly according to the Book of Common Prayer. The governor was one of the constituent parts of the General Assembly. The others were the Council, consisting of twelve men appointed by the Crown and two ex-officio members, and the Commons House of Assembly, an elected body of nineteen members. Other officials appointed by the Crown included the attorney general, secretary, provost marshal, and naval officer.

Reynolds established the machinery of royal government in Georgia with little difficulty, but, in the opinion of most historians, he failed to use it effectively to solve the problems of the colony. The situation demanded wise, tactful, energetic leadership which Reynolds, unfortunately, was unable to supply. The most important acts passed during his tenure dealt with printing paper money, taxing owners of Negroes and large tracts of land, and establishing an elaborate slave code. But other critical needs were neglected. Since another war with France was imminent, improving Georgia's defenses was the most pressing issue Reynolds faced. Although he managed to reorganize the militia, his elaborate defense plans were so costly that the British government refused to pay for them. Moreover, his failure to secure either the friendship of the neighboring Creek Indians or a defensive alliance with South Carolina further jeopardized the colony's security.

A poor politician, he squandered numerous opportunities to provide constructive leadership and within two years was detested by the people who had welcomed him so enthusiastically. His blunt and condescending manners offended Patrick Graham, James Habersham, Noble Jones, and other prominent leaders, and soon he alienated both the Council and the Commons House. Instead of seeking to conciliate those with whom he differed, Reynolds came to rely almost exclusively on William Little, his private secretary and shipmate of twenty years. Reynolds appointed Little, a naval surgeon, to seven offices, including clerk of the general court, clerk of the Commons House, and commissioner of Indian affairs. Soon Little was accused of committing illegal and unethical acts. Reynolds ignored petitions calling for the removal of Little, but the Board of Trade could not ignore the mounting criticism of Reynolds's administration. In August of 1756 it recalled him, and in February 1757 he surrendered the government to his successor, Henry Ellis.

A decent, honest man, Reynolds's talents were better suited for a career in the navy than for the position of colonial governor. In his excellent short book of 1959, *The Royal Governors of Georgia, 1754–1775*, W. W. Abbot observed that as governor Reynolds "never came down from the quarter-deck." Aside from his brief tenure as governor, Reynolds spent his entire adult life in the British navy. Born in 1713, he entered the navy at age fifteen and became an officer six years later. In 1745 he commanded the *Scipio*, a fireship on the home station, and in subsequent years spent considerable time in American waters. After leaving Georgia he was allowed to resign his gubernatorial commission and to resume his rank in the navy. In 1759 he was captain of the *Firm* but did not participate in any major engagement during the Seven Years War. During the next fifteen years he commanded seven different ships; when on shore, he lived at Newington Butts with his wife and children. He became a rear admiral in 1775 and was promoted to vice admiral in 1778. Though incapacitated by a paralytic stroke, he was promoted to admiral shortly before his death on 3 February 1788.

Henry Ellis
1757–1760

He was an eccentric scientist

Henry Ellis—explorer, author, geographer, scientist, and dilettante—served for three years as Georgia's second royal governor. The antithesis of Reynolds, he was tactful and conciliatory, and under his capable leadership the colony established an effective constitutional government.

Ellis, the second son of Francis and Joan Maxwell Ellis, was born on 29 August 1721 in the town and county of Monaghan, Ireland. At about the age of twenty, to escape the poverty of his area and the control of his overbearing father, he went to sea. Eventually the stern father became reconciled to the sensitive son, and when the elder Ellis died in 1773 he left his entire estate to Henry, which made him a wealthy man. Having previously sailed in the tropics, the West Indies, and the polar regions, in 1746 Ellis joined an expedition seeking a northwest passage to Asia. Though failing in the attempt, Ellis wrote a book about the experience, *Voyage to Hudson's Bay, . . . for Discovering a North West Passage*, which was well received and resulted in his election as a fellow of the Royal Society. Through the influence of the Earl of Halifax, he was selected as the successor of Governor Reynolds.

Landing in Charleston in January of 1757, he spent several days socializing with Governor William Lyttelton of South Carolina and arranging for a regular correspondence, which continued until both men left America in 1760. Reaching Georgia's capital on 16 February, Ellis was warmly received by a large crowd of Savannahians. After paying formal respects to Governor Reynolds, he took the oaths of office and received custody of the Great Seal. Though doubtlessly enjoying the celebrations held on his behalf, Ellis recognized the difficult situation he had inherited. Shortly after arriving he observed: "I found the people here exceedingly dissatisfied with each other, and an almost universal discontent arising from the late proceedings, and persons in power. Few approached me that were not inflamed with resentment and liberal in invectives; urgent that I should take some immediate and very violent steps, such as a total change in public officers, and the dissolution of the Assembly."

Instead of taking drastic action, Ellis proceeded cautiously—listening, sympathizing, soothing—promising nothing and learning much. After analyzing the situation, he concluded that the most critical problem facing the colony was improving its defenses. Before that problem could be dealt with effectively, however, he realized he must unify the people and gain their goodwill. By exercising restraint, treating all impartially, showing deference to the Council, and demonstrating his concern for the public good, he gained the colonists' respect and affection.

With a deft sense of timing, he delayed convening the General Assembly until 16 June, when he was prepared to present his legislative program. To strengthen the colony's defenses, he suggested that the labor normally spent on improving the roads be diverted to building wooden stockades at strategic points. In August and September of 1757 the men of the colony worked twelve days putting a palisade around the town of Savannah and building a log fort north of Augusta and three south of Savannah. Realizing that Georgia's meager resources were inadequate for a proper defense, he continued to request that troops and equipment be sent from England and eventually was provided 500 muskets and 100 troops.

At the governor's suggestion, public finances were strengthened by doubling the general tax on land and slaves. Georgia's economic problems stemmed largely from its inadequate population; therefore, to attract new settlers, a law was passed promising protection for any debtor from his creditor if he could get across the Savannah River without being caught, unless the creditor was a South Carolinian. The passage of these laws indicated that the colony was attempting to solve its fundamental problems of inadequate defense, insufficient wealth, and too few settlers.

With a skillful pilot guiding the ship of state and a cooperative General Assembly working harmoniously with him, numerous other laws were passed. Perhaps the most significant was the law of 17 March 1758, establishing the Church of England in Georgia. The law divided the colony into eight parishes and empowered the wardens and vestrymen of each parish to assess taxes for the relief of the churches, the relief of the poor, and for other parochial services.

Always concerned about improving Georgia's defenses, Ellis fitted out a ship to patrol the coast at his own initiative. Exercising the utmost tact and diplomacy, he maintained amicable relations with the Spanish in Florida and improved relations with the Creeks. Using the carrot-and-stick approach, he went to great lengths to impress the Indians with the power of the English while at the same time he granted them presents, offered them hospitality, and treated them with respect. His efforts achieved results in November 1757 when twenty-one Creek headmen signed a treaty of friendship and alliance. Indian relations were further enhanced when Ellis settled the long-standing claims of Mary Musgrove Bosomworth. Mrs. Bosomworth, a remarkable Indian woman, had served as James Oglethorpe's interpreter in the 1730s and had created much discord ever since. The Creeks previously had granted the islands of Ossabaw, Sapelo, and St. Catherines to the English, but Mrs. Bosomworth's claims to the land clouded the issue. With the approval of the Board of Trade, Ellis granted her St. Catherines Island and promised her £2,000 for the renunciation of all other claims. By this transaction a disruptive issue finally was settled. Georgia obtained undisputed title to the three islands and gained in Mrs. Bosomworth a valuable ally for future negotiations with the Creeks.

Governor Ellis found the climate of Georgia most disagreeable. His natural curiosity and scientific interest in natural phenomena led him to test the temperature frequently. He did this by dangling a thermometer by a thread from his umbrella to the height of his nostrils as he walked the sandy streets of Savannah in midsummer. On the basis of his observations, he concluded that the inhabitants of Savannah breathed "a hotter air than any other people on the face of the earth." In 1759 he published "An Account of the Heats and Weather in Georgia" in the *London Magazine*. Claiming that the insufferable heat had ruined his health, he asked to be recalled in November 1759. Since Ellis had spent considerable time in the tropics, apparently without ill effect, one suspects that boredom or simply a desire to return to England and the Continent were stronger motives for leaving Georgia than the climate. His request was granted, and James Wright was commissioned lieutenant governor on 13 May 1760 and arrived in Georgia in October. On 2 November 1760, Ellis departed from Georgia amid expressions of deep regret, leaving the colony in much better condition than he had found it three years before.

When he reached England he learned that Lord Halifax had named him governor of Nova Scotia. In poor health, he remained in England while his deputy performed the duties of the office. Regarded as an expert on American affairs, Ellis became a key advisor to British ministers, especially the Earl of Egremont, secretary of state, southern department. As the Great War for the Empire drew to a close, the key decisions that were made by the great lords of state were based on the advice of a very few individuals, and Henry Ellis was "prominent among them," observed Edward J. Cashin, Ellis's recent biographer. According to Cashin, he exerted considerable influence in establishing the terms of the Treaty of Paris, the Proclamation of 1763, and numerous other policies.

Generously rewarded for his service, Ellis retired from active government service in 1763, having secured several offices in Canada that returned him a total stipend of £1,012 annually. In addition he was confirmed as provost marshal and marshal of the admiralty for Granada, St. Vincent, Dominica, and Tobago, which paid £1,650 annually. While the duties of these posts were performed by deputies, Ellis, a bachelor, spent his retirement in elegant self-indulgent idleness. Usually spending his summers in London rather than on his estate in Ireland, he moved to France when the temperature dropped and then proceeded southward to the Mediterranean for the coldest winter months, usually staying at Marseilles or Pisa. During the spring he often returned to his friends in London, a pattern he followed for many years. During the French Revolution he was marooned in Italy where he had been observing Napoleon's Italian campaigns. He died in Naples in 1806, more than four decades after leaving Georgia in "ruined health."

Fig.1. James Wright

James Wright
1760-1782

An aristocratic servant of the king

James Wright, the last royal governor of Georgia, served as governor longer than anyone in Georgia's history—twenty-two years in form, fifteen in fact. Lacking the charm of his predecessor, he tended to be more formal, aloof, and dignified, but he too was a competent administrator who showed genuine concern for the welfare of the colony. Holding the typical eighteenth-century conservative view that government was the prerogative of the "better sort of people" who understood the needs of the rest of society, he developed a close working relationship with the more prestigious and affluent members of the province. Though he had little direct contact with the masses, he commanded their respect if not their affection, and even his political opponents—and they were numerous in the 1770s—never questioned his integrity.

Wright was born in London on 8 May 1716, the son of Robert and Isabella Wright. When his father was appointed chief justice of South Carolina, the family moved to Charleston in 1731. Wright studied law at Gray's Inn in London and was admitted to the bar. Returning to South Carolina, he became attorney general, a position he held until 1757 when he was sent to London as South Carolina's colonial agent. He married Sarah Maidman in 1742, and they had eight children. While still in London he was named lieutenant governor of Georgia on 13 May 1760 and took the oaths of office on 31 October. In April 1761, upon the resignation of Governor Henry Ellis, he was appointed governor, a position he retained until it was abolished in 1782.

Wright took office at an opportune time. Under the royal governors the colony's economy had begun to improve, and, when a peace treaty was signed in Paris early in 1763 removing the Spanish from Florida and the French from Alabama, Georgia was able to expand to the south and the west. From his long experience in South Carolina, Wright was thoroughly familiar with local problems. For Georgia to prosper he knew that peace must be maintained with the Creeks and that the population must be increased to stimulate agricultural production. He made land grants easier to secure and did all that he could to attract settlers to Georgia. He particularly sought small farmers who would protect the frontier and attempted to discourage large speculators. Shortly after arriving in Georgia, he sold his South Carolina property and invested in Georgia lands, thus demonstrating by personal example his confidence in the colony's future. By 1775 Wright had become one of the largest and wealthiest planters in the province, owning eleven plantations, more than 25,000 acres, and 523 slaves.

To entice more settlers to Georgia, he made good farmland available. Securing additional land and maintaining peaceful relations with the Indians required careful diplomacy, which Wright provided. He worked closely with John Stuart, the Indian superintendent for the Southern colonies, who the Indians trusted. Both Stuart and Wright agreed that treaty obligations applied to whites as well as Indians. They tried to keep traders from cheating the Indians and insisted that whites not settle on land owned by Indians. Despite occasional clashes, on the whole, Indian relations on the Georgia frontier remained good during Wright's tenure, and the Indians made two large cessions, in 1763 and 1773.

Wright actually had little to do with the cession of 1763, which was part of a general peace ending the French and Indian War, although he did attend the conference at Augusta where it was arranged. At the meeting with Stuart and the Southern governors, the Indians were impressed by the fact that the Spanish no longer owned the Floridas nor the French Louisiana. Consequently, with the removal of the two European powers, the Creeks were more willing to accede to the desires of the British. The Creeks ceded all lands between the Ogeechee and Savannah Rivers from Ebenezer to the Little River above Augusta and a strip of coastal land about thirty miles wide between the Altamaha and St. Marys Rivers. This cession more than tripled the area in Georgia open to white settlement.

Since most of the land acquired in 1763 was granted to settlers within a few years and the Creeks were heavily in debt to traders, Wright desired additional land. While in England from 1771 to 1773, he personally arranged for a second large land cession in 1773. Under the terms of the treaty, Georgia obtained from the Creeks and Cherokees over 1.6 million acres between the Savannah and Ogeechee Rivers north and west of the 1763 cession, and about 500,000 acres between the Ogeechee and Altamaha Rivers west of a strip ceded in 1763. Instead of granting these lands free to settlers, as had been the custom, Wright secured approval to sell them in order to pay the Indian debts to the traders and to finance frontier defenses. The governor was gratified when settlers flocked in, bringing Georgia needed settlers and revenues.

Even though Wright was deeply committed to Georgia and labored tirelessly on behalf of the colony, his first loyalty remained with the Crown. At first this attitude did not pose a problem, and Wright enjoyed nearly universal esteem. But the new colonial policy, adopted after the French and Indian War, created friction between the governor and the people of Georgia. The Sugar Act of 1764 and the Stamp Act of 1765, both designed to raise revenue in the colonies, seemed to represent a new departure in British-American relations. Many colonists bitterly resented Parliament's attempts to tax them. Wright also questioned Parliament's judgment in passing the taxes, but he felt duty-bound to enforce them. When the stamp distributor, George Angus, arrived in December 1765, Wright protected him and thereby enabled him to implement the law briefly. By prearrangement with Wright, the local merchants had agreed to pay the tax on the cargoes of the sixty vessels in Savannah harbor awaiting clearance. These stamps, it turns out, were the only ones sold in any of the colonies which later rebelled. Having enforced the unpopular measure against the determined opposition of the Sons of Liberty and at considerable danger to himself, Wright was disappointed when Parliament repealed the Stamp Act early in 1766. Repealing a law because of mob pressure seemed foolhardy to him. He believed that such action would merely weaken British authority and encourage the colonists to use similar tactics in the future. Following the repeal of the law, tensions subsided for a while, but Wright never again received from the people the wholehearted support he had enjoyed before the passage of the Stamp Act.

In the late 1760s and early 1770s conditions in Georgia remained relatively quiet, but beneath the surface revolutionary ideas were fermenting. In his lengthy correspondence with London, Wright insisted that Georgians basically were loyal to the Crown and content with British rule. Unfortunately, outside influences, especially from South Carolina, continued to stir up opposition to British policies. There was some truth in Wright's argument, but no matter how hard he tried, he could not isolate Georgia from the other colonies. In Georgia, as in other colonies, opponents of British rule made headway in the lower house of the legislature, which was an elected body. In 1771 Governor Wright rejected the Commons House's choice of Noble W. Jones as speaker. The friction between the governor and the lower house continued when the Commons House next selected Archibald Bulloch, who was as anti-British as Jones. Irate over the choice of Jones, Wright then adjourned the Assembly, a tactic he often employed when trouble erupted, and departed for England and thereby left the problem with James Habersham, the acting governor. During Wright's stay in England, King George III made him a baronet on 6 December 1772, as a reward for his work in Georgia.

Conditions in Georgia remained relatively quiet for more than a year after Wright returned in February 1773, but news of the Boston Tea Party, followed by the passage of the Intolerable Acts, prompted Georgians to protest. Although slow to revolt against the mother country, by 1775 Georgia was drawing closer to the other protesting colonies. A provincial congress of patriots, which met in Savannah in January, soon emerged as the viable government in Georgia. Wright, who had repeatedly sought additional British troops, tried every means at his disposal to uphold the authority of the Crown, but his efforts failed. By the summer of 1775 he realized that most of his authority had evaporated. The first armed clashes in the colony took place the following January when British vessels attempted to secure provisions in Savannah. Patriots then arrested the governor and other royal officials. Wright broke his parole on 11 February, boarded the British ship *Scarborough*, and fled to England.

Following the capture of Savannah by British troops in December 1778, the British attempted to reestablish royal government in Georgia. Wright and other civilian leaders returned to Savannah in July 1779 and resumed their duties. For the remainder of the war Georgia was badly divided between the royal government headquartered in Savannah and the patriots who controlled much of the interior. Wright continued to send urgent requests for more troops, as he had done for years before the war, but his efforts were unavailing. On 14 June 1782, he received orders to abandon Georgia, and a week later he left.

In England he spent his last three years trying to obtain financial compensation for himself and other loyalists who had lost their fortunes. He submitted claims for more than £33,000 for property lost in Georgia but received a pension of only £500 a year, a sum he considered woefully inadequate for his long and faithful service to the Crown. A tired and embittered old man, he died on 20 November 1785 and was buried in the north cloister of Westminster Abbey.

Archibald Bulloch
1776–1777

He was president and commander-in-chief of Georgia

The departure of Governor Wright and the collapse of royal government necessitated the creation of a new government, and, on 15 April 1776, Georgia's provincial congress issued a temporary state constitution known as the Rules and Regulations of 1776. It established three branches of government—a unicameral legislature, which had the real authority; a Council of Safety, consisting of thirteen members appointed by the legislature; and an executive called the president and commander-in-chief, who was appointed by the legislature for a term of six months. The first president selected under this government was Archibald Bulloch, who thus has the distinction of being the first republican governor of Georgia.

An early and consistent leader of the revolutionary movement in Georgia, Bulloch was a native of Charleston, South Carolina. His father, Reverend James Bulloch, was a Scottish Presbyterian clergyman, and his mother, Jean Stobo, was the daughter of a Scottish Presbyterian clergyman. About 1758 the family moved to Georgia, where Bulloch became a lawyer and planter. On 9 October 1764, he married Mary de Veaux, daughter of Judge James de Veaux of Shaftesbury, Georgia, and they had four children: James, Archibald, Jane, and William.

Bulloch's political career began in 1768 when he was elected one of the four delegates from Savannah to the Commons House of Assembly. Possessing recognized leadership ability, he served continuously in that body until 1773. In his first term he was appointed to a committee to correspond with Benjamin Franklin, Georgia's agent in London. The next year he was named to a commission to choose vestrymen for the parishes. When Governor Wright disapproved the election of Noble W. Jones, Bulloch became speaker of the assembly in 1771. From the beginning, Bulloch was part of the small group of patriots or Whigs who challenged Governor Wright and the new imperial policy that attempted to tax colonials. He served on a committee appointed to sympathize with the people of Boston who were punished by the Intolerable Acts. When Jonathan Bryan was removed from the Council, Alexander Wylly from the clerkship, and Noble W. Jones from the speaker's chair, Bulloch, along with Jones, George Walton, and John Houstoun, boldly signed a

Fig.2. Archibald Bulloch

notice in the *Georgia Gazette* that urged Georgians to attend a meeting at the liberty pole at Tondee's Tavern in Savannah on 27 July 1774 to consider the "critical situation" in the colonies. Early the next year, a provincial congress representing five parishes named Bulloch, Jones, and Houstoun delegates to the Continental Congress which was to convene in Philadelphia in May. The delegates declined to serve, however, since only a minority of the colony had selected them. A second provincial congress, with representatives from all of the parishes, met on 4 July 1775 and made Bulloch its president by unanimous vote. Three days later the congress chose Bulloch as one of the five Georgia delegates to the Continental Congress.

Upon assuming the executive power as president and commander-in-chief, Bulloch's modesty and republicanism contrasted starkly with

Governor Wright's royal rule. When Colonel Lachlan McIntosh, the commander of the Continental battalion in Savannah, posted a sentinel at Bulloch's door as he customarily had done for Wright, he received a note from the new governor stating: "I beg you will immediately order the sentinel to be withdrawn from my door; the grenadiers are already removed, in consequence of my orders. I act for a free people, in whom I have an entire confidence and dependence, and would wish upon all occasions to avoid ostentation." Bulloch was not only modest, but capable, popular, and energetic as well. He made sensible recommendations for improving Georgia's defenses, fostering trade, developing domestic manufacturing, and regulating the courts. He supervised the confiscation of estates of wealthy Tories and the arrest of harmful persons. In addition to his civil duties, he also led a detachment of militia and Creek Indians that destroyed the British and Tory base on Tybee Island on 25 March 1776. Reflecting his religious heritage, he issued a proclamation against swearing on the streets of Savannah and set aside a day of prayer to restore the enemy to reason and justice and to relieve the country from the distresses of war.

Bulloch seemed to be the only leader around whom all the various Whig factions could unite. The Council of Safety held him in such esteem that on 22 February 1777, it authorized him "to take upon himself the whole executive powers of government." Before the end of that month, however, he died suddenly and mysteriously. His death at age forty-seven was a disastrous blow to the Whig cause, and his leadership was sorely missed in the troublesome years ahead. According to nineteenth-century historian William B. Stevens, Bulloch was "just the man for the critical time in which he lived, and for the responsible station which he held." Contemporary scholars concur in that judgment. Professors George Rogers and Frank Saunders state that Bulloch "skillfully grappled with the problems that confronted the infant commonwealth" and that he "appeared singularly qualified to harmonize and hold in check the factions and ambitious rivalries that later fractured the patriot cause."

Bulloch was buried in the Old Colonial Cemetery in Savannah. A county in the southeastern part of the state bears his name.

Fig.3. Button Gwinnett

Button Gwinnett
1777

He signed the Declaration of Independence

Button Gwinnett, one of three Georgians to sign the Declaration of Independence, was born in 1735 at Down Hatherley, Gloucestershire, England, the son of Samuel and Anne Emes Gwinnett. His father was a clergyman and his mother was from a well-to-do family. In 1757 Gwinnett married Ann Bourne of Wolverhampton, and they had three daughters: Amelia, Ann, and Elizabeth Ann. For several years he was engaged in the exporting business with his father-in-law.

Gwinnett arrived in Savannah in 1765 and attempted to support his family as a merchant. Failing in that endeavor, he borrowed money and purchased St. Catherines Island, a thirty-six square-mile tract which lies off the coast of Georgia near the port of Sunbury. Unsuccessful as a merchant, he was equally unsuccessful as a planter and was plagued with financial worries the remainder of his life. But he was a skilled political organizer, and through the friendship of Dr. Lyman Hall he soon became active in local politics. He served as a justice of the peace in 1767 and 1768 and became a member of the Commons House of Assembly in 1769.

Gwinnett was so deeply in debt that for the next five years politics had to give way to the struggle for financial solvency. Hounded by creditors, he borrowed from one to pay another. A low ebb was reached when his personal property was seized and sold, and St. Catherines Island was placed on the block. Despite his financial reverses, he emerged as one of the more popular patriot leaders. His fiery personality seemed to be well suited to his locale, for the Congregationalists of St. John's Parish were the most defiant patriots in Georgia. He attended the public meeting at Tondee's Tavern in July of 1774 which questioned Parliament's right to tax the colonies and objected to the unpopular Intolerable Acts. When Lyman Hall went to Philadelphia as a delegate to the Continental Congress in 1775, Gwinnett inherited control of the radical faction, which was determined to wrest control of the colony from the more conservative coalition of Christ Church Parish, Savannah. In order to gain power, he sought to ally the rural backcountry Whigs with St. John's Parish. The success of his efforts became apparent in 1776 when Georgia's provincial congress chose Gwinnett as the commander of the state's Continental battalion. Many in the Christ Church faction refused to accept this result, so, in an effort to keep peace, Gwinnett yielded the military position and accepted election to the Continental Congress. Arriving in Philadelphia in May, he served on several committees but apparently did not participate in any of the debates. On 4 July he voted for the Declaration of Independence, and on 2 August he joined his Georgia colleagues George Walton and Lyman Hall in signing that historic document.

Back in Savannah by August, Gwinnett hoped to be appointed general of the Georgia brigade but was passed over in favor of the more conservative Lachlan McIntosh. Blaming the Christ Church coalition and the army for Georgia's political, financial, and military failures, he launched a campaign to give his party control of the legislature. When the provincial congress met, Gwinnett's supporters held the majority and elected him speaker. He also chaired the committee that wrote the ultra-democratic Constitution of 1777 which favored his rural allies. Shortly after the provincial congress adjourned in mid-February 1777, Governor Bulloch died suddenly, and the Council selected Gwinnett to succeed him. When the first assembly under the new constitution met in Savannah in May 1777, Gwinnett expected to continue as governor, but the Assembly chose John Adam Treutlen instead.

During his brief tenure as governor, Gwinnett, who was as eager for military glory as he was for political fame, used his executive powers to interfere with General Lachlan McIntosh's planned attack upon the British at St. Augustine. Then, using his authority as commander-in-chief, he called out the militia and led an invasion of Florida without requesting aid from McIntosh or the Continental army. Cooperation between the two headstrong rivals was impossible, and the ill-planned, ill-executed invasion of Florida was a complete fiasco. The Assembly conducted an investigation to determine whether Gwinnett or McIntosh was more culpable. McIntosh was incensed not only by the criticism of his military leadership and Gwinnett's interference, but also by the arrest of his brother, George, on suspicion of treason. When the legislative inquiry sustained Gwinnett, McIntosh called the governor a "scoundrel and a lying rascal" to his face. To obtain satisfaction Gwinnett immediately challenged him to a duel. The long-standing feud climaxed when the two political and military rivals met at dawn outside Savannah on 16 May 1777. Shots were fired simultaneously, and both men were wounded. McIntosh recovered, but three days later Gwinnett died.

A man of striking contrasts, Gwinnett exemplified, as recent biographer Harvey H. Jackson observed, "some of the best and the worst traits of Georgia Revolutionary Whigs." Of his patriotism and devotion to the cause of American freedom there can be little doubt. But his ambition and intolerance of opposition contributed to the extreme partisanship between Whig factions in Georgia, which weakened the cause he sought to advance and ultimately led to his own death.

Since he died so soon after signing the Declaration of Independence, Gwinnett's signature is quite rare and therefore extremely valuable. His name on a letter brought $14,000 in 1927; in 1979 his signature brought $100,000—then a world record auction price for any autograph.

Gwinnett County is named for him and is adjacent to Hall and Walton counties, which are named for the other Georgians who signed the Declaration of Independence.

Fig.4. John Adam Treutlen

John Adam Treutlen
1777-1778

He was a courageous patriot

John Adam Treutlen, the first governor of Georgia elected under the Constitution of 1777, was born in southwest Germany about 1730. The Treutlens were among the thousands of Protestant Germans who fled from the Salzburg area to escape persecution from a Roman Catholic archbishop. John Adam Treutlen's father attempted to take his family to Pennsylvania in 1744 but failed when the Spanish captured his ship and carried the passengers to Spain. He died in captivity, but eventually his widow, Maria Clara Treutlen, and her two surviving sons, John Adam and Frederick, were transported to Georgia at the Trustees' expense. The penniless Treutlens were indentured to a prosperous Swiss inhabitant of Vernonburg.

In spite of poverty, the widow Treutlen sent John Adam to school at Ebenezer, where he received an excellent education from Reverend John Martin Bolzius. The Salzburgers at Ebenezer were Lutherans, and, according to Reverend Bolzius, John Adam "grasped the Christian dogma very thoroughly." Unlike most of the Salzburgers, he also mastered English, a skill which enabled him to become familiar with English law. Advancing from humble beginnings, Treutlen prospered as a merchant and gradually amassed enough money to buy land and slaves. He became a respected planter with thousands of acres of land, a leading citizen of Ebenezer, and one of the most influential political leaders in the state. According to George Fenwick Jones, Treutlen's careful biographer, he had two wives (the first named Margaret) and five children: Christiana Elizabeth, Jonathan (died in infancy), Dorothea, Hannah, and John Adam. The first Mrs. Treutlen died while he was governor, and he married a widow, Mrs. Annie Unselt, on 14 January 1778.

Although a prosperous planter, Treutlen championed the yeomen farmers and small planters, and, as the agitation for independence increased, he became a fervent patriot as well. One of only thirty-six men who served in both the royal and revolutionary legislatures of Georgia, he was a member of the provincial congress which met on 4 July 1775. He advanced to the Council of Safety the next year. His appointment, along with Button Gwinnett and five others, to the committee which wrote the Constitution of 1777 indicates that contemporaries recognized his political prominence. His selection as governor by a wide margin on 8 May 1777 confirms that conclusion.

Under the new constitution the governor's powers were strengthened somewhat, but he still remained little more than a puppet of the uni-cameral legislature. The governor's term was extended from six months to one year, but he could not veto legislation, address the Assembly in person, or act without the consent of the Executive Council. At this time Georgians deeply distrusted a strong executive, so they placed most of the power in the popularly elected legislature. The Assembly consisted of seventy-two members elected annually, but after the Executive Council was chosen the total dropped to sixty. In place of the old parishes the constitution established the following eight counties: Chatham, Glynn, Effingham, Richmond, Burke, Liberty, Camden, and Wilkes. The consti-tution declared the people sovereign and proclaimed the separation of powers in the first paragraph, only to violate that doctrine in the articles that followed. Governor Treutlen routinely referred matters to the As-sembly and consulted with the Executive Council, as the constitution stipulated. In normal times the system functioned reasonably well, but in times of emergency it broke down. Consequently, on two occasions when military forces threatened the state, the Executive Council requested Governor Treutlen to take the whole executive power until the danger passed. This procedure led to greater efficiency, but, as historian Kenneth Coleman has pointed out, it was unconstitutional.

The most pressing problem that Governor Treutlen faced in his brief term was conducting the war. In many ways the weakest of the thirteen states, Georgia had financed most of her defense measures without assis-tance from the Continental Congress, but the effort had severely strained the state's economy. As the state issued more bills of credit than its credit could sustain, its currency depreciated in value. The crisis occurred in the summer of 1777. By then the treasury was empty, and the state no longer could supply its troops. To keep Georgia's troops in the field, Congress responded to Governor Treutlen's appeal by appropriating $400,000 to redeem Georgia's bills of credit and $300,000 for future expenses.

Another problem Treutlen encountered was a determined effort by South Carolina to annex Georgia. Late in 1776 the South Carolina Assembly proposed the union of the two states and sent William Henry Drayton to Georgia to promote it. Arriving in Savannah in January 1777, he presented elaborate arguments explaining why the two states should join. Claiming that union would end the existing jealousy, improve trade, raise land prices, and make Savannah a great port, he gained some adherents in Georgia, but not Governor Gwinnett or Governor Treutlen. Even though a convention rejected Drayton's proposal, he continued to agitate. Finally, on 15 July, Governor Treutlen, with the backing of the Executive Council, issued a proclamation offering a reward of £100 to anyone who would apprehend Drayton or anyone working with him. From the safety of South Carolina, Drayton continued to agitate and criticize Treutlen, but the movement for union soon died.

Few accurate records remain to document Treutlen's life after he left office on 8 January 1778. With the military situation in Georgia deteriorating with the fall of Savannah and Ebenezer to the British at the end of 1778, Treutlen moved to a family plantation near Orangeburg in upcountry South Carolina. There he was brutally murdered in the spring of 1782. According to legend, Tories hacked him to pieces, but that story cannot be documented. Evidence is also lacking as to where he was buried. Thus neither the birthplace nor final resting place of the first man elected governor of the state of Georgia is known. A courageous patriot and capable leader, John Adam Treutlen remains one of Georgia's more obscure and neglected governors.

In 1917 a county in middle Georgia was named for him.

John Houstoun
1778–1779, 1784–1785

He was a bold patriot

John Houstoun, one of Georgia's foremost patriots, was born in Georgia circa 1750. Both his father, Sir Patrick Houstoun, Baronet, Registrar of Grants and Receiver of Quit Rents, and his mother, Priscilla Dunbar Houstoun, were natives of Scotland. In 1775 John married Hannah Bryan, daughter of Jonathan Bryan, a wealthy merchant and member of Governor Wright's Council. Apparently John and Hannah had no children.

Little is known of Houstoun's early career except that he read law under a prominent attorney in Charleston and began his practice in Savannah in 1771. Despite his father's standing in the royal government, Houstoun became a zealous advocate of the patriot cause and rose quickly to a position of leadership. Along with Noble W. Jones, who also was the son of a prestigious member of Wright's government, Archibald Bulloch, and George Walton, he published a notice in the *Georgia Gazette* calling for a public meeting at Tondee's Tavern on 27 July 1774, for the citizens to consider their rights as American subjects. Governor Wright objected to that meeting and to the next one scheduled for 10 August, but the patriots attended in spite of his decrees and passed a series of resolutions protesting the Intolerable Acts. At the second meeting Houstoun was appointed to a committee to provide relief for Boston, whose port had been closed by the Intolerable Acts in retaliation for the famous Tea Party. Early in 1775, Houstoun, Bulloch, and Jones were selected as delegates to the Continental Congress, but they declined to go because the provincial congress that appointed them represented less than half of the colony's parishes. On 4 July 1775, a provincial congress having greater representation named Houstoun a delegate to the Continental Congress. With fellow delegates Archibald Bulloch and Reverend John J. Zubly, he travelled to Philadelphia and participated in the session of September 1775. Returning to Georgia, he attended the Council of Safety meetings which decided that Governor Wright should be arrested. Although the provincial congress which met in January 1776 elected Houstoun as a delegate to the Continental Congress, he remained in Georgia to counteract the influence of Zubly who opposed independence. As a result, he missed the opportunity to sign the Declaration of Indepen-

Fig.5. John Houstoun

dence. When news of the signing reached Georgia, Houstoun participated in the public celebration of that event. On 8 May 1777 he became a member of the Executive Council, and on 10 January 1778 he was elected governor.

Early in his term Georgia's third annual military expedition against the British at St. Augustine was planned and by April about 2,000 troops had been assembled. Governor Houstoun, who had no military experience, took the field determined to lead Georgia troops to victory, having been granted full executive power by the Executive Council which realized that in battle quick decisions would be necessary. In addition to the Georgia militia under Houstoun, the expedition consisted of the Georgia and Carolina Continental troops commanded by General Robert Howe, South Carolina militia under Colonel Andrew Williamson, and naval units under Commodore Oliver Bowen. Howe, the Continental commander of the Southern department, claimed the right of command, but Houstoun refused to take orders from him, and Bowen refused to take orders from either Howe or Houstoun. Internal dissension and lack of a concerted plan of attack doomed the invasion to failure. Although the Whigs had twice as many troops as the British, the expedition went no farther than the Georgia-Florida border where, after accomplishing practically nothing, it was aborted.

Personality differences and lack of coordination soon contributed to more disastrous defeats. After General John Burgoyne's surrender at Saratoga, New York, in October 1777, the British focused their attention on the South. A large British expedition commanded by Lieutenant Colonel Archibald Campbell arrived at Tybee Island on 23 December 1778 and landed unopposed below Savannah a week later. Savannah was poorly defended because Governor Houstoun and Colonel George Walton, commander of the Georgia militia, did not coordinate their activities. Nor did they cooperate with the Continental commander, General Robert Howe, who attempted to defend the main road to the city. The British easily went around his forces and completely routed the disorganized American forces. Taking full advantage of American mistakes, the British captured Georgia's capital and most important town. Campbell reported that he captured 450 Americans and killed about 100 others and acknowledged British losses of seven killed and nineteen wounded. A week after the fall of Savannah, Houstoun's term ended.

In August 1779 Houstoun was again selected as a delegate to the Continental Congress, but he did not take his seat. Instead, he joined

General Lachlan McIntosh's staff in Charleston. In 1782 he was elected to the House of Assembly as a representative from Chatham County. After the evacuation of the British, Houstoun returned to his plantation, White Bluff, and later built a mansion on a spacious lot he owned in Savannah. In January 1784 he was elected governor for a second time. His second administration dealt with a boundary dispute with South Carolina, the perennial Indian problem, and granting land to Georgia soldiers who had fought in the Revolutionary War. In addition, the legislature set aside 40,000 acres of land for the support of a state college and named Houstoun one of the seven trustees of the institution which became the University of Georgia.

After concluding his second term as governor, Houstoun remained active in Georgia's public affairs. In 1786 Governor Edward Telfair appointed him chief justice, but he declined the offer. He subsequently served as a Christ Church vestryman, justice of the peace in Savannah, mayor of Savannah, and judge of the Superior Court of the Eastern Circuit. Resigning from the bench in 1793, he devoted himself to his law practice and family business until his death, which came on 20 July 1796.

A bold advocate of colonial rights, Houstoun served with distinction in numerous positions of trust and must be classed among the most competent of Georgia's leaders in the Revolutionary War era. The state has perpetuated his memory by naming a county in middle Georgia for him.

John Wereat
1779-1780

He was president of the Supreme Executive Council

When Savannah fell to the British at the end of Governor Houstoun's term, the Whig government fled to Augusta where it attempted to reorganize itself. Unfortunately for the patriots, the legislative assembly that was elected in December 1778 and scheduled to meet the following January to choose a governor was so scattered that a quorum could not be assembled. Thus, when Houstoun's term expired the state had no executive head. Before the end of the year, however, it would have three governors—each claiming to be the legitimate executive of Georgia. In January the British seized Augusta, forcing the remnants of the Whig government to flee again. After the British withdrew in mid-February, scattered patriots began to return. By July enough of the Assembly had returned to elect—out of desperation—a Supreme Executive Council of nine men to exercise the executive power. In effect, these nine men— Joseph Clay, Joseph Habersham, Humphrey Wells, William Few, John Dooly, Seth John Cuthbert, William Gibbons, Sr., Myrick Davies, and John Wereat—were temporary dictators of the state. The Supreme Executive Council was an illegal and unconstitutional body, but the alternative seemed to be no Whig government at all. On 6 August 1779, the members of the Supreme Executive Council unanimously elected John Wereat president.

Born in the western part of England circa 1730, Wereat had by 1758 entered a partnership with William Handley, a merchant who had lived in Savannah since 1754. Wereat's wife, the former Hannah Wilkinson, was related to Handley, and it was with his encouragement that the young couple immigrated to Georgia early in 1759. Like Button Gwinnett, another young English merchant, Wereat experienced financial problems for many years. To satisfy creditors he had to dispose of 3,000 acres during the 1760s, but he retained his "best lands." These lands, along with his slaves, served as collateral for securing additional loans that were used to improve his holdings. Despite his financial reverses as a merchant, Wereat established himself in the plantation society of the low country and by 1775 owned substantial property.

Fig.6. John Wereat

In the British-American conflicts of the early 1770s, Wereat sided with his adopted country in preference to his native land. He served in each provincial congress that assembled from 1775 to 1777, first as a representative from St. Andrew's Parish and after January 1776 as a member from Savannah. In February 1776 he was elevated to the Council of Safety but shortly afterwards was appointed Continental agent for Georgia. In that capacity he was responsible for provisioning American vessels that called in Georgia ports, disposing of captured enemy ships, and furnishing cargoes for the *Georgia Packet*, which sailed regularly between Savannah and Philadelphia.

Recent research by Edward Cashin, George Lamplugh, and Harvey Jackson has emphasized the factionalism and rivalries among Georgia Whigs. The Revolution, it seems, was a struggle not only to gain independence from Britain, but also to control the government of Georgia. The celebrated Button Gwinnett-Lachlan McIntosh feud was one aspect of the factional divisions among the Georgia Whigs. Gwinnett led the more radical or democratic elements from St. John's Parish and the inland areas, while McIntosh was backed by the more conservative groups whose power was centered in Savannah. Wereat, a close friend of McIntosh, became the leader of the conservative faction. He had little use for Gwinnett, John Treutlen, or the Constitution of 1777 that, he stated, was drawn up by a small clique "at a nightly meeting in a Tavern." Wereat complained that by increasing county representation and reducing property requirements for voting, the constitution had rendered helpless the "best part of the community" and thereby had produced a situation in which "neither Liberty, or property are secure."

With the establishment of the Supreme Executive Council, the reins of government shifted from the radical to the conservative Whig faction. To demonstrate their selfless patriotism, in contrast to the greed and opportunism of their radical opponents, they agreed to serve without pay. Wereat's government suffered from a critical shortage of funds, military reverses, and opposition from the radical faction. Being an extralegal government, it could not secure the $500,000 appropriated by Congress for Georgia even though Joseph Clay, the state's Continental paymaster, was a member of the Council. The Franco-American siege of Savannah raised patriot hopes only to see them dashed when Count d'Estaing's grand assault on 9 October resulted in a dismal failure. When his fleet sailed away, Savannah remained firmly controlled by the British. Returning to Augusta, a disappointed Wereat set 1 December 1779 as the date for the election of a new assembly. Before the election could be held, the radical faction, now led by George Wells, Richard Howley, and George Walton, assembled their supporters in Augusta, called themselves the "House of Assembly," and on 4 November elected George Walton governor. In the meantime James Wright had returned to Savannah as the royal governor; thus Georgia had three men claiming to be governor at the same time, a phenomenon that would be repeated in 1947.

Although elected to the Assembly in December 1779, Wereat was discouraged by the resurgence of the radicals. He felt that the conservatives were powerless "to check and discourage the wicked and designing whose principles and policy is to raise themselves to wealth and opulence on the ruins of honest and inoffensive individuals and of the whole state." He continued to defend the reputation of Lachlan McIntosh and, ironically, was united with his friend in a British jail late in 1780 as a result of American military defeats. McIntosh became a prisoner of war in May when Charleston fell to the British, and Wereat was captured a few weeks later when British troops occupied Augusta. Released in the summer of 1781, Wereat went to Philadelphia to settle his accounts as Georgia's Continental agent. Returning to Georgia, he served from 1782 to 1793 as auditor-general, a position that brought him more power and prestige than any he held during the war. He also had the distinction of presiding over the Georgia convention that unanimously ratified the Constitution of the United States. After retiring from politics, Wereat engaged in land speculation. Acting on behalf of three Pennsylvanians, he made a bid for a tract of the western territory. When his offer was rejected by the notorious "Yazoo legislature," he helped form the Georgia Union Company, but his associates were unable to raise enough hard money to convince the legislature to approve their bid. After the Yazoo controversy, Wereat retired to his Bryan County home, where he died on 25 January 1799.

A consistent conservative, Wereat held several significant positions in Georgia during a turbulent era. Although unsuited by temperament for the give-and-take of politics, in the words of biographer George Lamplugh, Wereat nevertheless "proved himself a capable, conscientious public servant."

GEORGE WALTON
1779-1780, 1789

He signed the Declaration of Independence

Best remembered as a signer of the Declaration of Independence, George Walton was one of Georgia's most esteemed and controversial political leaders. In a political career that spanned three decades, he served as representative to Congress, United States senator, circuit court judge, chief justice of Georgia, and governor of Georgia.

Born in Goochland, later Cumberland County, Virginia, in late 1749 or early 1750, Walton was the son of Robert and Mary Hughes Walton. His parents died when he was quite young, and he grew up in the household of an uncle. Apprenticed to a carpenter, he worked industriously at his trade during the day and studied borrowed books at night. Such diligence impressed the carpenter, who encouraged him to pursue his education. In 1769 he moved to Savannah where he studied law. Though small of stature, Walton was handsome, dignified, and earnest, and he quickly established a flourishing law practice.

As opposition to British policies mounted, Walton emerged as a patriot leader. He was unanimously elected secretary of the July 1775 provincial congress and six months later was chosen president of the Council of Safety. Elected a delegate to the Continental Congress, Walton arrived in Philadelphia just in time to sign the Declaration of Independence. At age twenty-six, he was the youngest of the signers. An active member of Congress, he served on the Executive Committee and was keenly interested in Continental affairs in Georgia and in Indian affairs.

Leaving Congress in October 1777, Walton was commissioned a colonel in the first regiment of Georgia militia and participated in the invasion of Florida in the spring of 1778 and in the defense of Savannah in December of that year. Wounded in the thigh, he was treated by British surgeons but walked with a limp thereafter. After his recovery, he was confined to the prisoner-of-war detention area at Sunbury until his exchange in October 1779. The British hoped to get a brigadier general in return for Walton, but they settled for a naval captain. Soon Walton was back in the midst of Georgia political factionalism.

At the request of Major General Benjamin Lincoln, Walton went to Augusta to establish a constitutional government for the state. With the

Fig.7. George Walton

assistance of George Wells and Richard Howley, Walton convened a new assembly which elected Walton governor in November 1779. The best-known action of the Walton government was a request to Congress that Brigadier General Lachlan McIntosh be relieved of his command in Georgia. Previously Walton had supported McIntosh and the conservatives, but now he was allied with the radicals. Largely as a result of Walton's efforts, Congress suspended McIntosh from command without a hearing. Later investigations revealed that McIntosh had been wronged.

In fact, the incriminating letter from the speaker of the Assembly which led to his dismissal had been forged, apparently by Walton.

Despite the criticisms stemming from the McIntosh affair, Walton served in the Continental Congress from early 1780 to September 1781 and then became the new chief justice of the state in 1783. In addition to his judicial duties, he maintained rice plantations on the coast which were unprofitable. Disposing of his land in Chatham County, he moved to Richmond County where he was instrumental in developing the town of Augusta. His farming efforts, however, were unsuccessful, and after his death the sheriff sold his property to clear his debts.

Although Walton's personal finances remained in a shambles, his political career flourished. One of six Georgians appointed to the Constitutional Convention in Philadelphia, he was too busy with judicial matters to attend; consequently, only two Georgians, William Few and Abraham Baldwin, signed that historic document. Walton, however, later served as a member of the Georgia convention which unanimously ratified the United States Constitution. In 1789, a decade after serving two months as governor, he was elected governor a second time. The most important development of this term was the adoption of a new state constitution. The briefest of Georgia's nine constitutions, the Constitution of 1789 was modeled closely after the United States Constitution. It provided for a bicameral legislature and a single executive. The governor was given increased powers and was elected by the Senate from three names submitted by the House. The governor's term was extended from one to two years, and he was given the power of veto and pardon. To qualify for the office, one must have lived in Georgia six years, be at least thirty years old, and own 500 acres of land or property worth £1,000.

After concluding his term as governor, Walton retired to his Augusta home. His retirement was short, however, for in 1790 he was elected judge of a superior court. He held that position until 1795 when Governor George Mathews appointed him United States senator to complete the unexpired term of James Jackson. In 1799 he was appointed judge of the Middle Circuit, a position he held until his death on 2 February 1804. Walton was survived by his wife, Dorothy Camber Walton, and one of their two sons. He was buried in Rosney Cemetery, but, on 4 July 1848, his remains were reinterred beneath a monument erected in Augusta to honor Georgia's signers of the Declaration of Independence. Walton County and Walton Way in Augusta are named for him.

Walton reached maturity at a time when Georgia society was in a state of flux. The removal of the old royal establishment created new opportunities for political, military, social, and economic advancement, and Walton, a bright and determined young attorney, thrived in the hectic and violent environment of the Revolutionary era. Although bitter disputes frequently marked his political career, the people of Georgia recognized his extraordinary abilities and consistently placed him in positions where his talents could be utilized. By overcoming the obstacles of poverty and orphanhood and rising to the state's highest political offices, Walton demonstrated that Revolutionary Georgia was indeed a land of opportunity for those individuals with drive and ability.

Richard Howley
1780

The governor who fled the state

Richard Howley, a farmer, lawyer, member of the Continental Congress, and governor of Georgia, was born in St. John's Parish, Georgia, about 1740. Little is known about his early years except that he practiced law at Sunbury and owned a small rice plantation which was worked by a few slaves. Hugh McCall, Georgia's first historian, observed that Howley's character was a mixture of "an uncommon portion of excentricity, with great talents." What the eccentricities were is not recorded. During the Revolutionary War he emerged as one of the leaders of the radical faction of Whigs. Together with George Walton and George Wells he organized the Assembly which met in Augusta in November 1779. It elected Walton governor and made Howley president of the Executive Council. This government, dominated by the radical or backcountry faction, was established in opposition to the conservatives' Supreme Executive Council headed by John Wereat. These rival governments were united when a new assembly was elected, and it selected Howley as governor on 4 January 1780.

Howley could not have taken office at a more inopportune time. The state's currency had become practically worthless; few troops remained in the field; Savannah and much of the coastal area had fallen to the British; political dissension continued unabated; and many of the state's citizens had fled to safer and more prosperous regions. On 1 February the Assembly, realizing that conditions might deteriorate further, resolved unanimously that "the Governor, or, in his absence, the President and Executive Council, may do and transact all and every business of government, in as full, ample, and authoritative manner, in any other State within the confederation, touching and respecting of this State, as though it has been done and transacted within the limits of the State." The next day Howley issued a stirring proclamation urging the people to stand firm against the British. At the same time, for reasons of safety, the Assembly moved the seat of government from Augusta to Heard's Fort in the backwoods of Wilkes County.

During Howley's brief term some constructive legislation was passed. In order to attract badly needed settlers from Virginia and the Carolinas,

Fig.8. Richard Howley

the Assembly liberalized the land-granting policies. By an act of 23 January 1780, 200 acres of land were offered to each head of a family migrating to Georgia, with fifty additional acres for each member of the family. In addition, 6,000 acres were promised to anyone who would erect an ironworks, 2,000 acres for a forge, and 2,000 acres for a furnace. This law, with its later modifications, facilitated the rapid expansion of the Georgia backcountry in the postwar period and contributed to the democratization of the state. Indeed, the new land policy was one of the most revolutionary features of the Revolution in Georgia. The Assembly also provided for the establishment of a new town of 100 lots in Wilkes County to be named for George Washington.

Shortly after Howley was inaugurated, the Assembly elected him as a delegate to the Continental Congress and decreed that in his absence the president and three members of the Executive Council had full powers of government. Howley continued to serve as governor for several months before leaving for Philadelphia. On 23 May the Executive Council requested him to retire to a place of safety in the Carolinas, for longer delay "might endanger the liberty of his person." Since the military situation had deteriorated with the fall of Charleston and the surrender of General Lincoln's army in May of 1780, Howley decided to follow his Council's advice. He fled to New Bern, North Carolina, taking the state's archives and a quantity of paper money with him. The archives subsequently were taken to Baltimore for the duration of the war; the money was spent as Howley proceeded northward. The state's currency had depreciated to such an extent that his expenses to Philadelphia reportedly cost the state $500,000. Finally, on the sixth of July, Howley took his seat in Congress. To forestall any attempts to negotiate a peace with Britain leaving Georgia in British hands, the Georgia delegation of Howley, George Walton, and William Few issued a small pamphlet which attempted to show that Georgia had been united in the cause, had sacrificed its blood and fortune in the war, was "a material part of the Union," and should not be given up. Howley also worked to secure additional financial assistance from France.

Upon his return to Georgia, Howley was elected to the House of Assembly. He was named pro-tem chief justice in October 1782, and the next year replaced Lyman Hall in the House of Assembly. During this period he increased his landholding in Chatham and Liberty Counties by purchasing confiscated property. He moved from Sunbury to Savannah, where he died in December 1784, survived by his widow and one of his two daughters.

Thomas Rodney of Delaware, who served with Howley in Congress, left this rather unflattering portrait of him:

> Governor Howley of Georgia is a man of great reading and knowledge which he generally displays without system or design, straying far from the object in question, so that he often leaves in doubt what side of the question he is on. He is loud but not very eloquent, therefore rather excels in Declamation than argument, and of course, is not closely attended to, but he entertains the House with strokes of wit or spouts of knowledge. He would shine in a more Democratic assembly.

Howley is best remembered as a staunch patriot who defended his state as governor and as delegate to Congress during a turbulent period when Georgia was overrun by the British and divided by rival factions.

Stephen Heard
1780–1781

He was a friend of George Washington

When the Assembly named Richard Howley as a delegate to the Continental Congress, it expected the executive power to devolve upon George Wells, president of the Executive Council and a leading radical. The fiery Wells, however, was killed in a duel by James Jackson on 16 February 1780. Two days later Stephen Heard of Wilkes County replaced Wells as president of the Executive Council. When Howley finally departed for Philadelphia, Heard became Georgia's chief executive, acting as governor from 24 May 1780 to 18 August 1781.

Heard was born in Hanover County, Virginia, in November 1740, the son of John and Bridgett Carroll Heard. The Heard family had lived in Virginia about twenty years, having migrated from Ireland around 1720. According to historian R. J. Massey, Heard's education was cut short when he joined George Washington's regiment in the French and Indian War. Promoted to the rank of captain, Heard and Washington became lifetime friends. In 1759 John Heard moved his family to Georgia, settling forty-five miles above Augusta on Fishing Creek. In 1760 Stephen Heard was granted 150 acres near the mouth of Little River. John Heard and his two sons, living on what was still Indian land until 1773, built Heard's Fort on Fishing Creek in 1773–1774.

During the Revolutionary War Stephen Heard supported the Whig cause and fought under Elijah Clarke at the Battle of Kettle Creek, where the Whigs stopped Colonel James Boyd's invasion. Heard, like many settlers in backcountry Georgia, suffered abuses from the enemy. While he was attending a military conference in Augusta, his wife Jane and their adopted daughter were driven from their home in the midst of winter and subsequently died from exposure. Before the siege of Augusta in September 1780, Heard, along with his father and brother, were captured by Tories and imprisoned in Augusta. During Heard's confinement a faithful slave, "Mammy Kate," visited him twice a week. She brought him food, washed his clothes, and, if traditional lore can be accepted, enabled him to escape. Supposedly the stout Mammy Kate concealed Heard in the large basket used to carry clothes and carried him unnoticed through the British lines.

Fig.9. Stephen Heard

As governor, Heard inherited an impossible situation. Nineteenth-century historian George White stated that Heard "did all in his power to inspire the desponding people with hope." But, regardless of his efforts, there was little hope at this time. British forces occupied or controlled much of the state, including Savannah and the coastal area. Only Wilkes County and a part of Richmond County remained under Whig authority, and those areas were raided periodically by Tories and Indians. From May 1780 until July 1781 the whereabouts and actions of the state government are conjectural. No assembly was elected and the governor apparently moved from place to place to avoid capture by the British. It seems certain that Heard fled into North Carolina as the backcountry of

Georgia and South Carolina was ravaged by war. In reality, state government existed in name only. As Kenneth Coleman, the chief historian of the Revolution in Georgia, observed: "Truly, state government was in default and it was every man for himself in Whig Georgia." Following the recapture of Augusta, a new assembly met there in August 1781. Heard served as a member of this legislature and the Executive Council until he resigned in August 1782.

After the war Heard settled down to the quiet life of a prosperous farmer. He built a beautiful home in a forest near Washington which he called Heardmont. A model of beauty and comfort with plastered walls and solid mahogany furniture imported from London, it was reputedly the finest home in Georgia north of Augusta. His landholdings were expanded with generous land grants from the state for his civil and military service during the Revolution. In 1784 he received grants that totaled 6,850 acres, mostly in what became Elbert County. At the time of his death he owned twenty-four slaves. In 1785 he married Elizabeth Darden of Virginia and they had nine children—Barnard Carroll, Patsy Burch, George Washington, John Adams, Bridgett Carroll, Jane Lanier, Permetia Darden, Thomas Jefferson, and Sarah Hammond. Three of their sons were named for the first three American presidents.

Heard remained active in politics, serving several terms in the Assembly as a representative from Wilkes County and Elbert County. (In 1790 his area of Wilkes County became part of the new Elbert County.) He served as foreman of the first grand jury to convene in Elbert County, helped select the site of Elberton, and for many years was a justice of the county court. Heard also served as a representative to the Georgia constitutional convention of 1795. A lover of books, he accumulated an excellent library and was a patron of the Moravian school for young women at Salem, North Carolina, and a trustee of the academy at Washington, Georgia.

Heard died at his home on 15 November 1815 and was buried in the family cemetery at Heardmont. Fifteen years after his death, a county in the western part of the state was named in his honor. On his monument at Heardmont is the inscription: "An honest man is the noblest work of God."

Nathan Brownson
1781-1782

He was a physician

Nathan Brownson, the first of three physicians to serve as governor of Georgia, was born in Woodbury, Connecticut, on 14 May 1742. The son of Timothy and Abigail Jenner Brownson, he was graduated from Yale College in 1761. He studied medicine and began his practice in his native town. In 1769 Dr. Brownson married Elizabeth Lewis, who died in 1775. The next year he married Elizabeth McLean, and they had two children, Nathan and Galen.

At the invitation of Dr. James Dunwoody of St. John's Parish, Brownson came to Georgia about 1774. He purchased a 500-acre plantation near Riceboro, where he grew rice using slave labor. Gaining a reputation for honesty, intelligence, and patriotism—as well as medical skill—Brownson soon became a leader in the Revolutionary cause. He was one of the eleven delegates who represented St. John's Parish at the second provincial congress which met in Savannah in July 1775. Twice elected to the Continental Congress, Brownson attended sessions in 1777. Fellow delegate John Adams of Massachusetts described him as a "worthy, Spirited, sensible Man." During the Revolution he served as a surgeon of a Georgia brigade in the Continental army. Congress appointed him deputy purveyor of hospitals in the South in March 1781.

After the Whigs recaptured Augusta from the British in June 1781, a new assembly was elected. Delegates from every county except Camden met in Augusta in August and attempted to restore state government. The Assembly, choosing a full slate of state officials, elected Brownson first speaker and then governor.

The restoration of state government, unfortunately, did not automatically solve the state's problems, and Brownson was able to accomplish little during the four and a half months of his administration. He was fortunate enough to escape capture by the British, unlike Myrick Davies, president of the Executive Council, who was murdered by a band of Tories. Both Brownson and the Council reportedly came armed to meetings to avoid such a fate. Georgia's financial condition remained desperate, for the war had exhausted the state's resources, troops, and credit. Concerned that many Georgians had fled the state, Brownson urged those in exile to

Fig.10. Nathan Brownson

return home, reclaim their citizenship, and defend the state. Refugees who failed to return within a period of months were subject to vastly increased real-estate taxes. The governor and Council devoted most of their efforts, however, to securing salt, food, and other necessities to relieve the distress of both soldiers and civilians. The government managed to obtain food and military supplies on credit by confiscating the property of Tories. No doubt Brownson was relieved when his term ended in January 1782 so that he could resume his position as deputy purveyor of hospitals under General Nathanael Greene.

After the Revolution, Brownson remained active in public affairs. He was appointed justice of the peace for Liberty, Glynn, and Camden Counties and in 1782 represented Glynn County in the House of Assembly. He served as a trustee for the proposed state college, was a member of the state convention that ratified the United States Constitution, and represented Effingham County in the convention that drafted Georgia's Constitution of 1789. Under that new constitution, Brownson served as the first president of the senate. He also served on the state commission that superintended the erection of public buildings at Louisville, the future capital of the state.

After five years of retirement from public affairs, Brownson died at his Liberty County plantation on 18 October 1796, at the age of fifty-four. Honored and respected by his contemporaries, he also has received praise from historians. Brownson's recent biographers, George Rogers and Frank Saunders, concluded that he was a man of integrity, talent, and leadership, who "served Georgia honorably during the Revolution and remained in the forefront during the formative years, 1783–95." Brownson's last words reveal something of his character and faith: "The scene is now closing; the business of life is nearly over. I have, like the rest of my fellow creatures, been guilty of foibles, but I trust to the mercy of God to pardon them, and to His justice to reward my good deeds."

John Martin
1782-1783

He was "Black Jack from the Northward"

John Martin, a transplanted New Englander and proven patriot, was elected governor by the Assembly which convened in Augusta on 1 January 1782. Although living conditions remained desperate, the people of Georgia were becoming more optimistic. They had good reason to be encouraged. By then the Whigs had gained control of a majority of the state, confining the British to the Savannah area. And, with General "Mad" Anthony Wayne's army moving into the state, the terrible war seemed to be nearing its end. Martin's inaugural address captured this expansive mood:

> I am extremely happy in finding that the virtuous struggles made by the good citizens of this State against our cruel and unnatural enemies have at length nearly secured to us those blessings for which we have so long contended and, I doubt not but by a continuance of those exertions and the support we have reason to expect, we shall in a short time reap the happy fruits of our labors.

Martin is another governor whose background is very obscure. A native of Rhode Island, he was born about 1730, but the exact date and place are unknown. Likewise, the name of his first wife and the date of their marriage are unknown. John Martin and his brother James arrived in Georgia in 1767 and purchased adjoining plantations; John purchased 1,000 acres and James 500 acres. Drawn into the conflicts over British policies, Martin became one of Georgia's most active patriot leaders. He served as a delegate from Savannah to the provincial congress in July 1775 and later that year as a member of the Council of Safety. Military duties soon took priority over civil responsibilities. In January 1776 he was appointed a first lieutenant of the Seventh Company of the Georgia Continental battalion; within months he made captain and in 1777 was promoted to lieutenant colonel. In 1781 he was appointed commissary in charge of military stores. He also served as sheriff of Chatham County from 1778 to 1779, justice of the peace in Chatham County in 1781, mayor of Savannah in 1778, and representative to the Georgia House of

Assembly from Chatham County prior to his election as governor on 2 January 1782.

Martin's first assembly, which lasted only twelve days, was concerned primarily with the state's deplorable financial condition. Although it failed to adopt a tax bill, it began an investigation of how public monies had been spent. Martin attempted to cooperate fully with General Wayne, but Georgia had been so ravaged by war that few troops could be raised. The governor had more success in luring away British soldiers than in raising new recruits. On 20 February he issued two proclamations from the temporary seat of government at Ebenezer. The first, written in German and addressed specifically to the Hessians, promised each man who would leave British service 200 acres of land with a cow and two swine. The other announcement promised full pardon and protection to loyalists who surrendered to General Anthony Wayne before 15 March. This policy, suggested by General Wayne, produced immediate results, as desertions increased.

Despite the improving military situation, food shortages continued to plague Georgia. The shortage of grain was so acute that on 12 March the Council urged Martin to send a special plea to South Carolina for relief. The governor secured a quantity of rice from South Carolina but had such difficulty getting it transported that he had to pay one-third of it to get the remainder transported to Augusta. Although Martin and other state officials were fed from public stores, the state's financial condition had deteriorated so badly that the governor was not paid his salary. Finally, when reduced to begging and borrowing and no longer able to purchase "the most trifling necessaries," he appealed to the Assembly for assistance. It responded by empowering him to take ten Negroes belonging to any person who had forfeited them. Despite the Assembly's inability to pay the governor, it nonetheless appropriated 5,000 guineas for the purchase of an estate for General Nathanael Greene and 4,000 guineas for an estate for General Wayne.

At Martin's call, the Assembly met again from 20 April to 4 May. With leadership provided by Joseph Clay and ex-governor Howley, it heard petitions concerning ownership of property, especially slaves, and passed a confiscation and banishment act against Tories. This act, together with the Confiscation and Banishment Act of 1778, identified 342 individuals by name. The general terms of punishment, of course, applied to many others, but the number of Tories actually driven out of the state is a matter of continuing debate. Kenneth Coleman, a very careful scho-

Fig.11. John Martin

lar, has estimated that "not more than 1,250 to 1,500 white loyalists left Georgia. This number plus approximately 3,500 slaves make a total of 4,500 to 5,000 persons who left Georgia because of their British loyalty."

On 11 July 1782, the last British troops left Savannah and General Wayne's army took possession of the city. Two days later the Assembly met in Savannah for the first time since 28 December 1778. Though a treaty of peace had not yet been signed, for all practical purposes the war in Georgia had ended. On 9 January 1783, Lyman Hall succeeded Martin as governor, and shortly afterwards Martin was appointed one of the commissioners to meet with the Creek and Cherokee Indians. Martin was elected treasurer on 31 January 1783 and held that position until he retired from public service on 17 March 1784.

On Christmas Day 1783, Martin married Mary Deborah Spencer. His second marriage was short-lived, for he died in January 1786. His will makes no mention of children.

Martin was a capable leader whose devotion to the patriot cause was unquestioned. He served ably in several government positions, achieved a good military record, and as governor during an extremely difficult period addressed the state's most pressing needs. Royal Governor James Wright referred to him as "Black Jack from the Northward."

Lyman Hall
1783-1784

He signed the Declaration of Independence

Lyman Hall, physician, minister, and one of Georgia's most capable statesmen, was born in Wallingford, Connecticut, on 12 April 1724. Both of his parents, John and Mary Street Hall, descended from families long prominent in New England affairs. Hall, who earned a bachelor's degree from Yale in 1747 and a master's degree in 1750, intended to become a minister. Indeed, he studied theology with the president of Yale and an uncle and was ordained into the Congregational ministry in 1749. But after pastoring a church in Bridgeport for a short time, he abandoned theology for medicine, a profession he followed until his death. On 20 May 1752, Hall married Abigail Burr, who died a year later. He then married Mary Osborne of Fairfield, Connecticut, and they had a son named John.

About 1757 Hall moved to Dorchester, South Carolina, a Congregationalist (Puritan) settlement near Charleston. Economic conditions in the 1750s drove many of the Congregationalists from Dorchester to Midway in St. John's Parish, Georgia; Hall joined that migration by purchasing a small plantation a few miles north of Midway, where his slaves raised rice while he tended the sick. He made his residence and practiced medicine in Sunbury, a town built by the New Englanders, which became Georgia's second busiest port. Although Hall had returned to South Carolina by 1762 and practiced medicine in the village of Pon Pon, he was back in Georgia by 1774.

In the early phase of the Revolution, Hall quickly emerged as a recognized leader of the most radical parish in Georgia. While others hesitated, the Puritans of St. John's Parish spoke out boldly for their rights as American subjects of King George III. Governor Wright correctly observed that the head of the rebellion was located in St. John's Parish where the "descendants of New England people of the Puritan Independent sect" reside. St. John's Parish became so frustrated by the lack of revolutionary fervor displayed elsewhere in Georgia that for a while it considered seceding from Georgia and becoming a part of South Carolina. When the First Continental Congress convened in Philadelphia, all of the thirteen colonies but Georgia were represented. Unwilling to wait for the rest of Georgia to act, St. John's Parish sent Lyman Hall to Philadelphia. Arriving there on 13 May 1775, he took his seat and participated in the debates but refrained from voting since he was not an officially designated representative of the entire colony. In 1776 a new provincial congress reelected Hall and also sent Hall's close friend and neighbor Button Gwinnett and George Walton to the Second Continental Congress. John Adams described the Georgia delegation to the Congress as "intelligent and spirited men, who make a powerful addition to our phalanx." Lacking oratorical skills, Hall took little part in congressional debate, but he supported the cause of revolution and signed the Declaration of Independence.

Although reelected to the Continental Congress through 1780, Hall made his last appearance there in 1777. He remained in Georgia as a staunch supporter of the radical or rural faction of Whigs. The British, invading the Georgia coast in 1778, soon gained possession of most of the state and in the process burned Hall's plantation house and his home in Sunbury. Forced to move his family to safety for the duration of the war, Hall fled first to Charleston and later farther north, perhaps to Connecticut. After the British evacuated in 1782, he returned to Georgia and made his home in Savannah, where he practiced medicine and attempted to recoup his shattered personal finances.

Elected governor on 9 January 1783, Hall faced the difficult tasks of restoring state government and rebuilding the state's devastated economy. Demonstrating rare executive ability, he made a number of farsighted and constructive suggestions. He advocated exiling troublesome Tories and confiscating their estates, while offering leniency to those who had fled to Florida during the war. He sought new land cessions from the Indians to reward soldiers and to lure more settlers to the state, but also tried to avoid war with the Indians by barring whites from their hunting grounds. Hall had only limited success in improving the state's finances and defenses, but near the end of his term news arrived of the signing of a peace treaty in Paris officially ending the war. In addition, "to cultivate principles of religion and virtue among our citizens," he called for the setting aside of land for the endowment of "seminaries of learning." The Assembly responded by providing land that subsidized academies in three counties. Abraham Baldwin, another Yale-educated New Englander, pursuing Hall's suggestion, secured a charter for the University of Georgia in 1785, making it the oldest chartered state university in the United States.

Fig.12. Lyman Hall

After concluding his term as governor, Hall continued to practice medicine in Savannah and served briefly in the Assembly and as a judge of the Inferior Court of Chatham County. In 1790 he moved to Burke County where he purchased a plantation for his retirement. He lived there only a few months before his death on 19 October 1790. He was buried on a bluff overlooking the Savannah River, but in 1848 his remains were placed under the monument in Augusta which honors Georgia's signers of the Declaration of Independence.

Though neither a soldier nor an orator, Hall, a tall and well-proportioned man, earned the respect and trust of the people by his intelligence, dignity, and force of character. His biographer James Harvey Young has maintained that Hall provides "one of the few examples of firm executive leadership during the state's early history." Few Georgians, it seems, have made more positive contributions to the state than this transplanted New Englander.

Samuel Elbert
1785–1786

He was a major general

In the years immediately following the Revolutionary War, Georgia elevated men from a wide variety of occupations to the governorship, including several lawyers, a physician, a merchant, an Indian fighter, a land speculator, and two military heroes. One of the latter was Samuel Elbert, who succeeded John Houstoun as governor on 6 January 1785.

The son of William and Sarah Elbert, Elbert was born in 1740, either in Savannah, Georgia, or in Prince William Parish, South Carolina. As a child Elbert lived in both Georgia and South Carolina, but after the death of his parents he settled in Savannah, where he soon prospered as a merchant and Indian trader. By the outbreak of the Revolution he had risen from obscurity to prominence as one of Savannah's leading citizens. In addition to his thriving import business, he also possessed several tracts of land and numerous slaves. His marriage in 1769 to Elizabeth Rae, daughter of an affluent merchant, enhanced his social and economic standing. Active in civic affairs, Elbert served on several grand juries, was a justice of the peace, and became a member of the colonial legislature. Although his father was a Baptist minister, Elbert became an Anglican and served actively in Christ's Church in Savannah.

When the Revolutionary War began, Elbert was recognized as one of the Whig leaders and was usually aligned with the conservative faction. A member of the first Council of Safety and the provincial congress that met on 4 July 1775, he served on the committee assigned the task of supplying Georgia with arms and ammunition. But it was in military affairs rather than in politics that Elbert would make his major contributions during the war. What education and military training he received is unknown, but he displayed an aptitude for the military and was a captain in the Georgia Grenadiers in 1774. When Georgia raised a battalion for the Continental army early in 1776, Lachlan McIntosh was appointed colonel and Elbert was named lieutenant colonel. He saw action in March of 1776 when the British attempted to secure food and supplies in Savannah in an engagement known as the "Battle of the Rice Boats." In September he was promoted to the rank of colonel in the Continental army.

In the spring of 1777, a bitter dispute between General McIntosh, the Continental commander, and Governor Button Gwinnett led to Elbert's being given the command of an ill-fated invasion of St. Augustine and East Florida. Elbert led his forces down the inland waterway to Amelia Island, intending to rendezvous with mounted militia commanded by John Baker. Unfortunately, Baker's troops had been defeated by British regulars by the time Elbert's boats finally arrived. With provisions running low and illness taking a toll in oppressive heat, Elbert abandoned the invasion. Most authorities agree that the invasion was so beset with problems from its inception that it had little chance of success. Returning to Savannah, Elbert assumed command of the Continental forces in Georgia following the departure of McIntosh, who had killed Gwinnett in a duel.

Elbert trained his forces and participated in sporadic skirmishes along the Georgia-Florida coast until General Robert Howe, Continental commander in the South, ordered an invasion of Florida. At Frederica, Elbert, with 300 men, captured the brigantine *Hinchinbrooke*, the sloop *Rebecca*, and a prize brig. That was the chief accomplishment of this invasion of Florida, which, like the previous invasion, floundered because of inadequate supplies, poor transportation, intense heat, disease, and internal dissension.

The British, continuing their advance into Georgia, attacked Savannah on 29 December 1778. Elbert, commanding the left brigade of Howe's army, was forced to retreat with heavy losses as British forces smashed through the American lines. Joining Brigadier General John Ashe in South Carolina, Elbert fought in the Battle of Brier Creek in March of 1779. Once again, superior British forces overwhelmed the Americans. Although the battle was a humiliating defeat for the Americans, Elbert's troops fought gallantly and earned the respect of their adversaries. Wounded and captured, Elbert remained a prisoner until June 1781, when he was exchanged for a British general. With his former command dispersed, Elbert fought under General George Washington and had the satisfaction of serving at Yorktown, where the British surrendered. In 1783 he was commissioned brigadier general in the Continental army; Georgia commissioned him major general of militia, the highest rank the state could bestow.

Returning to Georgia in 1782, Elbert was in poor health and his business affairs were in disarray. Nevertheless, he continued to serve the public. In 1783 he was elected surveyor of Chatham County and vestryman for Christ's Church. He also served on a commission that negotiated

Fig.13. Samuel Elbert

a treaty with the Cherokees at Augusta. Although he refused to serve as a delegate to Congress in 1784, he accepted the position of governor the following year, when the legislature selected him by nearly unanimous vote. Despite declining health, Elbert provided strong executive leadership. He dispatched militia to subdue a lawless band who had ravaged the area between the St. Marys and Satilla Rivers, and he gave much attention to improving Indian relations. During his term, treaties with the Creeks were signed at Galphinton and Shoulderbone, and Congressional agents negotiated a treaty with the Cherokees at Hopewell.

Perhaps Elbert's most important accomplishment as governor was the passage of an act chartering the state university. The act of 24 January 1785, established "The Senatus Academicus of the University of Georgia," which was to provide general supervision over all educational activities in the state, from the university down to the academies and lower schools. The Senatus Academicus consisted of two bodies: a Board of Visitors composed of the top state officials, and the Board of Trustees, initially composed of thirteen prominent Georgians, including former governors Brownson and Houstoun. Despite the establishment of this organization, sixteen years would elapse before the first students would attend classes at the University of Georgia.

Before yielding the governorship to Edward Telfair, Elbert had the pleasure of informing Count d'Estaing that the legislature had granted him 20,000 acres of land for his "meritorious services" to Georgia.

After leaving office, Elbert was elected to the General Assembly. He also served as vice president of the Society of Cincinnati and as grand master of the Masonic order in Georgia. Elected sheriff of Chatham County in December 1787, he served until the following September when poor health forced him to retire. Like so many governors of this era, his life ended before reaching the proverbial three score years and ten. He died on 1 November 1788, at age forty-eight. Survived by his wife and six children, he was buried at Rae Hall, his home near Savannah. In 1924 the remains of Elbert and his wife were reinterred in the Colonial Cemetery in Savannah. Elbert County, carved out of Wilkes County in 1790, and Elberton, its county seat, are named for this governor who was recognized in his lifetime as one of Georgia's most capable military leaders and esteemed for his integrity, courage, and patriotism.

Edward Telfair
1786-1787, 1789-1793

He was a wealthy merchant

Probably no Georgian in the Revolutionary era was entrusted with more important positions or discharged his duties with greater ability than did Edward Telfair. After proving his worth in numerous posts during the war, he was elected to the state's highest office three times for a total of five years—a feat unequalled until Joseph E. Brown's tenure during the Civil War period.

Born at "Town Head," Scotland, in 1735, Telfair attended grammar school at Kirkudbright and received thorough commercial training which later enabled him both to accumulate a large personal fortune and to administer effectively the financial affairs of Georgia. After residing briefly in Virginia and North Carolina, in 1766 he settled in Savannah, where he soon became a member of the small merchant community. With his brother William, who had preceded him to the colony, Telfair formed partnerships with numerous firms which became the principal commercial houses of colonial Georgia. His firms dealt with European products, East Indian goods, and slaves; he also invested in shipbuilding and amassed extensive landholdings. In 1774 he married Sally Gibbons, the daughter of a prominent attorney, and they had three sons and three daughters— Josiah, Thomas, Alexander, Mary, Sarah, and Margaret.

While little is known about the role Telfair played in the early protests against British policies, by 1774 he had become an active patriot, in contrast to his brother who remained loyal to the king. On the night of 11 May 1775, after the news of the Battles of Lexington and Concord reached Georgia, Telfair, along with Noble W. Jones, Joseph Habersham, and a few other Liberty Boys, broke into the king's magazine in Savannah and seized 600 pounds of gunpowder. According to tradition, part of this powder was shipped to Boston and used in the Battle of Bunker Hill. Prior to that episode, Telfair had participated in the public meeting that denounced the Intolerable Acts and had served in the provincial congress. In June of 1775 he was one of three future governors elected to the sixteen-member Council of Safety. In July he again served in the provincial congress and in December was reelected to the Council of Safety.

During the Revolution, Telfair held a variety of state and local offices, and from 1778 to 1782 he represented Georgia in the Continental Congress where his sound judgment and business training were sorely needed. In Congress Telfair spoke infrequently, but he served on several committees and was one of Georgia's signers of the Articles of Confederation. Later he supported the Federal Constitution, which replaced the Articles, and voted to ratify it in the state convention. After the war he refused to return to Congress, preferring to serve in the Georgia legislature as a representative of Burke County and in various local capacities. He also served on several committees and commissions involved with settling boundary disputes with South Carolina and with directing Indian affairs.

Having achieved an enviable reputation, Telfair was elected governor on 9 January 1786. When he took office the state had not yet recovered from the devastation of the war and its finances remained chaotic. In an effort to improve the state's credit and establish more uniformity, Telfair called in the different liabilities—auditor's certificates, Continental certificates, governor's warrants, and speaker's warrants—and issued new paper currency backed by adequate resources.

Another controversial issue he faced was the effort by influential Savannahians, including Joseph Clay, William Gibbons, and James Jackson, to retain the state's records in the old capital rather than to allow them to be moved to the new capital at Augusta. The Savannahians argued that the constitution authorized each county to be the custodian of its own records. But where did Chatham County records end and state records begin? Telfair and his Council took a dim view of these affairs "tending to anarchy" and summarily dismissed from office the chief justice (ex-governor Houstoun), as well as all the assistant justices and justices of the peace of Chatham County. Telfair secured the records, which were transported to Augusta in two covered wagons protected by four armed guards, but in the process he incurred the ill will of the people of Savannah.

Telfair was the first governor elected under the Constitution of 1789, which extended the term of office to two years. Reelected to a third term, he served from November 1789 until November 1793 and continued policies established in his first administration. He urged the legislature to tax the people sufficiently to support the government, reform the judiciary, revise the land act, and secure the frontier settlements. The frontier certainly was in jeopardy because the Treaty of New York, which guaranteed the Creeks permanent occupancy of the western part of Georgia, so shocked Georgians that war nearly erupted. In fact, Governor Telfair had assembled a council of war and had begun preparations for raising 5,000 infantrymen and cavalrymen to crush the Creeks when President George Washington, who objected strenuously to such an action, intervened. In deference to the first president, who was held in great esteem by the people of Georgia, especially after his triumphant visit to the state in 1791, the war was called off. Frontier conditions, however, remained unsettled for many years.

Typical of the Georgia governors in the post-Revolutionary period, Telfair granted land in a careless and fraudulent manner. In disregard of the law, he signed warrants to Daniel Beall for 246,000 acres of land in Franklin County, to James Montfort for 244,000 acres in Liberty County, and to Patrick Crookshanks for 237,000 acres in Washington County. The last was by no means the largest grant in Washington County, for Thomas Davis received 318,000 acres and Richmond Dawson received 495,000 acres. In making such grants it apparently never occurred to Telfair that he was granting more land than the state possessed. Strangely enough, the land speculation mania had so gripped the people that few objected to this policy which, extravagant as it was under Telfair, reached even more fantastic proportions under his successor, George Mathews.

After leaving the governor's office, Telfair spent his remaining years in Savannah, managing his private businesses and devoting much time to civic and charitable endeavors. He died on 17 September 1807 and was buried in the old Colonial Cemetery, but his remains later were removed to Bonaventure Cemetery in Savannah.

One of the wealthiest men in the state, Telfair left a fortune which has benefited numerous public institutions in Savannah, including the Telfair Academy of Arts and Sciences, the Telfair Hospital, the Mary Telfair Home, the Georgia Historical Society, and the Independent Presbyterian Church.

A county in south Georgia, which later became famous as the home of Governor Eugene Talmadge, was created in 1807 and named for Edward Telfair, one of Georgia's most renowned citizens.

George Mathews
1787–1788, 1793–1796

He was a fiery frontiersman

In the unsettled conditions of the post-Revolutionary period, dynamic new leaders were called upon to govern Georgia. One of the most remarkable characters ever to hold the office of governor was George Mathews. A short, stout man with florid complexion and light red hair, he wore knee britches, a three-cornered hat, high boots, a full ruffled shirt, and sometimes a long sword at his side. Acknowledging only two superiors, George Washington and the Lord Almighty, he looked as if he knew no fear. Although Mathews had a shrewd mind and an excellent memory, he lacked formal education. He spelled coffee *kaughy*, knock *noc*, laugh *laf*, and revenge *ravange*. Fortunately, after writing his speeches, he had them "grammared up" by a schoolmaster.

Governor George Gilmer recorded the story of Mathews being nominated as governor of the Mississippi Territory in 1798, only to have his nomination withdrawn by President John Adams. Mathews went straight to Philadelphia, barged into the President's home, and informed him as follows: "Sir, if you had known me, you would not have taken the nomination back. If you did not know me, you should not have nominated me to so important an office. Now, Sir, unless you can satisfy me, your station of President of these United States shall not screen you from my vengeance." Adams placated the fiery frontiersman by promising to appoint his son, John, supervisor of public revenue in Georgia.

Of Irish ancestry, Mathews was born in Augusta County, Virginia, on 30 August 1739, the son of John and Betsy Ann Archer Mathews. Very little is known of his early years, but he married Anne "Polly" Paul in 1762, and they had eight children. After her death he married Margaret Cunningham Reed, a widow from Staunton, Virginia. In 1793, after three years of marriage, she asked to visit her friends and relatives in Virginia. Mathews objected, but she went anyway, alone. After completing her visit, she wrote for Mathews to come after her, as she did not want to make the return trip alone. He answered that he did not take her to Virginia and was not going to bring her back. The separation continued, and in 1797 the legislature granted them a divorce. Mathews married a third time in 1804, to Mary Flowers Carpenter of Mississippi.

By 1762, Mathews, with the assistance of one of his brothers, had established himself as a prosperous merchant in Staunton, Virginia, having previously gained local fame as an Indian fighter. He served as a local vestryman, warden, justice of the peace, and tax collector, and in 1776 was elected to the House of Burgesses. At the outbreak of the Revolutionary War, he joined Washington's forces as a lieutenant colonel and was promoted to colonel the next year. He saw action at Brandywine and was wounded and captured at Germantown in October 1777. Exchanged in December 1781, he fought under General Nathanael Greene in the South until the end of the war. As a reward for his military service, the Georgia legislature granted him thousands of acres of land in Wilkes County. In 1784 or 1785, Mathews settled on a tract along the Broad River in what is now Oglethorpe County and induced many of his Virginia neighbors to migrate with him. Less than three years after making Georgia his home, he was elevated to the governorship by the General Assembly on 5 January 1787. During his first term of slightly more than one year, Mathews strengthened the militia for use against the Indians, resolved a long-standing boundary dispute with South Carolina, and conducted negotiations with the Spanish over the problem of runaway slaves and border raids into Florida but failed to reach an agreement.

A staunch supporter of efforts to strengthen the Union, Mathews, as a delegate to the state convention from Wilkes County, voted to ratify the United States Constitution. He was an Indian commissioner in 1788 and 1789 and served in the convention that produced the Constitution of 1789. Following the ratification of the Constitution, Mathews was elected to the first session of the House of Representatives. Although he had received more votes than Georgia's other congressmen, James Jackson and Abraham Baldwin, he was out of place among the more sophisticated and educated representatives. The Georgia voters must have realized Mathews's inadequacies, for he was overwhelmingly defeated in the next election. More comfortable in the Georgia environment, he served several terms in the legislature as a representative from Wilkes County and on 5 November 1793 was selected for a second term as governor.

When Mathews took office, war with the Creeks and Spain seemed imminent. Citizen Genet, minister plenipotentiary of France to the United States, had engaged American citizens in a projected invasion of Spanish Florida, but mounting pressure brought about his recall early in 1794 and ended this threat. The Indian problems, however, were more serious. A major war nearly had erupted in Governor Telfair's administration, and tensions remained high. Improving Georgia's weak defenses became Mathews's top priority. After long and diligent efforts, he was able to secure federal assistance in the form of troops, supplies, and fortifications along the frontier. Elijah Clarke, however, complicated matters when he led an army into Indian territory and established a settlement across the Oconee River. When Mathews learned of this "Trans-Oconee Republic," he ordered General Jared Irwin to remove the settlement. Soon Mathews was notified that Clarke had abandoned the area and that the settlement had been destroyed. Mathews then had the pleasure of informing the secretary of war that "the posts are all burnt and destroyed and the whole business happily terminated without the loss of blood."

At this time Georgia's most valuable possession was land, and the state's political leaders seemed determined to dispose of it as quickly as possible. Like his predecessors and successors, Mathews made liberal grants of land to encourage settlement of Georgia's undeveloped frontier regions. But he was more generous than the others, and ultimately his excesses destroyed his popularity. Speculators and corrupt politicians—not the yeomen farmers—were the chief beneficiaries of this largesse. Four men were given 2,642,000 acres in Franklin County in 1793–1794. Between 3 November 1794 and 3 January 1795, Mathews granted nearly 3 million acres to thirty-five persons who paid only the processing fees. By 1796 Georgia's twenty-four counties contained less than 9 million acres, yet more than 29 million acres had been granted to speculators. This land speculation culminated in 1795 when the legislature, in the notorious Yazoo Act, granted Georgia's lands west of the Chattahoochee River, more than 30 million acres, to four companies for $500,000. Although there is no evidence to implicate Mathews in any of the fraud or corruption associated with that act, he signed the bill and tarnished his reputation thereafter.

Mathews had become wealthy from land speculation and wise investments, but in retirement he continued to live in the simple log cabin he had built in Wilkes County many years before. In 1797 he moved to the Mississippi Territory. Despite advancing age, he served on a diplomatic mission for the federal government in Florida from 1810 to 1812. When a change in policy led to his abrupt dismissal, the old soldier became so enraged that he decided to thrash President Madison. He was en route to Washington for that purpose when he fell ill and died on 30 August 1812, his seventy-third birthday. He was buried in St. Paul's churchyard in Augusta, Georgia.

George Handley
1788–1789

He signed Georgia's only patent

George Handley, described by William Stevens as "a soldier of prowess and a civil officer of merit," is one of Georgia's most obscure governors. Yet, during his brief career he impressed his contemporaries and made notable contributions to his state. Handley is not well remembered because he served only one year as governor, whereas Walton, Telfair, and Mathews, who preceded and followed him, served longer terms and overshadowed him. Also, in contrast to the other governors of this era, he lived a short life of only forty-one years.

Little is known about Handley's life prior to his arrival in Savannah in May 1775, except that he was born near Sheffield, Yorkshire, England, on 9 February 1752. He immediately took the side of the Liberty Boys in the tense struggles then raging with the mother country. Within a year of his arrival, Handley joined the Continental army as a lieutenant. Promoted to captain in October 1776, he displayed conspicuous bravery in the major engagements in Georgia and South Carolina. Captured in July 1780, he remained a British prisoner until his exchange, probably in 1782. He retired from military service as a lieutenant colonel and after the war became a member of the Society of the Cincinnati.

Handley made Augusta his home in 1783 and soon became active in politics. A popular young man with a commendable military record, his marriage to Sarah Howe, a niece of Governor Samuel Elbert, doubtlessly enhanced his political career. He was a justice of the peace in Richmond County from 1783 to 1787 and a secretary of the Executive Council in 1785 and 1786. The legislature appointed Handley inspector-general of the militia and one of Georgia's commissioners to the state of Franklin (now part of eastern Tennessee) in 1787. In January 1788, as a delegate from Glynn County, he voted to ratify the United States Constitution. Of the twenty-six delegates at the ratifying convention in Augusta, six served the state as governor—Wereat, Brownson, Telfair, Mathews, Irwin, and Handley. On 24 January 1788, the House of Assembly named Handley governor when James Jackson declined the offer. He served until 6 January 1789.

Early in Handley's term the legislature granted and he signed the only patent ever issued by the state of Georgia. It went to William Longstreet and Isaac Briggs for "a newly constructed steam engine, invented by them." Shortly afterwards the federal government assumed the responsibility for issuing patents. Longstreet failed to secure state aid and spent many years seeking financial backing to build a steamboat. Finally succeeding, his steamboat moved about five miles upstream in the Savannah River in 1807. Unfortunately, a few days earlier, Robert Fulton had launched the *Clermont* in the Hudson River. The Georgia vessel, not a commercial success, went largely unnoticed; when it blew up, Longstreet gave up his steamboat dream and concentrated on other inventions.

The most important achievement of Handley's term was the drafting of a new state constitution. On 21 January 1788, the Assembly appointed "three fit and discreet persons for each County" to consider "the alterations and amendments that are necessary to be made in the Constitution of this State." After the United States Constitution was ratified, Governor Handley called the proposed state constitutional convention, which convened in Augusta in November. Handley, a delegate from Glynn County, served as president of the convention—quite an honor since the convention also included William Few, George Walton, Edward Telfair, and other Georgia luminaries. After meeting sixteen days, the convention brought forward a new constitution modeled closely after the United States Constitution. A second convention convened on 4 January 1789, for the purpose of ratifying or rejecting the work of the previous convention. It did neither; instead it made a few changes in the proposed document. Only five of the thirty-one members of the second convention had served in the first one. Handley was one of the five. He did not, however, serve in the third convention which ratified the constitution on 6 May 1789, by vote of twenty to three.

President Washington appointed Handley collector of ports at Brunswick, a position he held until his death on 17 September 1793. Since he also was sheriff of Richmond County from 1790 until his death, he evidently had homes in both Augusta and Glynn County. He died at Rae's Hall, Georgia, at age forty-one.

Fig.14. Jared Irwin

Jared Irwin
1796-1798, 1806-1809

He helped to write three state constitutions

Jared Irwin, who served Georgia faithfully as soldier, legislator, and governor, was born in Mecklenburg County, North Carolina, in 1750. When he was seven, his parents, Thomas and Rebecca Lawson Irwin, moved the family to St. George's Parish (later Burke County), Georgia. Although documented evidence about Irwin's youth is meager, records show that he became an ardent patriot and fought in the Revolution. With his father and three brothers, he participated in engagements in Georgia and the Carolinas and attained the rank of colonel. As a reward for their military service, Irwin and his brothers received extensive land grants in Washington County in 1784. After the war, Irwin was called on frequently to defend settlements on the Indian frontier, serving in the Georgia militia as a brigadier general. Having achieved an enviable military reputation, Irwin turned to politics and gained even greater distinction in that field. In addition to holding many local offices, first in Burke County and after 1787 in Washington County, he served several terms in the state legislature, negotiated treaties with the Indians, served in the convention that ratified the United States Constitution, was a member of the state constitutional conventions of 1789, 1795, and 1798, and was twice elected governor.

He first became governor during a time of great turmoil. The convention of 1795 had adopted six amendments to the Constitution of 1789 which went into effect in October. In addition to apportioning the House of Representatives, reducing Senate terms from three years to one year, and transferring the seat of government from Augusta to Louisville, the amendments provided for the Assembly to meet on the second Tuesday in January instead of the first Monday in November. Since Governor Mathews's term expired on 6 November 1795, the state technically was without an executive for two months until Irwin was elected on the eleventh of January. This interregnum happened to occur when the whole state was aroused over the sale of Georgia's western lands, known as the Yazoo fraud. In fact, Yazoo had been the only significant issue in the election.

Since a majority of the new legislators were staunchly anti-Yazoo, resolving the fraud became the first and most important order of business. After the legislature heard numerous petitions and grand jury presentments, it elected a committee to determine the validity and constitutionality of the Yazoo sale. Three of its nine members later served as governor —James Jackson, David B. Mitchell, and David Emanuel. Jackson, the resolute leader of the anti-Yazooists, served as chairman. Despite threats of violence and assassination, the committee promptly delved into the records and on 22 January declared that "the fraud, corruption, and collusion, by which the said act was obtained, and the unconstitutionality of the same, evinces the utmost depravity in the majority of the late Legislature." The public good, it continued, "was placed entirely out of view, and private interest alone consulted." On 13 February the legislature, by vote of 44 to 3 in the House and 14 to 4 in the Senate, passed the Rescinding Act, which declared the sale null and void. Governor Irwin signed the bill the day it was adopted. Not content merely to nullify the Yazoo Act, the legislature cut out from the state's official records all references to the odious sale and burned them in a solemn ceremony before Governor Irwin and the entire legislature on the capitol grounds at Louisville. As the messenger of the house dropped the pages into the flames he spoke these words: "God save the State! And long preserve her rights! And may every attempt to injure them perish as these corrupt acts now do!"

Burning the Yazoo Act was not the only famous Georgia fire in 1796. In Savannah a disastrous fire destroyed two-thirds of the buildings in Georgia's largest town before the newly organized fire department managed to extinguish it. To "check the repeated and nefarious attempts to lay in ashes that City," Governor Irwin ordered one-half of the militia of Liberty, Bryan, and Effingham Counties to be held in readiness. To provide relief for the suffering, Georgia set aside part of the tax imposed on the importation of slaves.

The constitutional convention of 1795 decreed that another convention should be held in 1798 to determine if additional alterations and amendments were necessary. Irwin, whose term as governor expired in January, was elected president of that convention which assembled in Louisville in May. It wrote a constitution that followed the basic outlines of the existing one. Under the new constitution the governor and other executive officials continued to be elected by the Assembly. With only twenty-three formal amendments, this constitution served Georgia until the Civil War.

When Governor John Milledge resigned on 23 September 1806, Irwin, then president of the senate, completed his unexpired term. The next year he was elected to a full term as governor, serving until 1809. In the fall of 1807, when Irwin unpacked his saddle bags at the governor's residence, a double log house, he became the first governor to reside in Milledgeville. A few days later his wife, who had been injured in an accident, arrived in an ox-drawn cart. The chief issues of his second administration were Indian troubles and settling pioneers on the frontier.

Although evidence is sketchy, Irwin apparently married twice and had nine children. His sons Jared Jr. and Thomas were among the earliest graduates of the University of Georgia. Irwin abandoned his Presbyterian ancestry and became a Congregationalist. He donated several acres of land near his home, Union Hill, in Washington County, for a church to be used by all denominations. He died at his home on 1 March 1818 and is buried there.

A man of strong character, Irwin served the public effectively in numerous positions and maintained the popular support of the people throughout his long political career. Irwin County in south Georgia, created in 1818, is named for him, as is Irwinton and Irwinville.

James Jackson
1798–1801

He was the prince of duelists

In the past two centuries only a handful of Georgians have held all three of the state's top political offices—U.S. representative, U.S. senator, and governor. James Jackson was the first to do so. In addition, he distinguished himself as a military leader, diplomat, constitution-maker, and political party organizer. No Georgian in the post-Revolutionary period exerted more influence on state affairs than Jackson.

Born in Moreton-Hamstead, Devonshire, England, on 21 September 1757, he was the son of James and Mary Webber Jackson. Arriving in Savannah in 1772, he studied law under Samuel Farley, one of Savannah's most successful attorneys, and lived in the home of a family friend, John Wereat. After the Revolutionary War, with George Walton as his mentor, Jackson developed an excellent legal practice which, by his own estimate, brought him "an ample fortune."

Although Jackson had been in Georgia only a few years when the war with Great Britain broke out, he supported the patriot cause with fervor. Always in the forefront of the action, he was among the group of intrepid patriots who seized the powder magazine in Savannah in 1775. At the Battle of the Rice Boats in 1776, Jackson, then a lieutenant, was one of the seven men who volunteered to set fire to the ships. For his courage in fighting the British at Tybee Island he received a commendation from Governor Archibald Bulloch. Jackson served throughout the conflict with the Georgia militia and saw extensive action in Georgia and the Carolinas. Although wounded in the British invasion of Savannah in 1778, he participated in Count d'Estaing's unsuccessful siege of Savannah in 1779, the Battle of Cowpens in 1780, and the reoccupation of Augusta in 1781 and of Savannah in 1782. In 1781, at age twenty-four, Jackson held the rank of lieutenant colonel and commanded his own "legion." Jackson's military career did not end with the British surrender. In 1784 he was commissioned colonel of the Georgia militia. Two years later he was promoted to brigadier general, and in 1792 became a major general, Georgia's highest rank.

As a reward for his heroic service, the legislature granted Jackson thousands of acres of land and a beautiful estate in Savannah, Bonaven-

Fig.15. James Jackson

ture, which formerly belonged to the loyalist Josiah Tattnall, Sr. Jackson resided at Bonaventure until the fire of 1796 destroyed his home; afterwards he lived at Cedar Hill, a plantation near Savannah. In 1785 Jackson married Mary Charlotte Young, the daughter of William Young, a prominent Savannah resident who had served as speaker of the house under Governor James Wright. Of their eight children, three girls died in infancy and one son died at age six, but four boys—William Henry,

James Jr., Jabez Young, and Joseph Webber—reached maturity and had distinguished careers in politics and education.

The people of Chatham County elected Jackson to the legislature throughout the 1780s and again in 1791, 1796, and 1797. The legislature elected him governor in 1788, but he declined to serve, claiming that he lacked sufficient age and experience. He then was elected to the first United States Congress, which convened on 4 March 1789. Defeated by General Anthony Wayne in a controversial and perhaps fraudulent election in 1791, he then entered the United States Senate in 1793. Resigning his seat in 1795 so that he could return to Georgia and lead the fight against the Yazoo Act, he became the prime mover in publicizing, investigating, and nullifying that infamous transaction. The legislature that had disposed of more than 30 million acres of Georgia's land for about $500,000 was utterly corrupt. The members had accepted bribes of money, slaves, and land, some reportedly getting as much as 100,000 acres for their vote. George Watkins, it appears, was the only member of either house who voted for the sale without profiting personally from it. An outraged electorate chose new leaders for 1796. With Jackson chairing the investigating committee, the new legislature rescinded the sale and removed all traces of the act from the state's records. Jackson was so incensed by the fraud that he considered it a personal insult for anyone thereafter to refer to the Yazoo Act.

Jackson became known as the "prince of duelists" because he reportedly met opponents on the field of honor on at least twenty-three occasions. In 1780 he faced his political opponent George Wells in a bitter duel without seconds. When associates later found the combatants, Jackson had wounds in both knees, and Wells, president of the Executive Council, was dead. Between 1796 and 1802 Jackson fought at least three duels and engaged in several street brawls with Yazooists. He clashed frequently with James Gunn, his former colleague in the United States Senate, and faced him in a duel over the Yazoo affair. If traditions can be believed, Jackson had three savage encounters with Robert Watkins. Their first meeting was more a brawl than a duel. In the second clash, Watkins attempted to gouge out Jackson's eyes, a common practice among Georgia frontiersmen of that day. Their third encounter took place in 1802 after Jackson had been governor. By legislative order Watkins had produced a *Digest of the Laws of the State of Georgia*, but Governor Jackson objected to his inclusion of the Yazoo Act and the Rescinding Act in the compilation. He refused to pay Watkins for his work and ordered another digest to be prepared. After Watkins' third shot seriously wounded Jackson, both headstrong statesmen seemed to realize the absurdity of their action. They finally ended their enmity and shook hands as gentlemen.

Although Jackson moved in affluent circles, he had compassion for the common man and embraced the doctrines of Thomas Jefferson. In the aftermath of Yazoo he built Georgia's first true political party. With opposition to Yazoo and adherence to Jeffersonian principles as the chief tests of party loyalty, he enlisted the support of many capable leaders including George M. Troup, William H. Crawford, David B. Mitchell, John Milledge, and Josiah Tattnall. The party leaders established slates for legislative elections and established newspapers in Savannah, Augusta, and Louisville. For a generation the Jackson party, which united the aristocrat and the yeoman farmer under the banner of Thomas Jefferson, dominated Georgia politics.

On 12 January 1798, Jackson became governor, ten years after he had declined the office. After a successful term he was reelected by a vote of 53 to 14. His term had several noteworthy accomplishments. A convention in 1798, which Jackson dominated, wrote a new constitution which served the state longer than any other constitution. The University of Georgia, although chartered since 1785, did not exist when Jackson took office. On 5 December 1800, he signed the University Act which decreed that the institution should be established and which named him to the Board of Visitors. In addition, tax collections were improved, an official digest of the laws was secured, and the foreign slave trade was prohibited. William Foster, Jackson's biographer, concludes that "all in all, Jackson probably rendered greater public service while in the governorship than in any other office."

Before his second term as governor had ended, the legislature elected him to the Senate by a vote of 58 to 9. Ironically, he succeeded James Gunn, his Yazoo opponent. He served in the Senate from 4 March 1801 until his death on 19 March 1806. He was buried in the Congressional Cemetery in Washington, D.C. A county in the northeastern part of the state, created out of Franklin County in 1796, was named for him.

David Emanuel
1801

*He was the first Jew to hold the office of governor
in any U.S. state*

When James Jackson vacated the office of governor to serve in the
United States Senate, David Emanuel, president of the Senate, became
the state's chief executive. He served from 3 March until 7 November
1801, when Josiah Tattnall was inaugurated governor. Emanuel, described
by George White as "a fine looking man, amiable, of good judgment and
inflexible integrity," is primarily remembered today as the first Jew to
hold the office of governor in the United States (although some sources
question whether he was of the Jewish faith). Despite the fact that Emanuel was a prominent leader on the state level, few records remain to
document his life.

Emanuel was probably born in 1744 in Pennsylvania. His father,
David Emanuel, Sr., moved his family to Virginia and then to St.
George's Parish, Georgia, where he became a successful planter. David
Emanuel, Sr. died in 1768, leaving substantial property to his children
Asa, Levi, David, Amos, Elizabeth, Rebecca, Martha, and Ruth. Like his
father, David Emanuel, Jr. was a planter in St. George's Parish. He mar-
ried Ann Lewis, the daughter of another St. George's Parish planter, and
they had at least six children: John, Eli, Lewis, Mary Martha, Asenath,
Ann, and possibly another daughter.

Joining the patriot cause, he fought in the Revolutionary War and
was captured by the British in 1781. According to legend, he was
stripped in preparation to being shot when he suddenly leaped behind a
horse and ran into the darkness. Eluding his pursuers, he eventually made
his way to General John Twiggs's army.

After the war Emanuel held numerous local offices in Burke County
and represented that county in the legislature for many years. An active
supporter of James Jackson, he served with him on the committee that
investigated the Yazoo fraud. Emanuel also served in the constitutional
conventions of 1789 and 1795.

Emanuel died at his home near Waynesboro on 19 February 1808.
Emanuel County, created from Bulloch and Montgomery counties in
1812, was named for him.

Josiah Tattnall
1801–1802

His father was a Tory

In America's Civil War, brothers often fought on opposite sides; in the Revolutionary War, fathers and sons frequently wound up on opposing sides. Men of wealth, prestige, and authority in the royal government tended to remain loyal to the British government, but their sons often sided with the patriots. Noble Jones, James Habersham, and Josiah Tattnall, Sr. were prominent Georgians who objected to certain British policies but refused to take up arms against the mother country. Their sons, Noble W. Jones, Joseph Habersham, and Josiah Tattnall, by contrast, became ardent patriots.

Josiah Tattnall, the youngest of that trio of patriot heroes, was born at Bonaventure, near Savannah, in 1764. Though only a youth when the war began, he already had developed strong sympathies for the patriot cause, and the passage of time only strengthened those beliefs. His father, a staunch loyalist, moved his family first to New Providence, Nassau, and then to England. In his absence Georgia confiscated his estates and later granted his home to James Jackson. Young Tattnall was enrolled at Eton School. When residence in England failed to shake the boy's enthusiasm for the cause of American independence, his father tried another approach —he placed him on a British man-of-war bound for India. The captain was a friend of Josiah's father, and the boy was assured of favor and rapid promotion if he remained in the navy. Tattnall's zeal for America still did not waver; in fact, it may have grown stronger. His outspoken support of the colonies eventually led to his wounding a man in a shipboard duel. For some unknown reason the destination of the ship was changed from India to America, and when it landed at Port Royal, South Carolina, Tattnall escaped. Homeless and penniless, the eighteen-year-old lad obtained some money from his godfather, who lived in South Carolina, and made his way back to Georgia. In July 1782 he joined General Anthony Wayne's forces at Ebenezer, just in time to participate in the victory celebration following the British evacuation of Savannah.

Opportunities for military service continued in the postwar years, and in 1787 Tattnall commanded a detachment of light infantry. He led his unit in a successful expedition commanded by Colonel James Gunn against a band of insurrectionary slaves on Abercorn Creek. In 1788 and 1793 Tattnall organized militia units in Chatham County which were sent into nearby Bryan, Liberty, and McIntosh counties to deal with the restive Creek Indians. Tattnall advanced in rank, becoming a colonel in 1792 and a brigadier general in the Georgia militia in 1801. His son, also named Josiah, later achieved even greater military distinction in the Civil War as commander of Georgia and South Carolina's naval defenses and as captain of the *Merrimac*.

Tattnall served several terms in the Georgia House of Representatives, where he became one of James Jackson's party leaders. In 1796 he was among the legislators who opposed the Yazoo Act. That same year he was elected to the United States Senate to succeed James Jackson, who had resigned. He served the remainder of that term and then retired to private life in 1799.

His retirement was brief, for on 7 November 1801 he became governor. During his term the Tattnall property which had been confiscated was restored to the family. In addition, in appreciation for Tattnall's service to the state, the legislature repealed the banishment of his father. Although invited to return to Georgia, the elder Tattnall remained in England.

Failing health forced Tattnall to resign as governor in November 1802 after serving only one year. Hoping that a change of climate would improve his health, he went to the Bahamas. But after battling his illness for seven months, he died at New Providence, Nassau, British West Indies, on 6 June 1803. His death at thirty-eight made him the shortest-lived governor of the state. His remains were returned to Georgia and buried in the family cemetery at Bonaventure, as he had requested.

A county in southeast Georgia, carved from Montgomery County in 1801, was named for him.

John Milledge
1802–1806

He provided a campus for the University of Georgia

John Milledge, one of Georgia's most respected and unselfish public servants, was the son of John and Anne Smith Milledge. His father and grandparents were among the first British settlers in Georgia, arriving on the *Ann* with James Oglethorpe in 1733. Although his grandparents died within two years after their arrival in Georgia, his father became one of the foremost leaders of the colony. The son born in Savannah in 1757 added luster to an already distinguished family name.

Committed to the patriot cause, Milledge was one of the Liberty Boys who seized 600 pounds of gunpowder from the royal magazine in May 1775. Seven months later he was a member of the group that captured Governor James Wright and held him prisoner. During the war he served as an aide to Governor John Houstoun in the abortive campaign against St. Augustine in 1778. He fought in Savannah, both when it fell to the British in 1778 and when the Franco-American assault failed to dislodge the British in 1779. Returning to Augusta, he served briefly as an assemblyman and as attorney general until the British captured the town. As a colonel in the Georgia militia he helped to recapture Augusta in 1781 and later fought under General Anthony Wayne until the war ended in Georgia.

Having studied law under James Hume, Milledge opened a practice in Savannah after the war. About 1786 he married Mary Galphin, daughter of the famous Indian trader George Galphin, and they had one daughter who died in childhood. In 1790 Milledge moved to Augusta, which remained his home thereafter. Like his father, Milledge began public service at an early age. He was only twenty-three when he was elected attorney general in 1780. He entered the legislature in 1789, and for the next twenty years held public office continuously, serving in both houses of the Georgia legislature, in both houses of the United States Congress, and two terms as governor.

Throughout his political career Milledge grappled with the twin problem of disposing of Georgia's western lands and protecting settlers on the frontier. In 1789, as a representative from Savannah, he opposed the first Yazoo Land Act, arguing that land should be sold not to specula-

Fig.16. John Milledge

tors but to citizens who would reside on the land and cultivate it. Since the state was heavily in debt, he also sought a reasonable price for the land. Elected to Congress in 1792, he urged the federal government to provide greater military protection to Georgia's borders. He insisted that a strong national military force was essential to protect Georgia settlers from the Creeks, the Cherokees, and the Spanish. Though Milledge befriended Thomas Jefferson and supported his party, he adamantly disagreed with him on the issue of national defense. Elected to the Georgia Senate in 1793, he vehemently opposed the granting of huge tracts of land to speculators and consistently sought to make land available to bona fide settlers. "A citizen who calls but a few acres his own," he said, "feels an independence and satisfaction which are not enjoyed by the unstable tenant." He worked closely with James Jackson in opposing the Yazoo fraud and after returning to Congress continued to speak out against the Yazooists. Milledge, along with Jackson and Abraham Baldwin, signed the Act of Cession and Agreement with the federal government in 1802, whereby Georgia ceded to the United States all her territory west of the Chattahoochee River. In return Georgia received

$1.25 million from the federal government and the promise that the Indians would be removed from the remainder of the state.

When Milledge resigned from Congress to become governor in November 1802, he inherited problems with the Indians. The Treaty of Fort Wilkinson, negotiated before he took office, gave Georgia additional lands but left the Creeks in a hostile mood. Milledge succeeded not only in having this cession surveyed but also in obtaining additional lands from the Creeks. He ordered several whites out of Cherokee land in north Georgia and obtained from the Cherokees a small section of land and the right-of-way for a road from Tennessee to Augusta. The new road, built cooperatively by Tennessee and Georgia, was opened in 1805.

During Milledge's term the land lottery was adopted as a method of distributing the new land. Milledge seemed to think the land was being sold too cheaply, but he signed the bill into law. He also signed the Militia Act, which reorganized the system, and signed bills creating Wayne, Wilkinson, and Baldwin Counties out of land acquired from the Creeks.

According to Barbara Brown, Milledge's most thorough biographer, he had extensive land holdings and was deeply involved in agronomy, horticulture, and animal husbandry. "He spent a lifetime experimenting with various types of cotton seed to determine which seed would grow best in the different soils of Georgia," stated Brown, and he shared his findings through publications and correspondence with those who were interested. Milledge also made significant contributions to education. He appointed public spirited men as trustees of the academies, served as president of the Senatus Academicus, and donated a 633-acre tract which became the campus of the University of Georgia. In 1804 the General Assembly decided to build a new state capital in Baldwin County. It was named Milledgeville in honor of the governor.

During Milledge's second term as governor his friend James Jackson died; in September 1806 Milledge was elected to fill Jackson's unexpired term in the United States Senate. A staunch supporter of President Jefferson, Milledge had advanced to the position of president pro tempore of the Senate when he resigned in 1809 because of his wife's serious illness. After her death he married Ann Lamar of Edgefield District, South Carolina, on 28 May 1812. They had three children: John, Ann, and Thomas. Declining further public service, he spent his last years in "elegant leisure" in Augusta. He died on 9 February 1818 and is buried between his two wives in the Summerville Cemetery near Augusta.

David Brydie Mitchell
1809-1813, 1815-1817

He had little use for Tories or Federalists

David B. Mitchell, an influential member of the James Jackson faction, became one of the most popular and successful Georgia politicians of the early nineteenth century. In addition to serving three terms as governor, he served in both houses of the General Assembly and was solicitor general, judge of the Superior Court, United States district attorney for Georgia, and federal Indian agent. Since Mitchell, a native of Scotland, did not arrive in America until he was seventeen, his political achievements are particularly impressive.

Georgia's last foreign-born chief executive, Mitchell was born in Muthill, Perthshire, Scotland, on 22 October 1766. He arrived in Savannah in 1782 to claim property left him by his uncle David Brydie. After reading law for several years under the guidance of respected Savannah attorney William Stephens, he began to practice law in 1789, the same year he became a United States citizen. His practice soon flourished, and he married Jane Mills in 1792.

Mitchell was active in military organizations, rising to the rank of major general in the state militia in 1806, but found his niche in politics. A vehement Jeffersonian, he had little use for Tories or Federalists. He once remarked, "If I ever find it in my heart to forgive an old Tory his sins, I trust my God will never forgive mine." His devotion to republicanism led to a duel in 1802 in which he killed William Hunter, an avowed Federalist. The fiery young Scotsman found a home in the James Jackson faction of Georgia politics. He served two terms from 1794 to 1798 in the lower house of the legislature and represented Chatham County in the Georgia Senate in 1804–1805. From 1798 to 1801, he was a judge of the Eastern Division of the Superior Court. He then succeeded an arch-Federalist as mayor of Savannah and in 1803 was selected as United States attorney for the Georgia district. In addition, Mitchell was active in educational and cultural movements, serving as an officer in the Grand Lodge of Masons, a steward of Saint Andrews Society, secretary and treasurer of the Union Society, and a trustee of both the University of Georgia and the Savannah Library Society. On 9 November 1809, the legislature elected him governor over Jared Irwin by vote of 61 to 41.

Mitchell's first address as governor stressed the need for improving the state's land and water transportation, especially in territory recently acquired from the Indians, as well as strengthening the state's militia and banking system. During his six years as governor, progress was made in all of these areas. At this time Georgia had few bridges or roads, and often the roads were little more than paths that became impassable in inclement weather. Thus, Mitchell had much support for making highway improvement a top priority. He secured legislation that made the legislature responsible for locating and altering the course of public roads. In 1810 he established the state's first permanent highway board to oversee the state's roads. That same year the legislature chartered the Bank of Augusta with a capital stock of $300,000. Governor Mitchell also attempted to revise the criminal code and extend the penitentiary system. In spite of his own background, he supported a state law which outlawed dueling.

Reelected in 1811 over Irwin by a vote of 81 to 30, Mitchell worked tirelessly to strengthen the state's defenses, as war with Britain seemed imminent. Shortly after war was declared in June of 1812, he promptly seized seventeen British vessels in the St. Marys River, an action Georgians applauded. He angered the Clarkites, however, by failing to appoint Major General John Clark as commander of forces that were sent to invade the Creeks. Instead, he appointed Brigadier General John Floyd, explaining that "in the field, brains and money are both indispensable to a commanding general and of the former it is thought Clark is miserably lacking."

Mitchell was not a candidate in 1813, but in 1815 was elected for a third term as governor, defeating Peter Early 76 to 49. During this term the penitentiary was completed and money was appropriated for removing obstructions in the Savannah and Oconee Rivers. Mitchell supported the incorporation of the Bank of the State of Georgia at Savannah and used the bank stock to provide the first regular income ($8,000 per year) ever allocated for the University of Georgia.

Mitchell resigned as governor in 1817 and accepted President Madison's appointment as United States agent to the Creek Indians. Although Mitchell negotiated a favorable treaty with the Creeks in 1818 and helped prepare for the Treaty of Indian Springs in 1821, his tenure as agent was marked by controversy and criticism from John Clark, General Andrew Jackson, and General Edmund Gaines. On 4 March 1821, Mitchell was dismissed on trumped up charges of misusing his power and illegally

Fig.17. David B. Mitchell

bringing slaves into the country. Mitchell defended his reputation in a published account, *An Exposition on the Case of the Africans Taken to the Creek Agency by Captain William Bowen on or about the lst December 1817.*

Retiring to Mount Nebo, his home near Milledgeville, he continued to be active in business, civic, and political affairs until his death. He returned to public office in 1828 as judge of the Inferior Court of Baldwin County, a position he held until 1837. He was serving as a state senator when he died on 22 April 1837, in his seventieth year. He was buried in Milledgeville.

Peter Early
1813–1815

"I never saw him smile"

In contrast to most Georgia politicians, who typically are friendly, outgoing, and gregarious, Peter Early was dignified, erect, and extremely serious—utterly devoid of humor. His face bore a sad and reflective expression. A friend once remarked: "I never saw him smile." By temperament and training Early seemed better suited to be a judge than a governor. He was, in fact, a judge, serving on the Ocmulgee Circuit for six years prior to his election as governor, and his knowledge of the law, firmness, and impartiality on the bench won the respect and esteem of those with whom he came in contact.

Peter Early, the son of Joel and Lucy Smith Early, was born on 20 June 1773, in Madison County, Virginia, where his family had lived for several generations. After receiving a bachelor's degree from Princeton in 1792 and studying law under Jared Ingersoll in Philadelphia, he began to practice law in Oglethorpe County, Georgia, in 1795, his family having previously moved to Georgia. In 1797 he married Ann Adams Smith who, like Early, was a native of Virginia. They had six children: Lucy, Augustus, Cynthia Anne, Thomas, Peter, and Francis.

Although Early was not eloquent, his speeches were so logical and thoughtful that they made an impact and enabled him to compete favorably with more famous and experienced lawyers. Having established a good reputation, Early was elected to the board of trustees of the University of Georgia in 1797 and became a commissioner of the Greene County Academy in 1801. When John Milledge resigned from Congress in November 1801 to serve as governor, Early was chosen to replace him in a special election. Elected to a full term in 1802 and reelected in 1804, Early quickly distinguished himself in Congress. He participated in debates over the slave trade, supported Georgia's claims for payment for militia service in 1793–1794, favored self-government for the residents of the District of Columbia, and served as one of the seven managers or prosecutors in the impeachment of Associate Justice Samuel Chase. *Niles' Weekly Register* reported that his fellow congressmen called him the "Orator of the West." After declining to run in 1806, Early became the first judge of the new Ocmulgee Judicial Circuit created by the legislature in 1807. He remained in that position until the legislature elected him governor on 4 November 1813.

The country was in the midst of the War of 1812 when Early took office, so military affairs quite naturally dominated his administration. He enthusiastically organized both the militia and volunteer forces and cooperated fully with the federal government. When military operations in the South were jeopardized by lack of money, the governor drew a warrant for $80,000 from the state treasury. When a critic suggested that the Union might be dissolved and the $80,000 lost, Early replied: "I trust to God that such will never happen. If it should, I have no wish that Georgia should survive the wreck. I want her to win with the Union or sink together."

Despite Early's popularity as Georgia's wartime commander-in-chief, his political downfall came suddenly over the controversial "Alleviating Act." First enacted in 1808 and extended each year thereafter, this law provided for the relief of debtors. Although its weaknesses were widely recognized, the General Assembly lacked the courage to repeal the law because of its popularity with the masses. Convinced that the law was unconstitutional and unwise, Early vetoed the reenactment bill on 11 November 1814. The concluding paragraph of his veto message clearly explains his position:

> Contracts between individuals are matters of private right, and no reason of State can justify an interference with them. They are sacred things, and the hand of Government can never touch them without impairing public confidence. The alleviating system is believed to be injurious to the moral principles of the community. It accustoms men to consider their contracts as imposing no moral obligations, and, by making *fraud familiar*, destroys the *pride of honesty*. On the ground of expediency also, then, I feel compelled to withhold my assent from the bill. These views are respectfully submitted to the Legislature, and the bill herewith returned to the branch in which it originated.

Early paid a penalty for his courageous act. The legislature overrode his veto, and in the next election chose former Governor David B. Mitchell over Early by vote of 76 to 49. The people of Greene County, where Early had lived since 1800, did not lose confidence in him. In November 1816, they elected him to the Georgia Senate. He died on 15 August 1817 at age forty-four. He was buried at his home at Scull Shoals but in 1914 was reburied in the town cemetery in Greensboro, Georgia.

Historian Kenneth H. Thomas describes Early as "one of Georgia's bright young stars at the beginning of the nineteenth century." In 1818, a county in the southwestern part of the state, carved out of lands ceded by the Creeks, was named for him.

William Rabun
1817-1819

He was a zealous Christian

When David B. Mitchell relinquished the governorship to become United States agent to the Creek Indians on 4 March 1817, the executive power fell to the president of the Senate, William Rabun. The following November the legislature elected Rabun to a full term as governor, by vote of 62 to 57, over John Clark.

Of English and Scottish descent, William Rabun, the only son of Matthew and Sarah Warren Rabun, was born in Halifax County, North Carolina, on 8 April 1771. In the post-Revolutionary period the availability of good farmland lured thousands of settlers from Virginia and the Carolinas to the Georgia piedmont. The Rabun family was part of that exodus, settling in Wilkes County in 1785 and relocating in Hancock County the following year. Matthew Rabun helped to lay out the town of Sparta, was one of the organizers of the Powellton Baptist Church, and was Hancock County's delegate to the Georgia constitutional convention of 1798. Despite his family's prominence, William received only a modest education and, like his father, became a planter. He married Mary Battle on 21 November 1793, and they had one son and six daughters. Owning 500 acres and fifteen slaves in 1812, Rabun was respected more for his strength of character than for his wealth. A man of large physique and pleasing personality, he flourished in the frontier environment and consistently maintained the trust of the voters in his district. From 1802 to 1810 he was one of the justices of the Inferior Court of Hancock County. In 1805 and 1806 he represented Hancock County in the Georgia House of Representatives, and from 1810 until his election as governor in 1817 served in the Georgia Senate. President of the Senate from 1812 to 1817, Rabun was a leader of the Crawford-Troup party in the legislature.

Governor Rabun took office at an opportune time. With the country now enjoying peace, new settlers flocked into the frontier regions of the state in a steady stream. The price of cotton, Georgia's chief export crop, was high, and the treasury was amply supplied with revenues from the sale of bank stocks and federal payments for the state's western lands. His first message to the General Assembly reflected the prosperity of the period. The governor pointed out that appropriations for the soldiers, their widows, and children had been paid; that the penitentiary, under construction since 1811, was completed and ready for occupancy; and that funds were available to improve the state's waterways and schools. In response, the legislature added $250,000 to the free school fund and $255,000 to the internal navigation fund, but no additional money for roads. It also incorporated a steamboat company, chartered three canals, and revised the penal code.

The accidental destruction of a friendly Indian village in 1818 involved Governor Rabun in a bitter dispute with General Andrew Jackson, with whom he exchanged four acrimonious letters. In 1816 and 1817 Seminoles and Creeks made occasional attacks on isolated farms in newly settled parts of south Georgia. In March 1818 Rabun asked Jackson, then invading north Florida, to station troops in that part of Georgia. When Jackson took no action and made no reply, Rabun commissioned Captain Obed Wright to lead two companies of Georgia's cavalry to punish the "miscreant" marauders. The governor specifically instructed the militiamen to attack the villages of Phillemmee and Hopaunee. Instead, Wright and his men attacked a friendly town, Cheha, on the Flint River. They sacked and burned the town and killed ten of the inhabitants. When Jackson learned of the incident, he exploded with fury, not because the Indians had suffered but because his honor was at stake since he had promised to protect Cheha. The governor's arrest of Wright for disobeying orders failed to satisfy the irate general. Jackson's intemperate language incensed Rabun, who replied: "You state in a haughty tone that I, as governor of a State under your military division, have no right to give a military order whilst you are in the field. Wretched and contemptible must be our situation if this be the fact. When the liberties of the people of Georgia shall have been prostrated at the feet of a military despotism, then, and not till then, will your imperious doctrine be submitted to." In this incident the governor ably defended the honor of the state and proved that his mettle was equal to that of the fiery general.

Shortly before his term was to end, Rabun contracted a "malignant autumn fever" and died at his home on 24 October 1819. At age seventeen Rabun had joined the Baptist Church and remained a zealous Christian thereafter. Indeed, he practiced his religion so ardently that critics accused him of changing the governor's residence into a house of prayer. He did not move his family to Milledgeville when he became governor, but rather commuted to his plantation in Hancock County on weekends, where he continued to serve as clerk of the Powellton Baptist Church. At the time of his death he was secretary of two missionary societies and clerk of the Georgia Baptist Association. Rabun's good friend, the distinguished Baptist minister Reverend Jesse Mercer, delivered his funeral sermon. Rabun was buried on his estate, but in 1985 his remains were moved a few miles north to the Powellton Baptist Church cemetery. The state legislature, which attended his funeral as a body, adopted the following resolution:

> The death of the late Governor Rabun deprives society of an ornament, the State of an undeviating and zealous patriot, and humanity of an unwavering friend, and we despair of doing justice to worth so seldom equaled. The eulogium of this excellent man is written in the hearts of the people of Georgia. Nature had endowed him with a strong and vigorous mind and a firmness of character which never forsook him. Love of order and of his country were conspicuous in his every action, and justice, he regarded, not only as a civil, but a religious duty. His acts were marked with an integrity which did honor to his station. His private virtues were of the highest order. Who can estimate the loss to society of such a man?

Two months after Rabun died, a county in the mountainous area of north Georgia was named for him.

Matthew Talbot
1819

The first Clarkite to serve as governor

The death of Governor Rabun on 24 October 1819 made President of the Senate Matthew Talbot the state's chief executive. The first Clarkite to hold the state's highest office, he served less than one month until the legislature selected John Clark as his successor.

Although Georgians normally support their political favorites with fervor, the bitter partisanship of this period has rarely, if ever, been equalled. The "parties" of the early nineteenth century actually were co-alitions loosely organized around a dominant leader. Although personal-ities seemed more important than issues, the more aristocratic elements gravitated to the faction of James Jackson, later led by George M. Troup and William H. Crawford, while many small farmers and frontiersmen found John Clark's leadership more appealing. To contemporary Geor-gians the political alignment must have seemed perfectly normal, but outsiders had trouble understanding it. The differences between the two groups often were blurred; popular Baltimore journalist Hezekiah Niles once remarked of the parties: "We know not what they differ about—but they do *violently* differ."

Matthew Talbot was born in Bedford County, Virginia, in 1762 to a wealthy and politically prominent family. His father, John Talbot, served numerous terms in the Virginia House of Burgesses, owned thousands of acres of land, and reportedly carried over 100 slaves to Wilkes County, where the family moved after the Revolutionary War. Though wealthy settlers from Virginia ordinarily supported the Jackson-Troup-Crawford faction, Talbot sided with Clark instead.

Continuing the family's political tradition, Talbot served as clerk of Elbert County 1790–1791 and then became a justice of the peace and the surveyor for Wilkes County, where he invested in a cotton mill in 1810. He was a delegate to the state constitutional conventions of 1795 and 1798 and served as a captain in the state militia. Talbot served almost continuously in the legislature from 1799 until his retirement in 1824, including several years as president of the Senate. He was regarded as an honest, dignified, and impartial presiding officer—not an easy accom-plishment in that highly partisan age.

Fig.18. Matthew Talbot

In addition to his brief tenure as governor, Talbot was considered for the office on several other occasions. In 1823, when John Clark refused to try for a third term, Talbot accepted the faction's nomination in a race against George M. Troup. The factions were so evenly balanced and the rivalry was so intense that the legislature balloted furiously for three days before finally selecting Troup by vote of 85 to 81. After this slugfest, the legislature changed the system of electing governors. Henceforth, governors would be elected by popular vote and only in unusual circumstances, such as the 1966 election, would the legislature make the decision. In 1827, after Clark had retired to Florida, Talbot again agreed to be a candidate for governor, but he died on 17 September, a few weeks before the election. Shortly after his death, a county in middle Georgia was named for him.

John Clark
1819–1823

He knew no fear

John Clark resembled Andrew Jackson in many ways. Both Clark and Jackson were hot-tempered, rugged frontiersmen who fought several duels and, though poorly educated, achieved success as soldiers, Indian fighters, and planters. In politics both men posed as representatives of the common people and shared a common dislike of coastal aristocrats, the Second Bank of the United States, and the presidential aspirations of William H. Crawford. A contemporary left the following description of Clark:

> He acquired no profession, followed no trade, and never labored in the field. His time was passed in rowdyism. He knew no fear, and never learned from his fighting with the tories to give quarter to his enemies. In his brawls he used knives and guns without regard to consequences. . . . His drunken, restless ways kept him perpetually in mischief. As long as the Indians continued to make inroads into the frontiers, he was ever ready for the foray. . . . Every associate was obliged to be for or against him. He suffered no one of any consequence to occupy middle ground. He had the temper of the clansman. He defended his friends, right or wrong, and expected the same fidelity to himself.

Born on 28 February 1766, in Edgecombe County, North Carolina, Clark was the son of Elijah and Hannah Arrington Clarke. His father brought his family to upcountry Georgia on the eve of the Revolution and became the leader of a partisan Whig band. John Clark received only a meager education because in his youth he fought alongside his father in both the Revolutionary War and in several Indian campaigns. He saw action at Kettle Creek, was wounded at Musgrove's Hill in South Carolina, and was serving under General Anthony Wayne at Savannah when the British surrendered. At age sixteen he had achieved the rank of captain. A grateful Georgia legislature granted Clark 800 acres of land as a reward for his military service. He continued to serve in the Georgia militia and by 1796 was a major general. By then he also had become a substantial landowner, owning more than 1,000 acres in both Washington and Franklin counties. From the infamous Yazoo Act he received an

Fig.19. John Clark

additional 28,000 acres. His marriage in 1792 to Nancy Williamson, the daughter of Colonel Micajah Williamson, further enhanced his standing in the community. Despite educational deficiencies, Clark emerged as a political leader of the backcountry farmers and frontiersmen largely as a result of his volatile personality and military reputation and his wife's family connections.

First elected in 1801 to represent Wilkes County in the General Assembly, Clark was frequently in the midst of controversy. Indeed, controversy, brawling, and dueling characterized his entire political career. Since Clark had invested in two of the Yazoo land companies, and several of his friends and relatives also had been tainted by Yazoo, he incurred the wrath of James Jackson. Moreover, Jackson, and later William H. Crawford, had support from the Virginians living in the Broad River valley, whereas settlers from North Carolina gravitated to Clark. The rivalry between Clark and Crawford led to a duel in 1802 in which Crawford killed Peter Van Allen, a Clarkite. The feud lingered, and Clark eventually met Crawford on the field of honor in 1806 and wounded him. Clark challenged Crawford to another duel in July 1807, but Crawford refused to meet him. Clark vented his anger by flogging Crawford's associate Judge Charles Tait in the streets of Milledgeville—an outburst that cost him a $2,000 fine. During the War of 1812 Clark was infuriated by Governor David Mitchell who refused to give him command of Georgia's troops. Fortunately, Governor Peter Early subsequently allowed him to command the forces along the coast.

As the acknowledged leader of one of Georgia's two political factions, Clark frequently was a candidate for governor. After losing to Peter Early in 1813 and to William Rabun in 1817, he defeated George M. Troup twice in bitterly fought contests.

In 1819 Clark won by vote of 73 to 60; in 1821 the margin was only two votes, 74 to 72. Clark's victories over Troup were more than personal triumphs, they also represented the victory of western farmers and frontiersmen over the more established and affluent easterners.

During Clark's administration, an 1821 treaty with the Creeks granted Georgia the land between the Ocmulgee and Flint Rivers, out of which five new counties were carved. The Creeks named Clark "E-cun-naw-au-po-po-hau," which means "Always asking for land." Clark, like Andrew Jackson and many other frontiersmen, insisted that the federal government ought to move the Indians west of the Mississippi River. He sought federal compensation for property losses inflicted by Indians and for militia expenses against Indians. Few complained when Clark provided $10,000 from the contingency fund for relief following a disastrous fire in Savannah in 1820, but his efforts to spend state money to secure more favorable treaties with the Indians produced strong opposition. At the governor's insistence the legislature did, however, establish a fund of $500,000 to be used for internal improvements and for schools.

After two turbulent terms Clark withdrew from politics, and a comeback effort two years later failed. Ironically, with the choice of governor now placed in the hands of the people, the "aristocratic" Troup defeated the "democratic" Clark by about 700 votes out of more than 40,000 cast. Two years after his defeat, Clark moved to Florida, where he accepted a post as federal Indian agent. Clark mellowed in his old age and forgave

George Michael Troup
1823-1827

The apostle of states' rights

In George M. Troup the Jackson-Crawford faction found a leader as staunch, fearless, and popular as John Clark. Compromise was never a part of Troup's makeup; nor was campaigning, which he considered degrading. Consequently, the proud aristocrat never canvassed for votes, though he served for many years as state representative, United States representative and senator, and governor.

Throughout his political career, Troup defended states' rights with uncompromising zeal. As governor his blunt insistence that the federal government remove the Creeks from Georgia without further delay nearly led to civil war. When the federal government annexed Georgia's lands west of the Chattahoochee River in 1802, it agreed to remove the Indians from Georgia "peaceably and on reasonable terms." Although Georgia had received several cessions since 1802, the rich lands between the Flint and Chattahoochee Rivers still remained in Creek hands when Troup became governor in 1823. With settlers flocking into the state in search of good cotton lands, pressure to oust the Creeks completely continued to mount, and a clash of some sort appeared inevitable.

Into this impasse stepped Governor Troup. Convinced that a "reasonable" amount of time already had elapsed, he demanded action from the federal government. Unimpressed by the federal government's explanations, he insisted that if the United States was not going to fulfill the terms of the treaty of 1802, then it should restore to Georgia the states of Alabama and Mississippi. "Is it discovered at last that Georgia has no claim upon the United States or upon Indians under the compact of 1802?" he asked Secretary of War John C. Calhoun with biting sarcasm. "Is all that a dream, with which the deluded people of Georgia have been plaguing themselves for twenty years?"

Responding to Troup's intemperate rhetoric, President James Monroe appointed two Georgians, James Meriwether and Duncan G. Campbell, to meet with the Creeks. The Creeks were divided into two groups: the warlike Upper Creeks, who refused to leave Georgia, and the less militant Lower Creeks, who were dominated by Chief William McIntosh, first cousin of Governor Troup. In 1825 McIntosh and 400 chiefs and head-

Fig.20. George M. Troup

men of the Lower Creeks signed a treaty at Indian Springs, which ceded the remaining Creek lands in Georgia in return for land in the West and $400,000. The treaty so enraged the Upper Creeks that they decreed death for McIntosh. Shortly afterwards, a band of 170 braves surrounded McIntosh's home and set it afire. When the flames forced him into the yard, they shot and stabbed him to death.

When John Quincy Adams became president less than a month after the treaty was signed, he withdrew it and negotiated a new treaty with the Creeks that did not cede all their Georgia land. Troup declared the Indian

Springs treaty valid, ordered all Creek land surveyed, and urged the citizens of Georgia to be ready for military action, if necessary. Troup gave no indication that he would yield to the federal government or moderate his stand, even if war resulted. In 1827 he sent the following message to Secretary of War James Balfour:

> You will distinctly understand, therefore, that I feel it to be my duty to resist to the utmost any military attack which the government of the United States shall think proper to make on the territory, the people, or the sovereignty of Georgia, and all the measures necessary to the performance of this duty, according to our limited means, are in progress. From the first decisive act of hostility, you will be considered and treated as a public enemy, and with the less repugnance, because you, to whom we might have constitutionally appealed for our own defense against invasion, are yourselves the invaders, and what is more, the unblushing allies of the savages, whose cause you have adopted.

President Adams, unwilling to call the governor's bluff, negotiated another treaty in which the Creeks yielded the disputed land.

While Indian affairs and conflicts with the federal government dominated Troup's administration, he also supported public education, judicial reforms, and a state system of canals, turnpikes, and river improvements, but the legislature adopted little of his progressive program.

An amazing and colorful character, Troup was eccentric in both appearance and manner. Short in stature but compactly built, he had red hair and deep blue eyes and dressed in a unique fashion, often wearing a blue coat with brass buttons, a buff vest, and a fur cap. Oblivious to weather conditions, he sometimes wore summer outfits on the coldest winter days, and in summer wrapped himself in a cloak.

The son of George and Catherine McIntosh Troup, he was born on 8 September 1780 at McIntosh's Bluff in a part of Georgia that later became Alabama. He spent much of his youth in Savannah until his father, a prosperous merchant, sent him to a prestigious academy in New York and then to Princeton, where he was graduated with distinction in 1797. Returning to Savannah, he studied law under John Y. Noel and was admitted to the bar in 1800 but never pursued that profession with any enthusiasm.

Possessing an ample fortune, he devoted much time to public service. After serving three terms in Georgia's General Assembly as a representative from Chatham County, he then served in the United States

House of Representatives from 1807 to 1815, where he denounced with equal vehemence British impressment of American seamen, Yazoo land claimants, and the recharter of the United States Bank. He was a member of the United State Senate from 1816 until 1818, when he resigned to battle the Clarkites for the governorship. Though Clark defeated him by thirteen votes in 1819 and by two votes in 1821, Troup defeated Talbot by four votes in 1823. In 1825, in the state's first popular gubernatorial election, he outpolled Clark, winning 20,545 to 19,682. In 1829 the legislature elected him again to the United States Senate. Because of poor health he did not want the position, but he served until 1833 when he retired from public service to manage his six plantations.

On 30 October 1803, Troup married Ann St. Clare McCormick, who died a year later at their home in Bryan County. On 8 November 1809, he married Ann Carter of Albemarle County, Virginia, a descendant of Robert "King" Carter, colonial Virginia's largest landowner. They had six children: Coralie, Florida, George, Oralie, and two others who died in infancy. Mrs. Troup died in 1828 and Troup, in declining health for many years, died on 26 April 1856. He was buried at his plantation, Rosemont, in Montgomery (now Treutlen) County. A county in west Georgia was named for Troup, "the apostle of states' rights."

John Forsyth
1827–1829

He was called the "best off-hand debater in the world"

When Governor Troup refused to seek a third term in 1827, his party selected John Forsyth as its candidate. Having served as solicitor general of Georgia, congressman, senator, and minister to Spain, he was, as Professor E. Merton Coulter has observed, "one of the ablest men the state ever produced." To oppose Forsyth, the Clark party nominated Matthew Talbot, who died only a few days before the election, giving Forsyth the office.

Compared to Troup's turbulent terms, Forsyth's administration was uneventful and noncontroversial. His message to the legislature in 1828 protested the protective tariff and the federal government's failure to remove the Indians from Georgia and called for improvements in the state's penal code and judicial system. Since the Cherokees in north Georgia claimed to be a nation, separate and apart from Georgia, Forsyth urged the legislature to dispel that notion by extending Georgia's laws over the Cherokee territory, which it did on 20 December 1828. Without the bellicosity of George Troup, Forsyth upheld the rights of Georgia with equal firmness. Despite the bitter Clark-Troup party feud, a consensus could be reached on some issues, and tactful leadership by the governor produced a more harmonious legislative session.

Forsyth was born in Fredericksburg, Virginia, the son of Robert and Fanny Johnston Houstoun Forsyth. His father, a veteran of "Light-Horse Harry" Lee's legion in the Revolutionary War, moved his family to Augusta in 1785, when John was five years old. After attending a local academy, young Forsyth enrolled at Princeton, where he was graduated in 1799. Returning to Augusta, he studied law and was admitted to the bar in 1802. His practice flourished, and in 1808 he entered public service as solicitor general of the Middle Circuit. Defeated in a race for Congress in 1810, he succeeded two years later and remained in public office for the next thirty years. Much of Forsyth's service was on the national level, in part because his wife disliked the Georgia climate.

After serving in the United States House of Representatives from 1813 to 1818, Forsyth advanced to the Senate. He had barely taken his seat there when he was appointed minister to Spain. The Adams-Onis

Fig.21. John Forsyth

Treaty, ceding Florida to the United States, was ratified while he was minister. Although opponents criticized Forsyth's diplomacy, the people of Augusta regarded him as a hero and returned him to Congress in 1823. Four years later he was elected governor. The day after his administration ended, 5 November 1829, the legislature elected him to the United States Senate to complete John M. Berrien's term, and in 1831 he was elected to a full Senate term.

In his early career, including his term as governor, Forsyth supported George M. Troup and the states' rights doctrine. In the tariff-nullification controversy, however, he sided with the unionists and backed President Andrew Jackson's nationalist stand. The tariff had been popular in the South, but as the rates on manufactured goods rose ever higher, the South, dependent upon exporting cotton, saw the tariff as an economic burden which reduced trade. John C. Calhoun of South Carolina estimated that the tariff cost the South $14 million annually. The tariff became so controversial that it transcended the Troup-Clark divisions and shattered party alignment in Georgia.

Since repeated legislative protests about the burdensome tariffs had accomplished nothing, many political leaders suggested that Georgia should disobey the law. Accepting the states' rights doctrine enunciated by Calhoun, they advocated nullifying the tariff. The issue generated so much excitement that an anti-tariff convention was held in Milledgeville in 1832 with sixty of the state's eighty counties represented. The nullifiers had able leadership in John M. Berrien and Augustin S. Clayton. Had Forsyth, who attended the convention as a delegate from Richmond County, joined their ranks, Georgia might well have nullified the tariff as South Carolina did. As governor, Forsyth had objected to the tariff of 1828, and in the Senate he voted against the tariff of 1832, but he refused to support nullification. "The doctrine was preposterous," he said. "It was a mere web of sophism and casuistry." In resolutely opposing nullification, Forsyth argued that its adoption would lead to a bloody civil war. Described by a contemporary as the "best off-hand debater in the world," he matched wits with Berrien in several days of debate. After making his points, Forsyth walked out of the convention, taking fifty-two delegates with him, an act that seemed to nullify the nullification convention. The remaining seventy-one delegates passed some face-saving resolutions but did not nullify the tariff. That distinction was reserved for South Carolina exclusively. In the Senate Forsyth voted for Jackson's Force Bill. Forsyth's nationalistic position alienated some of his Georgia supporters who demanded his resignation, but it pleased President Jackson, who appointed him secretary of state on 1 July 1834. He held that prestigious post for seven years, and for more than a century was the only Georgian to have that honor until President John F. Kennedy named Dean Rusk to the post in 1961.

In addition to his lengthy record of public service and his oratorical skills, Forsyth was noted for his personal attractiveness, classical features, courtly manners, and keen sense of humor. On 12 May 1802, he married Clara Meigs, daughter of the president of the University of Georgia, and they had eight children—Julia, Mary, Clara, John Jr., Virginia, Rosa, Anna, and Robert. On 21 October 1841, the day before his sixty-first birthday, Forsyth died at his home in Washington, D.C. and was buried in the Congressional Cemetery there.

Historian Ed Cashin summarized Forsyth's career: "Politically he generally followed a moderate path, refusing to be drawn into extreme sectional positions. Forsyth fell short of reaching his full potential because of three shortcomings: too many social activities, a lack of 'sustained aggressiveness,' and a failure to identify more closely with the needs and aspirations of his constituents." A county, a town, and a park in Savannah are named for him.

George Rockingham Gilmer
1829–1831, 1837–1839

He was a hypochondriac

As settlers continued to move into the rich cotton lands of the Georgia piedmont, the state capital was moved successively westward from Savannah to Augusta, Louisville, and Milledgeville. George R. Gilmer, the first of eight governors to live in the governor's mansion in Milledgeville, was, appropriately, a westerner, born in Wilkes (later Oglethorpe) County on 11 April 1790. His parents, Thomas and Elizabeth Lewis Gilmer, had emigrated from Virginia to Georgia in 1784, lured by the fertile free land. Like most Virginians in the Broad River valley, the Gilmers supported the aristocratic Crawford-Troup faction in state politics. George, their fourth son in a family of nine children, never enjoyed robust health. Because of his frail constitution, his parents allowed him to neglect farm chores in order to develop his intellectual gifts. After acquiring all the education available in his area, he read history and literature at home and then received four years of rigorous training in the classics at Moses Waddel's famous academy in Willington, South Carolina. Years later, Gilmer was instrumental in securing Waddel as the president of the University of Georgia. After completing his education at age eighteen, Gilmer taught school briefly, studied law under Stephen Upson at Lexington, and served as a first lieutenant in the War of 1812. In 1818 he began a successful law practice in Lexington that provided his main source of income throughout his life, as he shunned wealth based on plantation slavery.

Gilmer's political career also began in 1818 with election to the state legislature. In 1820 he won election to Congress, where he expressed the militant states' rights position. He returned to the state legislature in 1824 to promote the presidential candidacy of William H. Crawford. In 1828 he had the unusual experience of being elected to Congress but not getting his seat because he failed to give formal notice of his acceptance. Upon arriving in Washington he learned that Governor Forsyth had ordered a new election. However, he was elected governor in 1829 and again in 1837. Between his two terms as governor, Gilmer served one more term in the United States House of Representatives from 1833 to 1835, where he supported the Jackson administration.

Fig.22. George R. Gilmer

During both of his administrations Indian relations dominated all other issues. The discovery of gold near Dahlonega in 1829 brought throngs of whites into the Cherokee territory, producing much turmoil and violence as well as serious legal and constitutional issues. In Hall County an Indian named Corn Tassel was convicted of murder and sentenced to be hanged. The case was carried to the United States Supreme Court on a writ of error, but Gilmer, claiming state sovereignty over Indian affairs in Georgia, ordered the sentence carried out in defiance of the court. The legislature, as determined as the governor to remove the Cherokees from the state, extended Georgia's laws over the Cherokee territory and required any whites living there to secure a permit. Eleven men, including three missionaries, subsequently were arrested for violating the law. By the end of Gilmer's first term, nine had accepted his offer of pardon, but two of the missionaries remained in prison and gained national attention during his successor's administration. By 1837, when Gilmer returned to office for a second term, the Cherokees, having exhausted all legal channels, had signed the Treaty of New Echota, agreeing to move to Oklahoma. The governor, resisting all efforts to delay Indian removal, dispatched state troops to assist the federal authorities in subduing hostile Cherokees. By the end of his term in 1839 the Cherokees were gone from Georgia, forced to trek west on what they called the "Trail of Tears."

Upon completing his term, Gilmer, physically exhausted from the strain of executive duties, retired to private life. Returning to Lexington, he spent his last years in happy retirement with his wife. In Eliza Frances Grattan, a Virginian and cousin of Thomas Jefferson, Gilmer found an ideal mate. Though childless, they enjoyed a happy marriage. A gentleman farmer in retirement, he practiced diversified farming and grew a variety of vegetables, grasses, and trees, and served as president of the Agricultural Association of the slaveholding states. A lifelong supporter of education, he served as a trustee of the University of Georgia for many years and made several bequests to that institution. In his last years he became a collector of minerals, books, and artifacts. In 1855 he published *Sketches of Some of the First Settlers of Upper Georgia*, an interesting and gossipy book about his neighbors and his own experiences, which revealed Gilmer's solid character, common sense, industrious habits, and fragile health. Plagued with numerous ailments, he claimed to have suffered pain every day of his life. He was afflicted with a toothache for "forty-five years" and was confined to bed "when life hung upon the slenderest thread" on more than one occasion. According to Gilmer, a physician, after examining him in 1834, "declared that evils numerous as those in Pandora's box had been fastened upon me." Yet, despite these maladies, he led a productive and seemingly happy life for sixty-nine years. He died at Lexington on 15 November 1859.

In an age of intense partisanship, Gilmer tried to be governor of all Georgians regardless of party affiliation. He urged the people to consider principles rather than men. Unwavering in his devotion to duty, his creed was: "Let me always do what is right, and I care not what the consequences may be."

A county in the north Georgia mountains, created out of Cherokee lands in 1832, was named for Governor Gilmer.

Wilson Lumpkin
1831–1835

He removed the Cherokees

Wilson Lumpkin, who served the people of Georgia as state legislator, congressman, senator, and governor, was born in Pittsylvania County, Virginia, on 14 January 1783. When he was only one-year old, his parents, John and Lucy Hopson Lumpkin, moved the family to an area in the Georgia piedmont that later became Oglethorpe County. Though Lumpkin was reared in a frontier environment, his education was not neglected. His father, a jurist and state legislator of some distinction, exposed his son to an abundant supply of newspapers and good books. Lumpkin read widely and became familiar with Josephus, Plutarch, Gibbon, Hume, Blackstone, Smith, Vattel, and Paley. On 20 November, 1800, he married Elizabeth Walker, who was his devoted companion for nineteen years until her death in 1819. Their children were Lucy, Ann, Pleiades Orion, Wilson, William, Elizabeth, and two sons who died at birth. On 1 January 1821, he married Annis Hopkins, and they had Samuel, John Calhoun, Martha, and a son who died in infancy.

At various times Lumpkin was a farmer, teacher, and lawyer, but he is best remembered for his public service. As governor, removing the Cherokees was the most pressing issue he faced. Indeed Indian relations were an overriding concern throughout his lengthy political career, which began in 1804 with his election to the state legislature. His first Indian assignment came in 1818 when President Monroe appointed him United States Commissioner to designate the boundary of the Creek treaty of January 1818. The next year he received a similar assignment for the Cherokee treaty of 1819, and two years later he surveyed the Creek cession of 1821. Having already served several terms in the General Assembly and one term (1815–1817) in Congress, Lumpkin withdrew from politics for three years. His retirement ended in 1825 when the legislature placed him on the new Board of Public Works, which was established to determine feasible routes for canals and railroads in Georgia. Accompanying the engineer, Hamilton Fulton, Lumpkin carefully studied the land from Milledgeville to Chattanooga and recommended a route for a railroad. In carrying out his duties he visited most of the Cherokee leaders and became convinced that the Cherokees had no future

Fig.23. Wilson Lumpkin

in Georgia. The only alternative to their extinction, he believed, was removal to an area beyond the Mississippi River.

Elected to Congress in 1826, Lumpkin served on the Committee on Indian Affairs where he emphatically advocated Indian removal. Such a policy, he argued, would benefit both Georgia and the Cherokees. Re-elected in 1828, he worked harmoniously with President Andrew Jackson, whose views on Indians nearly coincided with his own. In 1830 Congress adopted a controversial bill authorizing Indian removal. Though preferring to remain in Congress to expedite the implementation of this policy, Lumpkin reluctantly yielded to pressure from the Clarkites (Union party) and announced his candidacy for governor in the spring of 1831. He defeated George Gilmer 24,731 to 23,428.

Governor Lumpkin, ignoring the Supreme Court's ruling that Georgia's laws were invalid in the Cherokee territory, proceeded to have the

Cherokee territory surveyed. After the survey was completed in May 1832, the state created ten new counties: Forsyth, Lumpkin, Union, Cobb, Cherokee, Gilmer, Cass, Murray, Floyd, and Paulding. The Cherokee territory, divided into forty-acre gold lots and 160-acre land lots, was distributed by lottery. In the meantime, the missionaries Samuel Worcester and Elizur Butler, who had been jailed a month before Lumpkin took office, became the focal point of national attention. A storm of protest arose demanding their release. Lumpkin, however, was unmoved by it. Instead of freeing the missionaries, he ordered their mail censored and the guard increased. "I suffered no court to determine for me, as the Executive of Georgia, what were my constitutional duties," he wrote. Eventually realizing that the governor would not yield to pressure, the missionaries directed their counsel to suspend their court action against Georgia. A week later, on 14 January 1833, Lumpkin freed them.

At this critical juncture the Cherokees were hopelessly divided. One group, led by Major Ridge, his son John, and his nephew Elias Boudinot, editor of the *Cherokee Phoenix*, decided that further resistance was futile and that their only salvation was to join their tribesmen in Oklahoma. Another faction, led by John Ross, adamantly opposed leaving Georgia. As Georgians continued to move into the new counties, conditions deteriorated. Laws providing severe punishment for offenses against the Indians were unenforced. Lawlessness, hunger, and destitution set in. Lumpkin, reelected over Joel Crawford in 1833, urged the legislature to pass additional laws to control the Cherokees, which it did. After various negotiations in Georgia, Tennessee, and Washington, the Ridge-Boudinot faction signed the Treaty of New Echota on 29 December 1835. The Cherokees received $5 million for their lands. President Jackson accepted the treaty and the Senate ratified it on 29 May 1836, but the Ross faction considered it illegitimate. A few years later after the tribe had moved to Oklahoma, the Ross faction got its revenge by brutally murdering Major Ridge, John Ridge, and Elias Boudinot.

Although Cherokee removal was not fully accomplished when Lumpkin's term ended, it had become a certainty; moreover, Lumpkin remained active in carrying it out. He served on the commission which had the impossible job of settling the debts and claims of whites and Cherokees arising from the execution of the Treaty of New Echota. From 1837 to 1841 he served in the United States Senate, where he resisted all efforts to delay or change the treaty.

Near the end of his career he commented, "I would put a higher estimate on the many years of toil spent in connection with Indian affairs than any one branch of my public career." Certainly that was his chief interest, but it was not his only interest. He emphatically opposed nullification and backed Governor Forsyth's stand. He called for major reforms in education and in the penitentiary, and avidly supported internal improvements, especially railroads. When the Georgia Railroad and Banking Company received a charter in 1833, Lumpkin served as a director. He had a keen interest in the Western and Atlantic, the state-owned railroad that eventually linked the Chattahoochee River with Tennessee, and after leaving the Senate in 1841 spent two years rehabilitating its affairs. When the W & A finally was completed in 1851, Lumpkin was gratified that it closely followed the route he had selected in 1825. The town that grew up at the southern terminus of the railroad, originally called White Hall and Terminus, was renamed Marthasville in honor of Lumpkin's daughter. Today it is named Atlanta.

After completing his duties with the railroad, Lumpkin, at age sixty, retired to his farm in Athens. He devoted his remaining twenty-seven years to farming, writing, and serving as an elder statesman and as a trustee of the University of Georgia. Outliving most of his contemporaries, he died on 28 December 1870, at the age of eighty-seven, and was buried in Oconee Cemetery.

A town in southwest Georgia and a county in the northern part of the state are named for him.

William Schley
1835-1837

He subdued the Creek Indians

In 1835 William Schley, the Unionist candidate, defeated Charles Dougherty of the States Rights party by a vote of 31,177 to 28,606. The *Southern Recorder*, a critical newspaper, accused Schley of being a Federalist of the John Adams type—a charge he quickly denied. Although not a Federalist, he did believe in preserving the Union and was an uncompromising critic of Governor Troup's extreme states' rights views.

When Schley succeeded his friend Wilson Lumpkin as governor, removing Indians remained a major concern for Georgians. Although the Cherokee situation had been resolved, the Creeks continued to pose problems. When bands of marauding Creeks went on a rampage of murder and destruction, terrorizing the white settlers on the western frontier along the Chattahoochee River, he organized militia units and personally took part in the campaign against them. He remained at the Columbus headquarters for six weeks, assisting General Winfield Scott, whose United States army troops easily routed the Creeks.

Schley's administration also faced a serious conflict with the state of Maine. Two men from Maine aided and abetted a group of slaves in an escape from Savannah to Maine. Schley expected Maine officials to extradite the abolitionists to Georgia for prosecution and to return the slaves to their owners. When Maine refused to cooperate, Schley became indignant. Several sectional conflicts already had erupted over the institution of slavery. Almost without exception Georgia political leaders praised the institution of slavery as a positive good both for whites and blacks. The sectional conflicts, they insisted, resulted from the outspoken attacks on the institution by abolitionists, such as William Lloyd Garrison. The Georgia legislature found Garrison's fanatical insistence on immediate emancipation so repugnant that it passed a bill offering a reward of $5,000 for his arrest and conviction. Schley not only signed the bill but also declared that Garrison and abolitionists were "a sect of crazed enthusiasts who are endeavoring to enlist insurrection and rapine, conflagration and massacre, under the banner of philanthropy."

Schley's message to the legislature in 1836 urged the state to undertake a comprehensive geological survey, maintain an asylum for the

Fig.24. William Schley

insane, organize a supreme court, improve river navigation, provide education for the deaf, and sell the Altamaha Canal. He strongly recommended the construction of the Western and Atlantic Railroad and had the pleasure of signing the bill authorizing its construction. He also had the responsibility of building the new executive mansion in Milledgeville. Projected to cost $15,000, it actually cost $50,000 when completed in 1838. Perhaps the most important accomplishment of his term was the compilation of a digest of English law for use in Georgia.

In 1837 Schley lost his bid for a second term to former Governor George Gilmer, the States Rights party candidate, by a margin of 700 votes. In a quiet and close election, Schley received 33,417 votes to

Gilmer's 34,178. Following his defeat he retired to private life and a career of business. He established and operated the Richmond Factory, which manufactured cotton and woolen products, and at the time of his death was president of the board of trustees of the Medical College of Georgia.

Schley's career followed the general pattern of governors of this period in that he was born north of Georgia, was reared in a frontier region, practiced law, and served in both the state legislature and Congress. The son of John Jacob and Anna Shelman Schley, he was born in Frederick, Maryland, on 10 December 1786. Educated at academies in Louisville and Augusta, he was admitted to the bar in 1812. He practiced law in Augusta until 1825, when he was elected judge of the Superior Court for the Middle District of Georgia. In 1830 he represented Richmond County in the state legislature; in 1832 he was elected to the Twenty-third Congress as a Democrat. Reelected in 1834, he resigned from Congress to run for governor. Also typical of Georgia governors of this period, he lived a full life of almost seventy-two years.

Schley married Elizabeth Sarah Hargrove on 2 April 1822, and they had four children: Anna Maria, William, George, and Henry Jackson. Mrs. Schley died on 11 February 1845, and a year later he married Sophia Kerr. He died at Augusta on 20 November 1858.

Less than a year before his death, Georgia honored Schley by creating a new county and naming it for him.

Charles James McDonald
1839–1843

He never bargained for an office

Whenever Charles J. McDonald was offered any kind of deal to advance his political career, his standard reply was "I have never bargained for any office, and if I do not receive it without conditions, I shall never reach it." A man of stern integrity and honor, he followed this creed in serving the people of Georgia in a variety of offices. Described by Professor James Z. Rabun as having "unruly red hair, bright blue eyes, a firm jaw, a resolute face, and an excitable temper," McDonald became a respected statesman and jurist.

McDonald was born in Charleston, South Carolina, on 9 July 1793. His parents, Charles and Mary Glas Burn McDonald, natives of Scotland, had settled in South Carolina before the Revolution, but in 1794, when Charles was one year old, they moved to Hancock County, Georgia. After studying at Reverend Nathan Beman's academy at Mount Zion, McDonald earned an A. B. degree at South Carolina College in 1816. He studied law under Joel Crawford at Sparta, was admitted to the bar in 1817, and opened what soon became an extensive law practice.

Political positions came in rapid succession. In 1822 the legislature elected him solicitor general of the Flint Circuit of the Superior Court, a post he held until 1825 when he became judge of that circuit. Active in the state militia, he was commissioned brigadier general in 1823, but relinquished that position when he was elevated to the bench. By 1825 McDonald had settled in the new town of Macon. In 1830 he resigned his judgeship in order to return to the practice of law, engage in land speculation, and operate a Bibb County plantation. In 1830 he served a one-year term in the Georgia House of Representatives and in 1834 and 1837 one-year terms in the Georgia Senate. As the Democratic (Unionist) candidate for governor in 1839, McDonald defeated Charles Dougherty, the States Rights (Whig) candidate, 34,634 votes to 32,807; and two years later won reelection by a wider margin over William C. Dawson.

McDonald took office at a time of economic distress caused by the Panic of 1837. The price of cotton, Georgia's chief export crop, had plummeted to four or five cents a pound, personal debt had increased to alarming proportions, and commerce had stagnated. Since 1835 the

Fig.25. Charles J. McDonald

legislature had allowed the counties to keep for their own use all of the state's property tax, while expenditures for state government were paid from dividends from stocks in Georgia banks and from the earnings of the Central of Georgia Bank. Consequently, the public debt had increased to $1,000,000, the state's credit had dropped to a new low, and the treasury was nearly empty. To complicate matters further, McDonald's party held only slight majorities in the legislature, and in 1840 the Whigs controlled the Assembly.

McDonald attacked the problems boldly. He convinced the legislature to resume collecting all of the property tax since the counties had frittered away the funds they had received. Next, he persuaded the legislature to repeal the Common School Act of 1837, explaining that Georgia could not afford schools for all. For temporary relief of debtors, the governor proposed a bill to postpone foreclosures and executions for debts. The Whigs, led by Robert Toombs, defeated his measure in 1840, but two years later it became law. When the legislature attempted to cut the general tax by 20 percent, he vetoed the bill and urged a tax increase instead. In his annual message of 1842 he said, "The public faith must be maintained, and to pause to discuss the question of preference between taxation and dishonour, would be to cast a reflection upon the character of the people whose servants we are." Given this unpleasant choice, the legislature seemed to prefer dishonoring the state, inasmuch as it defeated the governor's bill providing higher taxation. With the session nearly over and the two houses unable to agree on a tax, McDonald ordered the state treasurer to pay the legislators' salaries last—after all other state expenses had been paid. The next day the enraged legislature, after denouncing the governor as a tyrant, raised the general property tax by 25 percent.

Improving the state's fiscal affairs clearly was McDonald's most important accomplishment as governor, but he sought other reforms too. He advocated the establishment of a supreme court, biennial sessions of the legislature, railroad construction, and improvements in education. Regarding the importance of education he stated, "The first thing to be regarded in a republic is the virtue of the people; the second their intelligence. Both are essential to the maintenance of our free institutions; the first inspires them with a disposition to do right, the second arms them with power to resist wrong."

After concluding his four years as governor, McDonald remained active in politics. A consistent believer in a strict interpretation of the Constitution, he switched from the Union party to the states' rights camp. As a Georgia delegate to the Nashville Convention of 1850, he served as vice president of the first session and president of the second session. A bitter critic of the Compromise of 1850, he defended the right of a state to secede from the Union. In 1851, as the gubernatorial candidate of the Southern Rights party, he was defeated by Howell Cobb by the overwhelming margin of 57,397 to 38,824. Appointed to the supreme court of Georgia in 1855, he served until declining health forced him to retire in 1859.

George Walker Crawford
1843-1847

He was Georgia's only Whig governor

George W. Crawford, one of Georgia's more neglected political leaders, had a long and eminently successful political career, both on the state and national levels. In addition to his political accomplishments, profitable business and professional endeavors brought him a considerable fortune, which enabled him to live luxuriously in a palatial estate at Bel-Air, near Augusta.

A cousin of William H. Crawford, George Crawford was the son of Peter and Mary Ann Crawford, born in Columbia County on 22 December 1798. His father, a Virginian and veteran of the Revolutionary War, acquired land in Georgia after the war and soon gained local prominence, serving ten successive terms in the state legislature. Utilizing his father's excellent library, Crawford secured a sound education at home and continued his studies at Princeton, where he was graduated in 1820. He studied law under Richard Henry Wilde, was admitted to the bar, and opened a law practice in Augusta in 1822. He married Mary Ann McIntosh on 4 May 1826, and they had four children: William Peter, Sarah, Anna, and Charles. Rising rapidly to eminence in his profession, Crawford, in 1827, was appointed solicitor general of the Middle Judicial Circuit of Georgia—a position he filled until 1831 when he resigned in order to devote more time to his lucrative private practice.

Like his famous cousin, Crawford was involved in a duel. Criticism of his father prompted the duel, which took place at Fort Mitchell, Alabama, in 1828, and resulted in the death of Congressman Thomas E. Burnside. Crawford deplored the unfortunate affair and later made anonymous financial contributions to Burnside's widow and children. In response to the incident, the legislature enacted a law barring future duelists from holding public office. The duel did not hinder Crawford's political advancement; the voters of Richmond County repeatedly elected him to the Georgia House of Representatives from 1837 to 1842, except for one year when he did not run. Upon the death of Congressman Richard Wylly Habersham in 1842, Crawford was elected to fill his unexpired term and served from 1 February to 4 March 1843. As the Whig party nominee for governor in 1843, Crawford defeated Mark A.

Fig.26. George W. Crawford

Cooper, the Democratic candidate, by vote of 38,813 to 35,325. The Whigs also gained control of both houses of the legislature. In 1845 Crawford was reelected by a margin of 1,751 votes over Matthew H. McAllister, an aristocratic lawyer-planter from Savannah.

The Whig party opposed the Central Bank of Georgia and advocated hard money and restraining state expenditures. With the support of the legislature, Crawford's administration was able to improve the state's fiscal affairs by discharging its debts and eliminating the inefficient Central Bank of Georgia. Crawford, even more frugal than his predecessor, reduced state expenditures more than $66,000 his first year in office. He nearly succeeded in paying in full a state debt of $500,000 to a London banking firm. While establishing sound currency and paying debts were priority items, Crawford also was instrumental in broadening educational opportunities, accelerating the construction of the state-owned railroad, and establishing a state supreme court. After decades of agitation, the Georgia Supreme Court became a reality during his term, finally bringing uniformity to Georgia's judicial decisions.

After completing his term as governor, Crawford served as secretary of war under Whig President Zachary Taylor from March 1849 to July 1850. In this position, as in his previous offices, Crawford discharged his responsibilities with integrity, diligence, and administrative skill. Following the death of President Taylor, he retired from politics. Apparently his abrupt retirement stemmed largely from mounting criticism over his role in the Galphin claim, a case that brought him $115,000 in legal fees after seventeen years of work. Although investigations completely exonerated him of any wrongdoing, the criticism continued.

Living with his wife and family at his Bel-Air estate, Crawford avoided politics but remained active in business, travelled extensively, and made profitable real estate investments in Georgia and in Texas. In January 1861 he came out of retirement to serve in Georgia's secession convention. Assembling in Milledgeville, the delegates, by unanimous vote, elected him permanent president of the convention. That was Crawford's last public service. He died on 27 July 1872. His funeral was held in Augusta's historic St. Paul's Episcopal Church, and he was buried in an unmarked grave in Summerville Cemetery, near his home. Few Georgians today remember the state's only Whig governor whose entire political career, his biographer Len Cleveland has observed, was "motivated by a traditional sense of duty rather than by deep political convictions."

George Washington Towns 1847–1851

He was handsome, suave, and courtly

George Washington Bonaparte Towns, lawyer, state legislator, congressman, and governor, was the son of John and Margaret George Towns, born in Wilkes County on 4 May 1801. About 1840 he dropped the name Bonaparte. His father, a Virginian and veteran of the Revolutionary War, settled in Wilkes County shortly after the war ended and subsequently moved his family to Greene and then to Morgan County.

Although Towns did not attend college, he read avidly and devoted much time to study. He considered studying medicine, but a severe injury resulting from being thrown from a horse forced him to abandon his plans. After regaining his health, Towns studied law in Montgomery, Alabama, and was admitted to practice in 1824. While living in Montgomery, he married Margaret Jane Campbell of Wilkes County. Margaret, who was in poor health at the time of the marriage, died a week later, on 5 November 1826. Despite its brevity, the marriage connected Towns with a prestigious Georgia family. One of Margaret's sisters married Governor Jared Irwin; her brother Duncan Green Campbell, a leader of the Clark faction, was nominated for governor in 1828; and her nephew John A. Campbell became a justice of the United States Supreme Court.

Returning to Georgia in 1826, Towns settled in Talbot County, where he became a popular political figure. After serving two terms in the Georgia House of Representatives and two terms in the Georgia Senate, he was elected to Congress and served from 7 December 1835 until 1 September 1836, when he resigned. Elected to the next session, he served the full term. In Congress he championed military preparedness, American interests in Texas, and removal of the Cherokees; he opposed the recharter of the Second National Bank, protective tariffs, and federal aid for internal improvements. Out of office for nearly a decade, he practiced law until he was again elected to Congress to fill the unexpired term of Washington Poe, who had resigned. Towns served from 27 January 1846 to 3 March 1847. He sought reelection but was defeated by the Whig candidate, John William Jones, by a margin of 180 votes. Towns's setback was temporary, for Georgia Democrats nominated him for governor in 1847. He defeated the Whig candidate, General Duncan L. Clinch,

43,220 votes to 41,931, and two years later won reelection over Edward Y. Hill by a wider margin.

During his first term the Whigs controlled the legislature, but in his second term the Democrats held slight majorities in both houses. By the end of his term the Democratic party once again had achieved dominance in Georgia politics, and no Whig would ever again occupy the executive chair. As governor, Towns oversaw the completion of the Western and Atlantic Railroad but failed to resolve a boundary dispute with Florida. He also sought reforms in the slave code, the adoption of ad valorem taxation, the use of tax revenue to support public schools, and a complete reorganization of the state militia. Regarding the last issue, he informed the legislature that "any change might be regarded as an improvement." Unfortunately, the legislature failed to enact Towns's sensible program of reform.

Deeply concerned over the growth of abolitionism, Towns, previously a Unionist, became a staunch defender of Southern rights and John C. Calhoun's interpretation of the Constitution. In accepting the nomination for governor in 1847, he denounced the Wilmot Proviso, which sought to outlaw slavery in any territory acquired from Mexico as "a strange amalgamation of religious fanaticism and political knavery." While he was governor, Congress passed the Compromise of 1850. In response to that measure, the Georgia legislature passed resolutions condemning portions of it, and Governor Towns called for an election of delegates to a state convention. The convention, which assembled in Milledgeville on 10 December 1850, was dominated by Unionists. Consequently it rejected the demands for secession and adopted instead the Georgia Platform, written by Charles J. Jenkins. That document, while insisting that the South had been mistreated, urged acceptance of the Compromise of 1850 to avoid the destruction of the Union. Towns, however, had become a fervent secessionist, favoring civil war as a last resort. In urging the state to upgrade its defense against northern extremists, his last message to the legislature asserted that "the state that arms its citizens, and gives warning to the aggressor to beware the next blow, will be respected."

After concluding his term as governor, Towns moved to Macon, where he resumed his law practice and operated a cotton plantation with many slaves. Though only fifty when he vacated the governor's office, his health declined and he remained incapacitated the last four years of his life. He died at his home in Macon on 15 July 1854, survived by his widow, Mary Jones Towns, a wealthy Virginian and daughter of John

Fig.27. George W. Towns

Winston Jones, a former speaker of the United States House of Representatives, and their five daughters and two sons. He was buried in Rose Hill Cemetery in Macon.

Towns was a handsome man, noted for his gracious manners and courtly bearing. Though not an eloquent speaker, he was regarded as an effective lawyer and a capable public servant. A man of firm convictions, his messages to the legislature were articulate and forceful, and his recommendations concerning slavery, education, taxation, and the militia were wise. His staunch defense of Southern rights was extreme, but he remained popular with his constituents until ill health and death silenced him in the prime of life. In 1856 the legislature named a county in the mountainous northeastern part of the state for Towns.

Howell Cobb
1851–1853

"He is the president as much as if he were sworn in"

Solicitor general, six times a member of Congress, speaker of the United States House of Representatives, governor, secretary of the treasury, president of the Provisional Congress of the Confederate States, and major general in the Confederate army, Howell Cobb compiled a record of political achievement that few Georgians have ever equalled.

Born in Jefferson County on 7 September 1815, he was the oldest son of John and Martha Rootes Cobb. The Cobbs were economically and socially prominent, and Howell Cobb increased his resources through his marriage to Mary Ann Lamar, the daughter of a wealthy middle Georgia planter. They had twelve children: John Addison, Lamar, Howell Jr., Mary Ann Lamar, Sarah Mildred, Andrew Jackson, Elizabeth Craig, and five who died in infancy. A graduate of the University of Georgia in 1834, Cobb studied law under General Edward Harden, was admitted to the bar in 1836, and opened a practice in Athens. With leisure and comparative freedom from financial worries, he devoted his life to public service.

Politics came naturally to the gregarious young attorney, and as a moderate Democrat Cobb rose rapidly in state and national party ranks. The state legislature elected him, at age twenty-two, solicitor general of the Western Circuit, a position he held for three years. He won four successive elections to Congress, serving from 1843 to 1851. He supported the Polk administration and became allied with the Martin Van Buren and Lewis Cass elements of the party. Despite his extensive investments in plantations and slaves, Cobb bitterly opposed John C. Calhoun and the states' rights doctrine. Cobb's moderation, coupled with his energy and ability, made such a favorable impression on his colleagues that they elected him parliamentary leader of the Democratic party in 1848. The next year, in a hotly contested race, he was elected speaker of the house on the sixty-third ballot. His moderation and support of the Union made the thirty-four-year-old Georgia slaveowner the most acceptable compromise candidate. In presiding over the House during the debates on the Compromise of 1850, Cobb played a major role in securing the enactment of that controversial legislation.

Fig.28. Howell Cobb

Passage of the Compromise of 1850 produced another party realignment in Georgia as the Whigs died out and the Democrats split into two factions. Supporters of the Compromise of 1850 formed the Constitutional Union party, while those opposing compromise and favoring secession established the States Rights party. Resigning from Congress, Cobb returned to Georgia to defend his role in adopting the compromise. In 1851 the Constitutional Union party nominated him for governor, and the States Rights party nominated former Governor Charles J. McDonald. Having previously served two terms as governor, McDonald seemed overconfident. After realizing his mistake, he campaigned vigorously but made little headway because he was a poor speaker. With the backing of Alexander Stephens, Robert Toombs, Charles J. Jenkins, and the moderate Democrats, Cobb trounced McDonald, 57,397 votes to 38,824. Cobb's total was the highest popular vote a Georgia governor had ever received, and also the greatest margin of victory.

Accustomed to a lavish and glittering lifestyle, Cobb found the town of Milledgeville "exceedingly dull." Consequently he disliked being governor and spent as little time as possible in the capital. But despite his long absences at his home in Athens, and in Washington, D. C. and New York, he had a reasonably productive two-year term as governor. Major legislation enacted included the creation of the position of school superintendent, the establishment of the Academy for the Blind, the expansion of the insane asylum, and the requirement that banks pay their liabilities on demand in specie. In addition, more than $500,000 was appropriated to finance repairs on the recently completed Western and Atlantic Railroad. To direct the affairs of that railroad, Cobb appointed William M. Wadley superintendent. A capable railroad executive, Wadley was a wise and popular choice.

Cobb's main legislative triumph, however, was in tax reform. Under the existing system, real property taxes had been levied according to the amount of land owned, but his new ad valorem system taxed personal and real property, including stocks and bonds. "Every citizen," he declared, "should be required to pay according to the extent and value of his property." Even though revenues increased from $291,077 in 1851 to $377,165 in 1853, they still failed to equal expenditures. Indeed, the state debt increased from $1.6 million to $2.6 million during his term. John Simpson, Cobb's biographer, has written that Cobb, "a spendthrift in private life" was "just as liberal with public funds."

Upon leaving office, Cobb rejected President Franklin Pierce's offer of the position of minister to Spain. Instead he practiced law for three years until he was reelected to Congress. In 1856 he campaigned extensively for his friend James Buchanan and served in his cabinet as secretary of the treasury. It was ironic that Cobb, an "irresponsible spendthrift" incapable of managing his own personal finances, was made keeper of the nation's purse strings. But, according to biographer Simpson, he surprised everyone by handling public money "with extraordinary caution and thrift." His power in the Buchanan administration was such that a critic wrote: "He is the president as much as if he were sworn in."

Cobb, who lusted for the presidency, sought his party's nomination in 1860. A leading contender, many considered him the logical successor to Buchanan. When he failed to secure the Democratic nomination, he resigned from the cabinet, abandoned his national stance, and advocated immediate secession. Instead of becoming president of the United States, he was elected president of the Provisional Congress in Montgomery which established the Confederate States of America. Though he had no military training, Cobb organized a regiment, fought at Seven Pines, Second Manassas, Harper's Ferry, and Sharpsburg, and ended the war with the rank of major general.

After the war he lived in Macon and formed a successful law partnership with James Jackson, who later served as chief justice of the Georgia Supreme Court. He opposed Congressional Reconstruction until his death, which came suddenly on 9 October 1868. Though Cobb had devoted the better part of three decades to public service, he was only fifty-three when he died.

Herschel Vespasian Johnson
1853-1857

He sought to preserve the Union

Three capable leaders—Howell Cobb, Herschel V. Johnson, and Joseph E. Brown—guided Georgia's ship of state in the 1850s. Johnson, like his predecessor, was a planter, lawyer, graduate of the University of Georgia, and statesman of national importance. The journalist-historian I. W. Avery regarded Johnson as Georgia's ablest political leader in the mid-nineteenth century. Writing in 1881 he stated: "There has been no public man in Georgia in the last quarter of a century the superior in brain power of H. V. Johnson. A powerful thinker, a strong speaker, possessor of an exquisite style of writing, the chastest and most vigorous master of language we have ever had in the state, he is one of our few public men that could be called great."

Born in Burke County, Georgia, on 18 September 1812, he was the son of Moses and Nancy Palmer Johnson. He was educated at Monaghan Academy near Warrenton, Georgia, and at the University of Georgia. Before earning his bachelor's degree in 1834, he married Ann Polk Walker, daughter of Judge William Polk of Maryland and the niece of President James K. Polk. A young widow, she reportedly was one of the most beautiful and intellectual women of her day. Her sparkling and gracious charm contrasted sharply with her husband's stern countenance and unsociable nature. They had nine children, four sons and five daughters. Johnson read law under William T. Gould, was admitted to the bar in 1834, and opened a practice in Augusta. In 1839 he purchased a plantation called Sandy Grove ten miles south of Louisville in Jefferson County, and thereafter divided his time between his planting interests, law practice, and political activities.

A gifted orator and staunch Democrat, Johnson received the Democratic nomination for a seat in Congress, but lost his first race to Absalom Chappell. In 1845 and 1847 he received serious consideration for the gubernatorial nomination, but willingly stepped aside for others. When Walter Colquitt resigned from the United States Senate, Governor Towns named Johnson to fill the vacancy. He served from 14 February 1848 to 4 March 1849. In the Senate he supported President Polk's policies in the war against Mexico and denounced the Wilmot Proviso.

Fig.29. Herschel V. Johnson

In 1849 the legislature elected Johnson to the judgeship of the Ocmulgee Circuit of the Superior Court, and he served in that position until his nomination for governor.

In 1853 the Georgia voters had two outstanding candidates for governor. By the narrow margin of 47,708 to 47,168 they selected Johnson over Charles J. Jenkins. Johnson later wrote that the support of Governor Cobb probably made the difference. Two years later Johnson defeated Garnett Andrews and B. H. Overby by a comfortable margin. With the Democrats controlling both houses of the legislature as well as the governorship, the state was becoming a one-party regime. Since Georgia enjoyed prosperity in the 1850s, Johnson's problems as governor were largely routine. He urged the legislature to establish a true free public school system, increase appropriations to the University of Georgia, enlarge the state capitol, and build a new penitentiary away from Milledgeville. The legislature, however, paid little attention to his recommendations.

Although a strong advocate of states' rights, Johnson also desperately wanted to preserve the Union. Consequently, he accepted the Compromise of 1850 and sought sectional reconciliation throughout the 1850s. He supported the controversial Kansas-Nebraska Act but deplored the violence that erupted in Kansas between the defenders of slavery and the free-soilers. Convinced that the Democratic party was the only national party, he opposed Republican party policies which were driving the South to secession. He understood that secession inevitably would produce a bloody civil war which the South could not win. The growing bitterness between North and South filled him with deep apprehension. In 1860 he reluctantly accepted the nomination for vice president on the Democratic ticket with Stephen A. Douglas. He did so "purely as a matter of patriotic duty," never expecting to win. Although he campaigned vigorously, in private correspondence he acknowledged that he could see "no prospect of Douglas being elected."

For accepting the vice presidential nomination on the Douglas ticket, Johnson was savagely assailed in Georgia. Despite the verbal criticism and burnings in effigy, Johnson steadfastly pursued his beliefs in a last-ditch effort to avoid the impending catastrophe. To a friend he confided: "I find myself alienated from many that I love best. But I feel that in the Union and its preservation lies the best future for me and my children and coming generations, and I will do what I can to preserve it." His message of conciliation, patience, and peace was lost in the emotional campaign of 1860. The breakup of the Democratic party gave the presidency to Abraham Lincoln, who received only 40 percent of the popular vote. Georgia, like most of the South, voted for John Breckinridge for president.

After Lincoln's election, Johnson continued to oppose secession until the state convention voted Georgia out of the Union in January 1861. He acquiesced in that decision but never expected the Confederacy to win the war. While most of Georgia's leaders greeted secession with enthusiasm and aspirations of military glory, Johnson, with greater realism, approached the future with deep foreboding. "I never felt so sad before," he wrote.

Despite his personal misgivings, he served loyally in the Confederate Senate from December 1862 until the end of the war. In Richmond he opposed conscription, the suspension of the writ of habeas corpus, the personal attacks upon President Jefferson Davis, and most of the financial measures undertaken by the Confederate government. In December 1864 General Sherman's troops sacked Johnson's home at Sandy Grove. After the war Johnson served as president of the state constitutional convention which produced the short-lived Georgia Constitution of 1865. In January 1866 the legislature elected him to the United States Senate, but the Senate, controlled by Radical Republicans, refused to seat him.

Before the war Johnson had been a wealthy man, owner of more than 3,600 acres of land valued at $25,000 and 117 slaves valued at $93,000. In 1860 his cotton and corn crop brought him $19,000. In addition to his plantation, he had derived a substantial income from his law practice, which by his own admission had been "lucrative" since 1844. The Civil War, which Johnson opposed so vehemently, ruined him financially, as it did many Southerners. Greatly embarrassed by his indebtedness, he made frequent references to this topic in his correspondence in the late 1860s. In 1867 he wrote to his son, Herschel, then a medical student in New York: "My profession is now yielding me almost nothing. Every branch of business is more depressed than I have ever known before. Money is extremely scarce." Two years later, to a friend in Washington, D.C., he stated: "I am totally ruined by the war and thus far I have been unable to rally." Despite this adversity, Johnson's faith in the Almighty, his confidence in his country, and his love for his family never wavered.

Johnson's financial condition improved in 1873 when Governor James M. Smith appointed him to the judgeship of the Middle Circuit of the Georgia Superior Court. He filled the position with conspicuous distinction until his death, which came suddenly on 16 August 1880. He was buried in the Old Louisville Cemetery in Louisville, Georgia. Newspaper obituaries praised him lavishly. The *Macon Telegraph* stated: "No man in Georgia was more beloved for the excellency of character and purity of life." The *Atlanta Weekly Constitution* ranked him among "the foremost of American statesmen." In 1858 the legislature honored Johnson by naming a county in middle Georgia for him.

Joseph Emerson Brown
1857–1865

He served four terms as governor

Joseph E. Brown, the only man who has served four terms as governor of Georgia, also served as circuit judge, state senator, United States senator, and chief justice of the Georgia Supreme Court. Like a hero in a Horatio Alger story, he rose from humble beginnings to become one of Georgia's wealthiest and most influential leaders.

Born at Long Creek, Pendleton District, South Carolina, on 15 April 1821, he was the son of Mackey and Sally Rice Brown. In his early youth his family moved to Union County, Georgia, a remote mountainous region with very limited educational opportunities. When Brown was nineteen, his father gave him a yoke of oxen so that he might further his education. When Brown arrived at the Calhoun Academy in South Carolina, he traded the oxen to a farmer for room and board and arranged to attend school on credit. Later he taught school and studied law in his spare time. After being admitted to the Georgia bar, he attended Yale Law School where he received a degree in 1846. Plain and practical, he opened a law practice in Canton which soon netted him $2,000 to $3,000 a year, enabling him to pay off his educational debts.

He married Elizabeth Grisham, daughter of a Baptist minister, on 13 July 1847, and they had eight children: Julius Lewis, Mary Virginia, Joseph Mackey, Franklin Pierce, Elijah Alexander, Charles McDonald, Sally Eugenia, and George Marion. Their son Joseph Mackey Brown followed his father's footsteps by serving as governor of Georgia.

In 1857 the Democratic party convention had become so hopelessly deadlocked after twenty stormy ballots that a committee was chosen to select a candidate. Unable to agree on any of the leading contenders, they chose Brown as a compromise candidate. The choice of the relatively unknown mountaineer dismayed Democratic party leaders. Although the thirty-six-year-old Brown had served one term in the Georgia Senate and had been judge of the Blue Ridge Circuit for two years, few politicians outside of the north Georgia mountains had heard of him. Robert Toombs was so aghast when he heard of his nomination that he reportedly exclaimed, "Who in the hell is Joe Brown!"

Brown faced a formidable opponent in Benjamin H. Hill, a popular and experienced leader and one of the best orators the state ever produced. By contrast, Brown was not an eloquent speaker and his voice was harsh and twangy. But the homespun mountaineer was courageous, intelligent, and forceful, and his unpretentious appearance and simple logic appealed to the common people who voted for him in overwhelming numbers. In a spirited campaign Brown defeated Hill by 10,000 votes.

Since Brown lacked the wealth, experience, and distinguished family ties of his recent predecessors, many expected him to seek guidance from the state's older respected leaders. That expectation never materialized, as the young governor showed surprising strength and independence in taking charge of state affairs. His boldness became apparent at his inauguration. A staunch Baptist, he put an end to the drinking and rowdiness at the ceremony which traditionally left the governor's mansion in a shambles every two years. Instead of an open-house melee, he held a series of orderly receptions. He displayed more independence when he vetoed legislative efforts to infringe upon the governor's pardoning power. He made the state-owned Western and Atlantic Railroad an important source of patronage, but also gave it efficient management by appointing Dr. John W. Lewis superintendent. Under his leadership it became a very profitable operation. Indeed by 1860 the Western and Atlantic was earning $500,000 a year. In 1858 Brown induced the legislature to set aside $100,000 annually from the profits of the W & A for public education. Under Brown's guidance the state finally made substantial progress toward establishing a comprehensive system of public education. Regrettably, the Civil War soon nullified those efforts.

After proving his ability in his first term, Brown easily was reelected in 1859 over Warren Akin, a Methodist preacher and lawyer from Cassville. In 1861, as the state prepared for war, he defeated Eugenius A. Nisbet, a distinguished lawyer and judge, by a vote of 46,493 to 32,802; and in 1863, with overwhelming support from the soldiers, he won a fourth term, receiving more votes than the combined total for Joshua Hill and Timothy Furlow.

An ardent states' righter, Brown became a rabid secessionist when Abraham Lincoln was elected president. Immediately after Lincoln's election, he began to prepare the state for war. Requesting a $1,000,000 appropriation to arm the state, Brown ordered munitions from other states and European countries. Before Georgia officially seceded on 19 January

1861, he seized Fort Pulaski, the federal fort near Savannah, and immediately after secession he captured the federal arsenal at Augusta. Using additional funds borrowed from banks, the governor prepared the coastal defenses, purchased lathes and boring machines, converted railroad machine shops to the manufacturing of gun barrels, established factories for making clothes, shoes, and blankets, and organized and equipped numerous battalions and regiments. Joseph H. Parks, Brown's excellent biographer, doubts if any Confederate official worked harder or more efficiently than Brown in preparing for Southern defense during the early months of the war. Brown continued to make strenuous efforts throughout the war to equip the soldiers in the field and to aid the needy, especially orphans and widows.

Soon Brown was in conflict with Confederate authorities over the recruiting of troops and the commissioning of officers, thus beginning a controversy that would continue throughout the war. During the war Confederate President Jefferson Davis suffered severe headaches. Brown must have caused some of them, for he quarreled publicly with Davis over conscription, jurisdiction of troops, suspension of habeas corpus, taxes, and confiscation of property without compensation. By the spring of 1863 Brown advocated the removal of President Davis from authority. According to Professor Parks, "Brown had built up an aversion to everything that emanated from Richmond." Brown clearly displayed greater loyalty to Georgia than to the Confederacy, and his vision rarely extended beyond the Savannah River. Though he rallied the people of Georgia and utilized the state's resources with unusual vigor, his fanatical devotion to state sovereignty undoubtedly weakened the Confederate war effort.

Following the Confederate surrender in April 1865, Brown was arrested and jailed briefly in Washington, D. C. until he was pardoned by President Andrew Johnson. Resigning as governor in June 1865, he urged the people to accept first the presidential plan of reconstruction and later the Radical plan.

Having a realistic grasp of the military-political situation, he explained that further opposition was futile and would only prolong military control of the state. If the Confederacy could not withstand the Northern onslaught when it had armies in the field, he reasoned, it certainly could not resist without troops. By late 1866 Brown even urged Georgia to approve the Fourteenth Amendment and accept universal suffrage. In urging such compliance at this time, he was almost alone among Georgia

Fig.30. Joseph E. Brown

political leaders. Consequently, he was bitterly denounced throughout the state as a selfish, scheming traitor to his state who had been bought by his former enemies. Brown's enormous popularity vanished quickly.

Holding no office, Brown was influential in the election of Rufus Bullock, a Republican, as governor. In 1868 Governor Bullock rewarded him with an appointment as chief justice of the Georgia Supreme Court. In May 1868 Brown went to Chicago as a delegate to the Republican national convention and assisted in the nomination of Ulysses S. Grant. In December 1870 he resigned as chief justice so that he could devote more time to his business interests. Now making Atlanta his home, he practiced law and made lucrative real estate investments in south Georgia, northwest Georgia, and in Fulton and DeKalb counties. He headed a company which leased the Western and Atlantic Railroad from the state from 1870 to 1890. In 1873 he formed the Dade Coal Company. He also became president of the Walker Iron and Coal Company and the Rising

Fawn Iron Company. These enterprises made him one of the state's wealthiest men, and it is difficult to determine whether Brown achieved more success in business or in politics.

By shifting his political allegiances to meet the existing conditions, Brown managed to remain in a position of power and influence almost continuously from 1857 to 1891. He was a Democrat until 1860, a Confederate during the Civil War, a Unionist in 1865, a Republican while that party was in power in Georgia, and a Democrat thereafter. When the Republican regime was driven out of the state in disgrace, Brown re-entered the Democratic party and soon became one of its most powerful leaders. In 1880 Governor Alfred H. Colquitt appointed Brown to the United States Senate, where he served until 1891. Together with John B. Gordon and Alfred H. Colquitt he formed the "Bourbon Triumvirate," which dominated Georgia politics in the 1880s.

In addition to his business and political pursuits, Brown was a philanthropist of note. He made donations of $50,000 to the University of Georgia and to the Southern Baptist Theological Seminary in Louisville, Kentucky. He also made numerous gifts to Mercer College and to various Baptist churches. His interest in education was a lifetime concern. Brown served on the Board of Trustees of the University of Georgia from 1857 to 1889 and on the Atlanta Board of Education from 1869 to 1888.

In poor health the last fifteen years of his life, Brown died on 30 November 1894. After his body lay in state in the capitol rotunda, he was buried in Oakland Cemetery in Atlanta. Estimates of his wealth range from $1.5 million to $12 million.

Recognized as a man of superior abilities, Brown was controversial in his own day and has remained so with historians since then. Critics refer to him as "the chameleon of Georgia politics" and regard him as a political and economic opportunist. Although numerous investigations failed to implicate him in any illegal activities, suspicions remained, and he has never received the esteem of the people of Georgia in any way commensurate to the offices he held. No county bears his name and few markers commemorate his achievements. The statue of Brown and his wife on Capitol Square, unlike all the other statues there, was not financed by public funds or popular subscriptions—it was placed there by members of his own family. Thus the powerful and influential Brown remains one of Georgia's most enigmatic statesmen.

James Johnson
1865

He was a courageous Unionist

James Johnson, who served briefly as Georgia's provisional governor in 1865, was of Scottish ancestry, born in Robinson County, North Carolina, on 12 February 1811. The son of Peter and Nancy McNeil Johnson, he attended the University of Georgia, aided by a loan from the Presbyterian Society of Athens. Earning a bachelor's degree in 1832, he shared first honors with Alexander Stephens and William H. Crawford, Jr. In 1834 he married Ann Harris of Jones County, and they had one son, Walter H. Johnson, who served for many years as United States revenue collector in Atlanta. Like Joseph E. Brown, Johnson taught school for a brief period while he studied law. Admitted to the bar in 1835, he opened a practice in Columbus and soon gained the respect of his peers.

A man of firm convictions, Johnson was not easily swayed by popular opinion and often took unpopular political positions. A staunch Whig, he was elected to the Thirty-second Congress (1851–1853), defeating Henry L. Benning. When he sought reelection two years later, he was defeated by Alfred H. Colquitt, who would later serve as governor and United States senator. In 1857 Johnson was a delegate to the state convention of the American party, and he supported Warren Akin in his futile race against Joseph E. Brown. An opponent of secession, Johnson remained loyal to the Union and did not participate in the Civil War. At the end of the war President Andrew Johnson attempted to implement his plan of reconstruction by elevating Unionists to positions of authority in the Southern states. On 17 June 1865, he named James Johnson provisional governor of Georgia. Though not related, the two Johnsons were friends, having served together in Congress. The appointment surprised most Georgians who expected Joshua Hill to be named, but the choice of the plain, unassuming, slightly bald Johnson was well received throughout the state.

Following instructions from the president, Governor Johnson called for the election of delegates to a state convention which was to meet in Milledgeville on the fourth Wednesday in October 1865. Since most of the state's top leaders had not yet taken the amnesty oath, they were ineligible to vote or serve in the convention. Upon opening the convention,

Fig.31. James Johnson

Johnson urged the delegates to comply with the president's requirements
for political restoration. With leadership provided by two anti-secession
lawyers, Herschel V. Johnson and Charles J. Jenkins, the convention
repealed the state ordinance of secession, abolished slavery, and repudi-
ated the state's $18 million war debt. Only the debt issue provoked much
controversy, and it was adopted on 7 November, the day before the convention adjourned. In addition, the convention also produced a new state
constitution. The Constitution of 1865 made few changes in the Constitution of 1861. The most significant ones prohibited slavery, limited the

governor to two successive terms, gave the legislature the power to select judges of both the supreme court and the superior courts, and had the supreme court meet at the seat of government. It retained universal white male suffrage with no disqualifications because of the war, and added a new clause prohibiting "the marriage relation between white persons and persons of African descent." The convention also ordered an election for governor and other officials.

On 15 November 1865, Charles J. Jenkins was elected without opposition. Though Johnson knew that his days in office were numbered and that the people were eager to be rid of him, his message to the new legislature offered sound recommendations for the welfare of the state. The legislature, which assembled on 4 December, followed his advice by ratifying the Thirteenth Amendment. On 19 December, Johnson relinquished his office to his successor, who had been inaugurated five days earlier.

At the president's suggestion Johnson sought a seat in the United States Senate, but the legislature selected Herschel V. Johnson and Alexander Stephens instead. As a reward for his loyal service, Johnson was appointed United States collector of customs at Savannah, a position he held from 1866 to 1869, when he became judge of the Superior Court of the Chattahoochee Circuit. In 1875 he retired from the bench and resumed his law practice in Columbus. His last years were spent in quiet retirement with his son. He died on 20 November 1891 and was buried in Linwood Cemetery in Columbus.

Being a Whig and a Republican in an overwhelmingly Democratic state, Johnson lacked the popular appeal of contemporaries, such as Stephens, Brown, Colquitt, and others. Consequently, his political impact was limited. Yet, when given the opportunity, he served the state well. A distinguished lawyer, he was recognized as an able and courageous judge; as provisional governor, he conducted the state's affairs impartially under adverse circumstances. In an obituary the editor of the *Columbus Enquirer-Sun* wrote: "Judge Johnson was a man of remarkable character, and although differing on the vital issues of the day with the vast majority of his people, always had their respect and esteem. He was a man of strong convictions, and was noted for his moral courage and his strict adherence to what he conceded his duty."

Charles Jones Jenkins
1865-1868

He defiantly opposed the Radical Republicans

Charles J. Jenkins, Georgia's first popularly elected governor after the Civil War, had a long and fruitful career of public service which spanned nearly half a century. The only son of Charles Jones Jenkins, he was born on the family plantation in Beauford District, South Carolina, on 6 January 1805. When Jenkins was eleven years old, his family moved to Jefferson County, Georgia. Studious and thoughtful, Jenkins was educated at Mt. Zion Academy in Hancock County, Willington Academy in Abbeville District, South Carolina, and the University of Georgia. Transferring to Union College in Schenectady, New York, after his sophomore year, he received his bachelor's degree in 1824. A member of Phi Beta Kappa, he was graduated third in his class. After reading law with John M. Berrien in Savannah, he was admitted to the bar in 1826 and began the practice of law in Sandersville, but moved to Augusta in 1829.

Like many talented young lawyers, he was attracted to politics. From 1831 to 1834 he served as solicitor of the Middle Circuit of state courts. In 1830 he was elected to the Georgia House of Representatives from Richmond County as a member of the Troup party and continued to serve intermittently throughout the 1830s and 1840s. Gravitating to the Whig party, he emerged as a leader, serving as speaker in 1840, 1843, 1845, and 1847. At the state convention of December 1850, Jenkins was largely responsible for the adoption of the "Georgia Platform," which offered a conciliatory program regarding slavery in the territories. Attracting national attention, he was offered the post of secretary of the interior by President Millard Fillmore, but declined it. Defeated in the gubernatorial race of 1853 by Herschel V. Johnson, he was out of office until 1856 when he was appointed to the Georgia Senate to fill the unexpired term of Andrew J. Miller, who had died. In 1860 Governor Brown appointed Jenkins associate justice of the Georgia Supreme Court, a position he held throughout the Civil War.

Although Jenkins upheld the right of secession, he believed that Georgia should not secede until the Lincoln administration committed some overt act. He considered secession a blunder but supported the Confederacy nonetheless. Pardoned by President Andrew Johnson, Jenkins, along with Herschel V. Johnson, dominated the state convention which wrote the Constitution of 1865. Elected governor without opposition, he succeeded Governor James Johnson on 19 December 1865.

Jenkins found the state in a deplorable condition when he became the chief executive. The war had devastated Georgia's economy. Few farms, factories, or railroads functioned effectively. The people were destitute, the state treasury was empty, and taxes had not been collected for a year. Securing loans of $400,000 from New York banks and issuing bonds of $3.6 million, Jenkins managed to put the Western and Atlantic Railroad in working condition, rebuild some of the infrastructure, and restore the normal functions of government. With modest tax increases he also provided relief for veterans and the poor.

Convinced that military rule in the South was unconstitutional, Jenkins refused to cooperate with Radical Republicans or acquiesce in congressional efforts to extend civil rights to freedmen, establish new political leadership in the South, punish Confederate leaders, and prolong military occupation. He filed unsuccessful suits in the United States Supreme Court to overturn military rule and to block the implementation of the Reconstruction Acts. He pleaded with federal officials for removal of Union troops and for relief measures to alleviate the suffering, but little aid was provided. The governor opposed ratification of the Fourteenth Amendment, and his view prevailed in the legislature with only two dissenting votes. Although his firm defiance brought few tangible results, it was popular with the people of Georgia.

Having been at loggerheads with the Radicals for two years, Jenkins's final act of defiance came in January 1868. Under the Reconstruction Acts, Georgia was ordered to write a new state constitution to incorporate the Fourteenth Amendment and Negro suffrage. Elections for that purpose were held in October 1867, and the convention, which assembled in Atlanta in December, eventually produced the new state constitution. When General George Meade, commander of the U.S. Third Military District, ordered the state to pay the $40,000 cost of the convention, Jenkins objected, pointing out that the legislature had not authorized such an expenditure. Besides, he added, since the federal government had called for the convention, it ought to pay for it. General Meade then ordered Jenkins removed from office.

In leaving the governor's mansion in Milledgeville, Jenkins carried with him $400,000 in state funds, the seal of the Executive Department, and the executive records of his term of office. During a self-imposed

Fig.32. Charles J. Jenkins

two-year exile from the state, he deposited the money in a New York bank, spent time in Halifax, Nova Scotia, and toured Europe before returning to Augusta in 1870. In January 1872, with Georgia finally in "safe" hands, he returned all of the state property intact to Governor James M. Smith, whom he considered the first legally elected governor since his dismissal.

Jenkins spent his remaining years in semiretirement at his home in Summerville, emerging for one last public duty—serving as president of the state constitutional convention of 1877. He served as president of the Merchants and Planters Bank and for many years was a member of the Board of Trustees of the University of Georgia. He died on 14 June 1883, at the age of seventy-eight.

On 24 May 1832, Jenkins married Sarah Jones of Burke County, and they had three children: Mary, Charles, and Sara. His wife died in 1849, and five years later he married Emily Gertrude Barnes of Philadelphia, Pennsylvania.

A man of impeccable integrity, Jenkins was respected by contemporaries as a Christian gentleman. In 1905 the state named a county for him.

Thomas Howard Ruger
1868

He had a distinguished military career

Brevet Brigadier General Thomas H. Ruger served as provisional governor of Georgia from 13 January to 4 July 1868. Although he had a long and distinguished military career, his impact upon Georgia was negligible. During the brief period he was the state's chief executive, political power actually resided with his superior officer, General George Meade, whose orders Ruger discharged "impartially and faithfully, to the satisfaction of his superiors."

Meade received a popular welcome in Georgia when he replaced General John Pope as the commander of the Third Military District in late December 1867, but his popularity vanished two weeks later when he removed Governor Jenkins from office. The state constitutional convention, which met in Atlanta from December 1867 to March 1868, was a strongly Republican, conservative body which avoided the excesses and corruption that plagued many Southern states in this period. In a businesslike manner the 169 delegates adopted numerous positive reforms in the Constitution of 1868. It abolished imprisonment for debt, granted women more rights, gave black men the right to vote, and made Atlanta the state capital. When Governor Jenkins refused to sign a warrant to pay for this convention, General Meade removed him, the state treasurer, the secretary of state, and the comptroller general from office, thus abruptly ending civil government. Meade appointed Ruger provisional governor, Captain Charles F. Rockwell treasurer, and Captain Charles Wheaton comptroller general and secretary of state. For the first time in history, Georgia was governed by army officers imposed upon the state by force.

Deposed Governor Jenkins sought an injunction against Generals Grant, Meade, and Ruger, but the United States Supreme Court refused to act. In the meantime General Meade set 20 April 1868 as the date for ratifying the new constitution and for electing state officers. The Republicans easily agreed on Rufus Bullock as their nominee, and he quickly received the backing of former governor Brown. The Democrats, now trying to rebuild their party, faced severe obstacles. Their first nominee, Judge Augustus Reese, was declared ineligible by Meade, as was their second choice, Judge David Irwin. Finally, Meade accepted their third nominee, General John B. Gordon, since he had not held political office before the war. The Democrats failed to defeat either the constitution or Bullock. The constitution was adopted by a majority of 18,000 votes, and Bullock defeated Gordon by a majority of 7,000.

Meade convened the newly-elected legislature which selected Joshua Hill and H.V.M. Miller as United States senators and ratified the Fourteenth Amendment. After Bullock was inaugurated as governor, Meade notified Washington that Georgia had complied with all of the demands of Congress. Meade had removed Ruger on 4 July to make room for Bullock, and on 30 July he withdrew military authority from Georgia's government.

Although essentially a caretaker during his five and a half months as provisional governor, Ruger inaugurated the infamous convict-lease system. Acting on an 1866 statute that gave the governor discretionary power to lease convicts and relieve the state of prison expenses, he leased one hundred prisoners to William A. Fort of Rome for work on railroad construction. Two days before leaving office, he executed a second lease. His successors expanded this policy in the years which followed. Friendly, considerate, and wholly without arrogance, Ruger, the last of the Milledgeville governors, was highly regarded by the people of Milledgeville.

Ruger was born on 2 April 1833 in Lima, New York, the son of Thomas Jefferson and Maria Hutchins Ruger. His father, an Episcopal minister, moved his family to Janesville, Wisconsin, when Ruger was thirteen. A quiet, diligent student, Ruger was graduated from West Point in 1854, third in his class. Resigning his commission a year later, he began the practice of law in Janesville.

When the Civil War began, he was made lieutenant colonel of the Third Wisconsin and served throughout the war, rising to brevet major general in November 1864. He saw action at Antietam and Gettysburg, helped subdue the draft riot in New York City in 1863, fought in the western theater under General William Sherman, and was in North Carolina when the war ended. Reverting to the rank of colonel after the war, he commanded the Department of North Carolina for a year prior to his appointment as provisional governor of Georgia.

In 1871 Ruger was appointed superintendent of the United States Military Academy and served for five years, during which time he earned a reputation for high scholastic standards and strict discipline. During the next two decades he held numerous commands in the South and West and attained the permanent rank of major general in 1895. He retired in

Fig.33. Thomas H. Ruger

1897 on his sixty-fourth birthday.

After traveling in Europe for two years with his family, he settled in Samford, Connecticut, where he spent his last years in quiet retirement enjoying his books and his garden. Ruger died on 3 June 1907, survived by his wife, Helen Lydia Moore Ruger, whom he had married in 1857, and their two daughters, Helen and Anna.

Rufus Brown Bullock
1868–1871

Georgia's first elected Republican governor

Rufus Bullock, Georgia's first elected Republican governor, was born in Bethlehem, New York, on 28 March 1834. When he was six years old, his parents, Volckert Vreeder and Jane Eliza Brown Bullock, moved the family to Albion, New York. After being graduated from Albion Academy in 1850, Bullock soon became an expert in the field of telegraphy and supervised the construction of telegraph lines in New York City, Buffalo, Albany, Philadelphia, and other Northern cities. In 1859, as an assistant superintendent of the Adams Express Company, he was sent to Augusta, Georgia, to expand lines and develop business in that area. By 1860 Bullock was directing the affairs of the Southern Express Company, which had purchased the Adams Express Company and was extending telegraph lines throughout the South. In 1860 he married Marie Elizabeth Salisbury of Pawtucket, Rhode Island, and they had four children: Volckert Vreeder, Rufus, Cornelia, and Hugh. Although opposed to secession, Bullock served the Confederacy loyally in a civilian capacity. As an adjunct to the Confederate Quartermaster Corps, the Southern Express Company built badly needed telegraph lines and transported packages throughout the South. In April 1865, Bullock, then an acting lieutenant colonel in charge of railroad transportation, surrendered with General Robert E. Lee's Army of Northern Virginia at Appomattox Courthouse.

Returning to Augusta after the war, Bullock realized that the South, though devastated by war and poverty, offered great opportunities for enterprising businessmen. By securing capital from New York, he organized the First National Bank of Augusta and soon became its president. Diversifying his interests, he also became president of the Southern Porcelain Manufacturing Company and the Macon and Augusta Railroad. Unable to rebuild the railroad for lack of capital, he again sought aid from wealthy interests in New York but was rebuffed. Georgia's unstable political situation restrained capitalists from making large investments in the state. Told that he could have all the money he wanted if he could bring Georgia back into the Union, Bullock entered the political arena. He later stated that he became involved in Reconstruction "with no other end in view except the hastening of Georgia's recovery from the effects of the war."

A large, handsome, affable man, Bullock became a staunch Republican, firmly committed both to economic expansion and to equal rights for all. Chosen as a delegate to the constitutional convention (December 1867 to March 1868), he emerged as a dominant political force. With the support of Republicans, blacks, the debtor class, and former governor Joseph E. Brown, he then defeated John B. Gordon in the gubernatorial contest of 1868 by a vote of 83,527 to 76,356. By order of Major General George C. Meade, Bullock replaced Thomas H. Ruger as provisional governor on 4 July and was inaugurated to serve his elected term on 22 July.

Taking office at a most inopportune time, Bullock faced intense opposition from the Democratic party, the old planter leadership, most of the legislature, and the Ku Klux Klan. To accomplish his goals—or even remain in office—he was utterly dependent upon the unwavering support of federal troops and the Congress, which, unfortunately, he failed to receive. His efforts to purge the legislature of those members not qualified under the Test Act were thwarted by General Meade, who refused to intervene. After the legislature ratified the Fourteenth Amendment, Meade reported to Washington that the state had complied with the demands of Congress, and on 30 July military authority was withdrawn. The legislature elected Joshua Hill and H. V. M. Miller as United States senators in preference to Bullock's choices, former governor Joseph E. Brown and Foster Blodgett, a political crony from Augusta. Over Bullock's strenuous objections, the legislature then expelled its black members—three senators and twenty-nine representatives. Losing control of the state government, Bullock sought the reinstitution of military rule. In testimony before Congress he asserted that Georgia had not complied with federal laws and that there was no "adequate protection for life and property, the maintenance of peace and good order, and the free expression of political opinion."

Congress did not respond immediately, but later events reinforced Bullock's position. The increased activity of the Ku Klux Klan, a race riot in Camilla, a sharp decrease in black voting in the 1868 presidential race, and the legislature's refusal to ratify the Fifteenth Amendment finally prompted Congress to act. After March 1869 Georgia's congressmen were excluded on a technicality, her senators were not seated, and the army was again given jurisdiction over the state with General Alfred H.

Fig.34. Rufus B. Bullock

Terry in command. The legislature that convened in January 1870 was more to Bullock's liking. With the assistance of the military, the black members were restored and Bullock's critics were purged. The legislature then approved the Fifteenth Amendment.

A controversial entrepreneur who shared Bullock's economic vision and cooperated with him to forge a new Georgia was Hannibal I. Kimball. At a cost of $600,000 he built the Kimball House, Atlanta's finest hotel, which became the city's business and social center. He helped finance Union Passenger Depot, served as president of Atlanta's first cotton factory, built another hotel, and profited handsomely when the state purchased his opera house to be used as the new capitol. During Bullock's administration the state legislature passed thirty-eight bills which authorized nearly $8 million in state bond support for railroads. As president of seven Georgia railroads, Kimball received the bulk of that state aid. When Kimball left the state in 1871 with a debt of $5 million owed primarily to New York banks, critics accused him of defrauding the public and misusing state funds. A state investigating committee charged him with conspiring with Bullock to swindle the state. It claimed that he had been paid for fifty railroad cars that he never delivered. In 1874 Kimball returned to Georgia, denied that Bullock and he were partners, and dared anyone to prove he had done anything illegal. Despite a diligent investigation, the state legislature found no evidence to indict him of any illegal activity. Bullock consistently defended his friend and claimed that no one in the past fifty years had done as much as Kimball to promote Georgia's prosperity.

On 15 July 1870, Congress decided that Georgia had been chastised sufficiently and now was entitled to representation. With the seating of Senators Hill and Miller and the congressional delegation, Georgia was again officially in the Union. Bullock, who barely held power with the support of federal troops, could not remain in office without them. The election of large Democratic majorities in both houses of the legislature convinced Bullock that when the legislature convened in November 1871, its first order of business would be his impeachment. To avoid that disgrace he secretly resigned on 23 October and fled the state.

Contemporaries criticized Bullock's administration with unrestrained bitterness, and Bullock himself became the most bitterly assailed and vilified governor in the state's entire history. He was condemned as a carpetbagger and scalawag who squandered the state's meager resources, lined the pockets of his friends, and attempted to impose a Republican despotism on the state. Writing in 1881, journalist I. W. Avery asserted that Bullock's administration was "continuously worthy of censure. It grew in its criminality. It was unbrokenly evil." The Avery interpretation of Bullock, with slightly more restraint, appears in practically all historical accounts of Reconstruction in Georgia, including modern scholarly accounts, such as *The Reconstruction of Georgia* (1966) by Alan Conway and *A History of Georgia* (1977), edited by Kenneth Coleman. Though

Bullock's opponents grossly exaggerated, state expenditures did rise significantly during his administration, especially the costs of operating the state-owned Western and Atlantic Railroad under the leadership of Foster Blodgett. With Bullock's support, the legislature in 1870 began the policy of leasing the railroad. The first lease awarded the state $25,000 a month for twenty years. Leasing proved so successful that the state has continued that policy to the present. Bullock admitted that the state debt had increased by $4.8 million during his administration, but he argued that the money had been wisely invested in redeeming prewar debts, improving public schools, moving the capital from Milledgeville to Atlanta, and constructing more than six hundred miles of railroad.

For several years Bullock remained in New York, a fugitive from Georgia justice. Finally, in 1876, he returned to Atlanta to face his accusers. After several delays, prosecutors tried Bullock in two separate cases, *State v. Bullock* and *State v. Bullock, Blodgett, and E. N. Kimball.* In January 1878 both juries returned verdicts of not guilty. The prosecutor admitted that "the most searching investigation failed to disclose any evidence of his guilt, and he was promptly acquitted by a Democratic jury." Despite those verdicts, subsequent historical accounts invariably have depicted Bullock in an unfavorable light. Even the above-mentioned Conway and Coleman books indict him as a lax or inept administrator who allowed corruption to flourish.

A more favorable interpretation of Bullock, however, has appeared in the recent work of Russell Duncan. In a thoroughly researched 1988 dissertation and in *Entrepreneur for Equality,* the first full-length biography of Bullock, he has argued convincingly that Bullock provided competent and principled leadership but was a victim of partisan politics. His "crime" was not in violating any law or in misusing his office, Duncan argues; rather, it was in attempting to implement unpopular Radical Reconstruction policies, including equal rights for blacks. Such policies were anathema to most white Georgians. Several years later, with blacks relegated to an inferior status and conservative Democrats firmly in control of state government, Bullock, then out of office and no longer a threat to Georgia traditions, could receive justice in a Georgia courtroom.

Continuing to reside in Atlanta, Bullock became one of the city's most prominent citizens, serving as junior and senior warden at St. Philip's Episcopal Church, president and director of Atlanta's first cotton mill, president of the Atlanta Chamber of Commerce, president of the Commercial Club, vice president of the Capital City Club, and member of the Piedmont Driving Club. He accompanied Henry Grady on his famous visit to New York City in 1889, served as a member of the official delegation that greeted President Benjamin Harrison when he visited Atlanta in 1891, and served as master of ceremonies for the Atlanta Cotton States and International Exposition in 1895. Clearly, by the end of the century, Bullock had become an accepted member of Atlanta's business and cultural elite.

In 1903, after withdrawing from his business interests, Bullock, then in declining health, moved from Atlanta to his former home in Albion, where he died on 27 April 1907. The *Atlanta Constitution*, which had criticized Bullock unmercifully when he was governor, acknowledged in an obituary that "few Georgians, whether by birth or adoption, did more real good for the state than he."

Bullock's life was a series of contrasts and contradictions. A Yankee by birth, he lived most of his adult years in the South. An opponent of secession, he served the Confederacy loyally. A friendly, kindly, generous man, he was bitterly hated in the Reconstruction era. Accused of gross misdeeds as governor, he was never convicted of any of them. Driven from the state in disgrace, he became one of Atlanta's leading citizens. Without question he possessed exceptional ability, and, thanks to the research of Duncan, it now appears that he has been unfairly maligned.

Benjamin F. Conley
1871-1872

He was Georgia's last Republican governor

The abrupt resignation of Rufus Bullock made President of the Senate Benjamin F. Conley the new governor. Sworn in on 30 October 1871, he immediately became embroiled in a controversy over how long he was entitled to serve. Conley claimed he was entitled to the remainder of Bullock's term, but the new legislature, which convened two days after he was sworn in, insisted that Conley's term already had expired, since he was no longer president of the Senate or even a senator. The legislature, now controlled by the Democrats, argued that L. M. Trammell, the new president of the Senate, should be the chief executive. The partisan battle finally was resolved by a compromise. A special gubernatorial election was set for the third Tuesday in December, and Conley was allowed to serve until the newly-elected governor was inaugurated. Conley vetoed the bill, but it was passed over his veto, and he served until James M. Smith was inaugurated on 12 January 1872.

Though a staunch Republican and a close associate of Governor Bullock, Conley was cast from a different mold. Born in New Jersey on 1 March 1815, he moved to Augusta, Georgia, when he was fifteen. Working as a clerk, he applied himself with such diligence that he accumulated enough capital to go into business for himself. His enterprise prospered, and he soon became one of the city's rising young merchants. In politics he also advanced rapidly. Regarded as one of the ablest leaders of the Whig party, he was a member of the city council of Augusta for twelve years before serving as mayor from 1857 to 1859. An uncompromising Unionist, Conley took no part in the Civil War, retiring to his plantation in Montgomery County, Alabama, for the duration of the fighting. Returning to Augusta after the war, he resumed his business interests and by 1868 had become president of the Macon and Augusta Railroad. An ardent supporter of Republican Reconstruction policies, he was a delegate to the constitutional convention that met in Atlanta from December 1867 to March 1868. The election in April ratified the state constitution, elected Bullock governor, and sent Conley to the state Senate. When the new legislature convened on 4 July, Conley, a political ally of Governor Bullock, was chosen president of the Senate by vote of 23 to 17. A sen-

Fig.35. Benjamin Conley

sible and fair man, he was regarded as an effective presiding officer.

As governor, Conley delivered a conciliatory message to the legislature, seeking to advance the interests of the state "without reference to race, color, or party alliance." The state, he continued, had had enough of "wrangling and strife," and needed "repose and quiet, which can never be promoted by continually fomenting political strife." Despite his efforts, political divisiveness continued. Opposed by a hostile Democratic legislature, Conley, a lame-duck governor associated with the unpopular Bullock regime, accomplished little during his two months and twelve days as governor. His vetoes of several minor bills were overridden by the legislature. His pardon of Foster Blodgett, the controversial superintendent of the Western and Atlantic Railroad, brought criticism, as did his disposal of 270,000 acres of land under the Morrill Act for only $243,000. Conley was by no means a popular governor, but he managed to avoid the scorn heaped on his predecessor and was generally respected by his opponents for his integrity and character. Writing in 1881, I. W. Avery, who rarely discerned any good in Republicans, admitted that Conley's administration was "a very great improvement on Gov. Bullock's." And the equally partisan Rebecca Latimer Felton noted that "nobody has charged any irregularity upon him, although he was a Republican."

After leaving office, Conley lived in Augusta until President Grant appointed him postmaster of Atlanta, a position he held from 30 July 1875 until 12 October 1883. A popular postmaster, he was regarded as one of Atlanta's leading citizens. Active in civic and religious affairs, he was the founder of the Washington Lodge of Odd Fellows and served as grandmaster of that organization. Deeply committed to the Christian faith, Conley was for many years senior warden of St. Philip's Church in Atlanta, having previously been warden of St. Paul's Church in Augusta. He delighted in doing works of charity, especially caring for the poor in his neighborhood. Growing feeble in his last years, he died suddenly at his home in Atlanta on 10 January 1886. Survived by his widow, Sarah Semmes Conley, and their two sons, John L. and Morris J., Conley was buried in the Magnolia Cemetery in Augusta beside his daughter Mary.

Despite holding views that were unpopular with the majority of Georgians, Conley's courage, honesty, and integrity were admired by his contemporaries, and his obituaries stress his strong character, love of family, and generous nature.

After the flight of Governor Bullock, a correspondent for the *New York Herald* made the following observation: "So far as Georgia is concerned there is no Republican party in the State. Bullock has `gone back on it'; Brown doesn't recognize it and all the other leaders, big fish and sardines alike, repudiate it." His words were more prophetic than he realized. Conley was Georgia's last Republican governor in the Reconstruction era, and for nearly a century thereafter the Republican party did not even exist in the state.

James Milton Smith
1872–1877

One of the boldest men in the history of Georgia

James M. Smith, a plain and practical man who for a time worked as a blacksmith, had the distinction of being elected governor without opposition. In the special election of December 1871 to fill the unexpired term of Governor Bullock, the Republican candidate withdrew from the race, thereby giving Smith the victory unopposed. His inauguration on 12 January was a time of rejoicing for most white Georgians, since it marked the return of the Democrats to power after five years of Republican rule.

A man of strong intellect and character, Smith was well-prepared for the challenges he faced. Born in Twiggs County on 24 October 1823, he was the son of James M. Smith, Sr., a poor farmer blacksmith, and Martha Smith. He attended school in Monroe County, studied law, and was admitted to the bar in 1846. Locating in Thomaston, he soon developed a large and lucrative practice. Attracted to politics, Smith was the Democratic candidate for Congress for the Third District in 1855, but was defeated by Judge Robert P. Trippe of the American party. Years later, when Smith was governor, he would appoint Trippe to the Georgia Supreme Court. At the outbreak of the Civil War, Smith enlisted in the Thirteenth Regiment of the Georgia Volunteer Infantry. He fought valiantly in the Army of Northern Virginia until receiving a severe wound at Cold Harbor in June 1862. Unfit for further combat, Smith, then a colonel, was elected to the Confederate Congress and served from 2 May 1864 until 18 March 1865. Resuming his law practice after the war, he formed a partnership with Colonel Peter W. Alexander, and together they built one of the outstanding firms in Columbus. An outspoken opponent of Radical Reconstruction, Smith was elected to the General Assembly in 1870 and rose to a position of leadership almost immediately. In December 1871 he was elected speaker of the house by vote of 135 to 21 and was nominated for governor by acclamation. After completing Bullock's unexpired term, Smith was reelected to a four-year term, defeating Dawson A Walker of Murray County by 60,000 votes.

Taking office after Bullock and Conley, Smith faced difficult problems—none more pressing than the state's financial condition. After studying the available records the legislature voided bonds worth $6.5 million, despite protests that honest debts were being repudiated. Pursuing a policy of fiscal restraint, Smith improved the state's credit, conducted state business efficiently without increasing taxes, and paid off a floating debt of $1.2 million. When Smith left office the bonded debt stood at $8,477,500 plus $2,688,000 in endorsed railroad bonds, and there was a cash balance in the treasury.

Appointing men of exceptional ability to high office was a characteristic of the Smith administration. When irregularities appeared in the Treasury Department, Smith replaced the popular treasurer, John A. Jones, with John W. Renfroe, who brought order and efficiency to that department. In 1874 the Department of Agriculture and the Office of State Geologist were formed. Smith named Dr. Thomas P. Janes to head the former and Dr. George Little the latter, and both provided capable leadership. Of even greater benefit to the state was Smith's choice of Gustavus J. Orr as state school commissioner. Orr served so effectively that he achieved national recognition. Smith also made admirable appointments to the Georgia Supreme Court, especially James Jackson and Logan Bleckley.

At the end of his term Smith sought a seat in the United States Senate, but the legislature chose Benjamin H. Hill instead. To appease the disappointed Smith, Governor Alfred Colquitt appointed him the first chairman of the Railroad Commission. At the expiration of that six-year term, Smith resumed his law practice in Columbus. In May 1887 Governor John B. Gordon appointed Smith judge of the Superior Court of the Chattahoochee Judicial Circuit, a position he accepted at a considerable financial sacrifice. The legislature elected him to a four-year term in November 1888, but long before completing that term he suffered a stroke. After being bedridden for weeks, he died on 25 November 1890.

Smith was married twice but had no children. On 8 June 1848, he married Hester Ann Brown, who died after a long illness on 31 July 1880. He married Sarah Marshall Welborn, a widow from Columbus, on 1 September 1881. Smith was buried in Alta Vista Cemetery in Gainesville beside his first wife.

Despite Rebecca Latimer Felton's charges that Smith was a governor who "knew his duty and did it not" and went out of office "unwept, unhonored and unsung," modern scholarly opinion holds that Smith had an honest and generally productive administration. Contemporary newspapers also praised him as a man of exceptional character and integrity.

Fig.36. James M. Smith

The *Atlanta Journal* declared his record as governor was "very credit-able," while the *Atlanta Constitution* described him as an honest man and "one of the boldest and most fearless men in the history of Georgia." Even more lavish in its praise was the *Columbus Enquirer-Sun* which stressed Smith's "intellectual ability and rugged honesty." It editorialized that Smith "never took a position without deliberation; but when he took it his convictions were unmovable and he had both the courage and the ability always to sustain them."

Alfred Holt Colquitt
1877-1882

Every act of his administration was attacked and falsified

Alfred H. Colquitt—lawyer, preacher, soldier, legislator, congressman, senator, and governor—was one-third of the "Bourbon Triumvirate," along with John B. Gordon and Joseph E. Brown. So completely did this trio dominate Georgia politics from 1872 to 1890 that they seemed to be playing musical chairs with the governorship and Georgia's United States Senate seats. The Bourbons were business-oriented Democrats who favored sectional reconciliation, industrialization, low taxes, and frugal government. These ideas, popularized by Henry Grady and the *Atlanta Constitution*, gained wide acceptance among Georgia voters, and politically the triumvirate was a winning combination. In simplest terms, Brown provided the brains; Gordon, the looks; and Colquitt, the religion. With Grady's talents the team was unbeatable.

Colquitt, the son of Senator Walter T. and Nancy Lane Colquitt, was born in Walton County on 20 April 1824. A graduate of Princeton in 1844, he studied law and was admitted to the bar in Columbus in 1846. After serving in the Mexican War as a staff officer with the rank of major, he settled in Macon and resumed his law practice. In 1848 he married Dorothy Tarver of Twiggs County. She died in 1855, and he then married his sister-in-law, Sarah Wimberly Tarver. From his first wife Colquitt inherited a plantation in Baker County which became his home thereafter.

A licensed Methodist minister, Colquitt was attracted to politics and, like his father, was a staunch pro-South Democrat. After serving as assistant secretary of the Georgia Senate, he was elected to Congress in 1852, defeating Unionist James Johnson, who later served as governor. Because of his wife's failing health he did not seek reelection in 1854. In 1859 he served in the state legislature and later was a member of the state secession convention. An advocate of secession, he immediately entered the Confederate army as a captain. He received numerous promotions and ended the war with the rank of major general. His most famous victory was at Olustee, Florida, in 1864, where his forces defeated a larger and better equipped Union army.

Fig. 37. Alfred H. Colquitt

After the war Colquitt farmed, practiced law, and opposed Congressional Reconstruction. In 1870 he served as president of both the state agricultural society and the Democratic state convention. In 1876 he was elected to a four-year term as governor, defeating the Republican candidate, Jonathan Norcross, by the largest majority recorded up to that time—111,297 to 33,443. In 1880, with the brilliant Henry Grady running his reelection campaign, he defeated Thomas Norwood of Savannah in a bitter fight to secure the Democratic nomination by a margin of 54,345 votes.

During his six years as governor Colquitt implemented the Bourbon philosophy and was particularly successful in strengthening the state's fiscal affairs. A general policy of government retrenchment saw reductions made in large expenditures as well as small ones, including postage, gas, printing, and stationery. His efficient administration reduced the public debt of more than $11 million to $9.6 million, paid the floating debt of $256,000, and lowered taxes. During Colquitt's term a convention, which met in Atlanta in July and August of 1877, wrote a new constitution that served the state until 1945. Although ex-governor Jenkins presided over the convention, Robert Toombs dominated the proceedings. Toombs, who was especially interested in safeguarding the state's finances, reportedly remarked that in the new constitution he had "locked the door to the Treasury and given the key to the people." One of the changes produced by the new constitution was reducing the governor's term from four years to two years. In December the voters approved the new constitution and selected Atlanta as the state capital in preference to Milledgeville.

Although the Colquitt administration adopted several constructive measures, the governor encountered strong opposition from members of his own party. According to journalist I. W. Avery, "every act of his administration was attacked and falsified." Colquitt made enemies by failing to satisfy job seekers. He claimed that 3,000 Democrats clamored for the thirty available jobs; thus he made thirty friends and 2,970 enemies. The governor was denounced so vehemently for endorsing bonds of the North-Eastern Railroad for $260,000 that he demanded a legislative investigation to clear his name. Although the committee reported that the charges against him were "vile and slanderous," suspicions remained. Additional investigations ultimately led to the impeachment and conviction of the comptroller and the impeachment and acquittal of the treasurer. The single event that aroused the most controversy was Colquitt's appointment of ex-governor Brown to fill the unexpired Senate term of General John B. Gordon, who resigned in May of 1880. Brown was still hated by many Georgians because of his stand on Reconstruction and Republican affiliation. When Gordon accepted a position with the Western and Atlantic Railroad, then leased by Brown, the cry of "Bargain and Corruption" filled the air.

At the end of his gubernatorial term Colquitt was appointed to the United States Senate to fill the unexpired term of Benjamin H. Hill, who had died in office. Colquitt served from 1883 until his death in 1894.

"Few men in any state have ever been called to meet and conquer greater trials in the executive chair," observed Senator John B. Gordon, and "none, perhaps, has ever emerged from a more critical and stormy administration to meet the almost universal and enthusiastic approval of the people and to be transferred by their votes to the Senate as a complete and triumphant vindication."

Like his father, Colquitt was a strong advocate of temperance and was interested in all religious and moral issues. An unpretentious and mild mannered Christian, he was president of the International Sunday School convention which met in Atlanta in 1878. His gentle nature and exemplary character made an impact on his contemporaries that seldom has been equalled. Regarded as one of Georgia's most outstanding political leaders of the nineteenth century, he died in Washington, D.C., on 26 March 1894. Colquitt was survived by his widow and six children—one son, Walter; three unmarried daughters, Hattie, Dorothy, and Laura; and two married daughters, Mrs. Marshall and Mrs. Thomas Newell. He was buried in Rose Hill Cemetery in Macon.

Alexander Hamilton Stephens
1882-1883

He was the vice president of the Confederacy

One of Georgia's most esteemed political leaders, Alexander Stephens held numerous public offices in a distinguished career that spanned nearly half a century. Of Scottish descent, he was born on a farm in Wilkes County on 11 February 1812, the son of Andrew Baskins and Margaret Grier Stephens. His mother died shortly after his birth, and his father and stepmother died when he was fourteen. Though poor, orphaned, and always in frail health, Stephens possessed a keen mind, an indomitable spirit, and a willingness to work—traits that enabled him to overcome these obstacles. He attended an academy at Washington, Georgia, where his admiration for his teacher, Reverend Alexander Hamilton Webster, led him to adopt Hamilton as a middle name. Citizens of Washington, expecting him to become a Presbyterian minister, financed his education both at the academy and at the University of Georgia, where he was graduated at the head of his class in 1832. He taught school for two years and repaid his benefactors before settling in 1834 at Crawfordville, where he soon developed a lucrative law practice.

Stephens's political career began with election to the Georgia House of Representatives in 1836. He served continuously until 1841 and then advanced to the Georgia Senate in 1842. In the legislature he supported construction of the Western and Atlantic Railroad, the creation of a state-supported system of public education, and more generous financing of the state university. Elected to Congress in 1843, he served for sixteen years and became one of the foremost Southern spokesmen. Although he supported the annexation of Texas, he detested President James K. Polk and opposed the Mexican War. He condemned the Wilmot Proviso and tried to block the acquisition of territory from Mexico, arguing that such territory would poison relations between the North and the South. Stephens backed Zachary Taylor until the president attempted to bring California and New Mexico into the Union as free states. He supported the Compromise of 1850 and, after becoming a convert to the concept of "popular sovereignty," also endorsed the Kansas-Nebraska Act of 1854. Originally a member of the States' Rights party of Crawford and Troup, he gravitated into the ranks of the Whigs, and in Congress was closely aligned with Henry Clay. With Robert Toombs and Howell Cobb, he helped form the Constitutional Union party to preserve the Compromise of 1850. When that party collapsed in 1852, he returned briefly to the Whig party, which disintegrated after 1854. The issue of slavery drove him into the Democratic party since it was the only national party disposed to protect Southern rights.

In 1859 Stephens retired from Congress, but the split in the Democratic party in 1860 brought him back into the political arena. With threats of secession filling the air, Stephens campaigned for the election of Stephen A. Douglas and decried disunion. The election of Abraham Lincoln convinced most of the state's leaders that Georgia should secede, but not Stephens. Having known Lincoln in Congress, he urged Georgians to be patient and give the Republican president a chance. Elected to the state secession convention, Stephens spoke against secession and voted against the measure. But, convinced that Georgia was going to secede anyway, he signed the ordinance of secession without protest. Despite his serious misgivings about secession, he was a delegate to the convention at Montgomery, Alabama, that organized the Confederate government. He helped write the provisional Confederate constitution and was chosen vice president of the Confederacy.

A moderate constitutionalist, Stephens was miscast in the role of revolutionary leader, and his unswerving devotion to states' rights and constitutional law led to numerous conflicts with President Jefferson Davis and the Confederate Congress. During the first year of the war he made patriotic speeches urging the people to do their utmost for the Confederate cause. But as the war progressed, he became increasingly disenchanted. He had a low regard for members of Congress and feared that President Davis was becoming a dictator. In the many controversies between Davis and Governor Joseph E. Brown of Georgia, Stephens usually sided with Brown. He publicly denounced major actions of the Confederate government, especially the conscription of troops, the suspension of habeas corpus, and proclamations of martial rule. From July 1863 to December 1864 he stayed away from Richmond, the Confederate capital. Unlike Davis, he willingly sought peace long before Appomattox. In fact, he was one of the Confederate commissioners at the Hampton Roads Conference on 3 February 1865, which discussed the possibility of peace with President Lincoln and Secretary of State William H. Seward. Stephens was arrested at his home, Liberty Hall, by Union troops on 11 May and imprisoned in Boston until 12 October, when he was

Fig.38. Alexander H. Stephens

released on parole.

Because he failed to understand that the war had changed the nation, its Constitution, and the South irrevocably, Stephens remained an "unreconstructed" rebel, observed Thomas E. Schott, his latest biographer. Denied a seat in the United States Senate, to which the Georgia legislature had elected him in January 1866, Stephens devoted much time during the Reconstruction era to writing about the Civil War and American history. The first thick volume of *A Constitutional View of the Late War Between the States* appeared in 1868 and the second in 1870. Though tedious by modern standards, the book was popularly received and brought Stephens $35,000 in royalties. He wrote hundreds of editorials in the *Atlanta Sun* and in 1872 published *The Reviewers Reviewed* and an American history text. His last work was *A Comprehensive and Popular History of the United States.*

In 1872 Stephens announced his candidacy for the United States Senate but lost to John B. Gordon. Four weeks after his defeat, however, he was elected to the House of Representatives. Although so crippled by rheumatism that he depended on crutches or a wheelchair, Stephens represented his constituents in Washington for a decade. Despite illnesses which often kept him from his seat, he spoke out forcefully on the need for monetary reform, the plight of farmers, and the injustices of the tax laws. After observing him in the House of Representatives, a Washington journalist was moved to write:

> How anything so small and sick and sorrowful could get here all the way from Georgia is a wonder. If he were to draw his last breath any instant you would not be surprised. If he were laid out in his coffin, he would not look any different, only then the fires would have gone out in those burning eyes. . . . That he is here at all to offer the counsels of moderation and patriotism proves how invincible is the soul that dwells in his shrunken and aching frame.

In 1882, at the age of seventy, he decided to retire. The Democrats in Georgia, then seriously divided, urged him to become their candidate for governor and thus unite the party. He consented to run and easily defeated former general Lucius J. Gartrell of Atlanta, candidate of the Republicans and the Independents, by vote of 107,253 to 44,896. Inaugurated on 4 November 1882, he served only 119 days. The demands of the job proved too strenuous for his feeble body. A trip to Savannah to participate in the 150th birthday celebration of the founding of Georgia led to his death on 4 March 1883. He was buried temporarily in Atlanta and later removed to Crawfordville.

"Little Aleck," Georgia's "Great Commoner," never married. A lover of children, good books, dogs, and the game of whist, he devoted his entire life to public service. A state park and a county in northeast Georgia are named for him, and in 1927 a statue of Stephens, sculpted by Gutzon Borglum, was placed in Statuary Hall in the United States Capitol.

James Stoddard Boynton
1883

He was a respected judge

James S. Boynton—highly esteemed by his contemporaries but little remembered today—was the seventh son and eleventh child born to Elijah S. and Elizabeth Moffett Boynton on 7 May 1833. His father, a native of Vermont of Scotch ancestry, was one of the first settlers in Henry County. His mother came from a South Carolina family, of French extraction. As a youth James worked on the family farm, attended the local "old field school," and had aspirations of attending West Point. The modest family income and the death of his father in 1849 prevented his going to West Point, but he was able to further his education at Hearn's School in Cave Spring and at the Georgia Military Institute in Marietta. After studying law for seven weeks with L. T. Doyall in McDonough, Boynton was admitted to the bar in October 1852, when he was only nineteen. He moved his few worldly possessions to Monticello, where he opened a law office. There the struggling young attorney fell in love with Fannie Loyall. They were married on 2 December 1852, and they had two sons, Jesse and Luther. With a keen mind, an upright character, a willingness to work, and the support of a loving wife, Boynton advanced steadily in his chosen profession. He practiced law in Monticello until 1858, when he moved to Jackson and formed a partnership with James R. Lyons. Two years later he was elected ordinary of Butts County.

When the Civil War began, Boynton enlisted as a private in the Thirtieth Georgia Regiment. Seven months later, when his regiment was reorganized, he was elected major. Displaying conspicuous valor and bravery in battle, he advanced to the rank of colonel. After serving in Savannah, Charleston, Wilmington, and Jacksonville, he fought in the arduous campaign in Mississippi and received a commendation for gallantry. He joined the Army of Tennessee shortly before the Battle of Chickamauga, and his regiment was in the thick of the fighting thereafter. While leading his men on an advance near Atlanta, he was severely wounded on 22 July 1864. When he rejoined his regiment six months later, he was still in a weakened condition, unable to walk without crutches, but he remained in command until his regiment was disbanded.

Fig.39. James S. Boynton

During the war Boynton had moved his family to Griffin, and after the war he established his practice there. He served as a judge of the county court, and from 1869 to 1872 was mayor of Griffin. In 1880 Boynton was elected to the Georgia Senate. When that body assembled, he was unanimously chosen president of the Senate—one of the very rare instances when a freshman legislator has been elected presiding officer by unanimous vote. "An admirable presiding officer," according to contemporary journalist I. W. Avery, he was reelected two years later.

When Governor Alexander Stephens died on 4 March 1883, Boynton became the acting governor. Immediately after taking the oath of office, he ordered an election for 24 April and summoned the General Assembly to meet, count the votes, and install the new governor. Eight candidates sought the Democratic nomination, but when the nominating convention convened in Atlanta, the field had been narrowed considerably. In the early balloting Boynton and A. O. Bacon, an experienced lawyer from Macon who had been speaker of the house since 1874, were the leading contenders. After seventeen ballots it was apparent that neither could secure the nomination, so a conference committee recommended Henry D. McDaniel as a compromise, and he subsequently was nominated and elected. Boynton remained in office a total of sixty-five days, until McDaniel's inauguration on 10 May 1883. For Boynton, the highlight of his brief tenure as governor came on 30 April when he married Susie T. Harris of Walton County in a gala ceremony.

After serving as governor, Boynton was twice elected judge of the Superior Court of the Flint Circuit, serving from 1886 to 1893 when he resigned to become division counsel of the Central of Georgia Railway Company. Against his wishes the voters of Spalding County elected him to the legislature in 1896. That was his last public office. Enfeebled in his last years, he died at his home in Griffin on 22 December 1902 and was buried with Masonic honors in Oak Hill Cemetery beside his first wife, who had died in 1877.

Through diligent application Boynton rose from humble circumstances to positions of considerable authority. A man of dignity, courage, and independent thought, he served the people of Georgia in a number of capacities and maintained throughout his lengthy public career the respect of his colleagues and the public. A devout Baptist, his character was above reproach, and he had little tolerance for sham, pretense, or deceit. He was highly esteemed as a lawyer, judge, and presiding officer of the Senate.

Henry Dickerson McDaniel
1883-1886

The guiding force behind the construction of the capitol

In the special election to fill the unexpired term of Governor Alexander Stephens, who died on 4 March 1883, the Democratic convention became hopelessly deadlocked. After seventeen ballots it was apparent that neither James Boynton nor A. O. Bacon could secure the nomination. Fearing that Bacon might become governor, Henry Grady guided the convention toward empowering a special committee to recommend a nominee. It suggested a compromise candidate, Henry D. McDaniel, who was then nominated by acclamation and elected. The new governor had a terrible stutter and sometimes could barely speak at all. Woodrow Wilson, then an unhappy lawyer in Atlanta, watched the crowds assemble for the inauguration of McDaniel and wrote down a vicious comment made by a Tennessean. Georgia, the Tennessean said, was exchanging a governor who could not walk for one who could not talk. Despite his handicap, McDaniel received all but 334 votes in the special election and in 1884 was reelected to a full term without opposition.

Scion of a prominent Walton County family, McDaniel was born in Monroe on 4 September 1836, the son of Ira Oliver and Rebecca Walker McDaniel. His father, a professor at Mercer Institute, moved his family to Atlanta in 1847, where he became a successful merchant and Henry attended the public schools. After graduating from Mercer with highest honors in 1856, Henry studied law for a year, gained admittance to the bar, and began to practice in Monroe in partnership with an uncle, Dickerson Holliday McDaniel. At age twenty-four, McDaniel was the youngest member of the secession convention. Though he doubted the wisdom of secession and voted against the initial resolution favoring it, he later sided with the majority. Entering the Confederate army on 3 July 1861, as a first lieutenant in the Eleventh Regiment of Georgia Infantry, he soon was promoted to captain and then major. At Funkstown, Maryland, as the Army of Northern Virginia retreated from Gettysburg, he was severely wounded in the abdomen on 10 July 1863 and was captured two days later. He was hospitalized and confined at Johnson Island, Ohio, until 25 July 1865. Returning to Monroe, he resumed his law practice, served in the state constitutional convention of 1865, and married Hester

Felker. Hester, daughter of a Monroe banker, would be his loving companion for sixty years.

After the General Amnesty Act went into effect, McDaniel was again called to public service. In 1872 he was elected to the General Assembly and two years later advanced to the Georgia Senate, where he served four successive terms without opposition. Noted for his intelligence, integrity, and business acumen, he chaired the Senate Finance Committee and Judiciary Committee. Although conservative by nature, he also sponsored reform measures, including the Railroad Tax Act of 1874 and the Railroad Commission Act of 1879.

McDaniel was a capable and honest executive whose most notable achievement was in improving the state's finances. By negotiating the sale of over $3.5 million in new bonds, strengthening regulations over the treasury, administering state revenues carefully, and raising taxes on railroads, he was able to save thousands of dollars, maintain a low millage rate, and reduce the bonded debt over a million dollars. McDaniel also was the guiding force behind the construction of a new capitol in Atlanta. As ex officio chairman of the Capitol Commissioners, he was instrumental in appointing the other commissioners, choosing the architect, hiring the contractors, and selecting the building materials. For the outside walls, calcitic limestone was used instead of the more expensive Georgia marble, despite considerable public pressure and lobbying. The governor inspected the construction site regularly to make sure that waste was kept to a minimum. Largely because of his efforts, the building was constructed within its original estimated cost of $1 million—a rarity among public buildings in America. Other measures passed during his administration include the establishment of the Georgia Institute of Technology; increased appropriations for the state institutions for the deaf, the blind, and the insane; and provision for annual pensions and other benefits for Confederate veterans. McDaniel's views coincided with the Bourbon concept of laissez faire, cheap government, and the encouragement of industry. Consequently, as historian Judson Ward has noted, his administration "met with the approval of the dominant Bourbon oligarchy." He differed from the Bourbons, however, by not exploiting the office for his own material advancement. Governor during a period of relative calm between the turbulent era of Reconstruction and the agrarian unrest of the 1890s, McDaniel was a popular and productive executive.

After leaving office, McDaniel withdrew from politics, resumed his law practice, and expanded his business interests. As successful in busi-

Fig.40. Henry D. McDaniel

ness as he was in politics, he amassed a considerable fortune through lucrative legal fees and wise investments. He was president of the High Shoals Cotton Factory and served for many years on the board of directors of the Georgia Railroad and Banking Company, the Walton Cotton Mill Company, the Monroe Railroad Company, and the Monroe Cotton Mills. He also devoted much time to education, serving on the boards of trustees of the University of Georgia and the Southern Baptist Theological Seminary in Louisville, Kentucky.

Growing feeble his last years, McDaniel died at his home in Monroe after a short illness on 25 July 1926. Almost ninety when he died, he had lived longer than any other Georgia governor. Survived by his widow and two children, Sanders and Gipsy, he was buried at Rest Haven Cemetery in Monroe. His tombstone bears the simple inscription "Christian, Soldier, Statesman." Though little remembered today, McDaniel was highly esteemed by his contemporaries.

John B. Gordon
1886-1890

He was the idol of Georgians

John B. Gordon, perhaps the most distinguished soldier Georgia ever produced, was the idol of the state for nearly forty years. Without any formal military training, he rose from captain to corps commander, a feat unmatched in the Army of Northern Virginia. Tall, straight, and powerful, with piercing gray eyes and abundant boldness and dash, he was a natural leader of men and an inspiring figure in battle. As one old veteran put it, "He's most the prettiest thing you ever did see on a field of fight. It'ud put fight into a whipped chicken just to look at him."

The son of Reverend Zachariah H. and Malinda Cox Gordon, he was the fourth of twelve children, born on 6 February 1832. His parents had migrated from Wilkes County, North Carolina, to Upson County, Georgia, shortly before his birth, and in 1840 they moved to Walker County, where John was educated in local schools. After attending Pleasant Green Academy, he entered the University of Georgia, where he compiled a commendable academic record but withdrew during his senior year without completing the requirements for a degree. In 1854 he settled in Atlanta, studied law under Basil H. Overby and Logan E. Bleckley, and after passing the bar joined their firm. On 18 September 1854, he married Fanny Rebecca Haralson, the charming daughter of General Hugh Haralson of LaGrange. Ironically, Gordon's two law partners married Fanny's sisters, Elizabeth and Caroline. Gordon's marriage was an unusually happy union that provided stability and much happiness in his life. Loving companions for nearly half a century, John and Fanny had six children—Hugh, Frank, Frances, Caroline, John, and Carolina.

Attracting few law clients in Atlanta, Gordon was engaged in coal mining operations in northwest Georgia when the Civil War began. An avid secessionist, he was elected captain of a company of mountaineers called the "Raccoon Roughs." Ordered to the front in Virginia, he soon displayed rare military talents. Whatever he lacked in training and experience he made up for in courage and leadership. Promotions came quickly. In less than two years he was a brigadier general, in May 1864 he became a major general, and during the last months of the war he commanded the II Corps of the Army of Northern Virginia. At Antietam he received two serious wounds but refused to leave the field. Continuing to lead his men into battle, he was shot three more times before he finally lost consciousness. His wife, who accompanied him throughout the war, nursed him back to health. In the thick of the fighting from Manassas to Appomattox, he fought at Seven Pines, Malvern Hill, Chancellorsville, Gettysburg, Spotsylvania, and Petersburg. With the possible exception of Nathan Bedford Forrest, Gordon is regarded as the greatest untrained soldier produced by the Confederacy.

Possessing an enviable military record, proven ability as a popular leader, courtly manners, and a strikingly handsome appearance, the young hero naturally gravitated into politics. An outspoken opponent of Radical Reconstruction and reputedly the head of the Ku Klux Klan in Georgia, he seemed to epitomize the Lost Cause. But his appearance was somewhat misleading. Though he used his looks and military reputation to advance his political career, and during his last years toured the country delivering a famous lecture on "The Last Days of the Confederacy," he did not dwell exclusively on the past. In fact, he looked to the future. A capitalist at heart, he continually engaged in business ventures and became one of the "Bourbon Triumvirate." The Bourbons, it was said, could look forward and backward at the same time. Certainly Gordon did. While extolling the virtues of the antebellum South of slavery, cotton, and plantations, he helped establish the "New South" of cities, factories, and railroads.

In 1868 Gordon received the Democratic nomination for governor, but since many Democrats had been disfranchised by the Radical Republicans who then controlled the state, he lost to the Republican candidate, Rufus Bullock. Five years later, after the Republicans were ousted, he was elected to the United States Senate, defeating the popular Alexander H. Stephens and Benjamin H. Hill. An articulate spokesman for Southern rights, he sought to end Reconstruction and restore self-government in the Southern states. In addition to his devotion to the South, Gordon also became a strong proponent of national reconciliation and received much praise in the Northern press. A New Yorker asserted that Gordon "did more by word and pen and deed than any other southern man to assuage the feeling of animosity and restore real harmony and fraternal good will between the north and the south." An opposition paper described him as "the ablest man from the South in either House of Congress."

Fig.41. John B. Gordon

On 15 May 1880, shortly after being reelected, Gordon abruptly resigned from the Senate to accept a business position. He first accepted an offer in Oregon, but when the Louisville and Nashville Railroad made a more appealing proposal, he accepted it and remained in Georgia. His resignation profoundly shocked the nation. When Governor Alfred Colquitt appointed Joseph E. Brown to succeed Gordon, surprise and regret turned to outrage and indignation. Brown, who ably led the state as governor during the Civil War, had earned the everlasting enmity of most white Georgians (especially Democrats) by accepting Republican rule and switching to that party during Reconstruction. They assumed that some type of corrupt bargain had taken place. Gordon, who had been notoriously unsuccessful in his business investments, explained that he had considered resigning from the Senate for financial reasons for some time. Denying the existence of any collusion, he, with his popularity intact, spent the next few years seeking the wealth that thus far had eluded him. Recent research by Harold Davis and Ralph Lowell Eckert, however, indicates that agreements were made by the three participants, plus Henry Grady of the *Atlanta Constitution* and H. Victor Newcomb, president of the Louisville and Nashville Railroad Company. Although their secretive correspondence was concealed from the public, apparently no laws were broken, and in time all of the individuals achieved their goals: Colquitt gained reelection as governor; Brown revived his political career; Atlanta became a rail center; and Gordon achieved wealth. Although Gordon, Colquitt, and Brown were all touched by the breath of scandal, each escaped relatively unscathed. Moreover, the public outcry drove them into a closer alliance known as the "Bourbon Triumvirate," which dominated state politics in the 1880s. Before the 1880 election, a Georgia newspaper correctly predicted that "Brown with his money, Gordon with his buttons, and Colquitt with his religion will make a combination than can not be broken."

After gaining a fortune and then losing it through unwise speculative ventures, Gordon reentered the political arena in 1886. His campaign manager, Henry Grady, persuaded Jefferson Davis to come to Atlanta for the unveiling of a statue of Benjamin H. Hill. Other Civil War luminaries joined the procession, and Gordon escorted the former president of the Confederacy at ceremonies in Atlanta and Savannah. With the multitudes going wild over the emotional reunion, Gordon announced his candidacy for governor. His opponent, A. O. Bacon, a competent legislator and de-bater, could not match Grady's publicity and Gordon's magnetism. After an extremely bitter campaign, the Democratic convention nominated Gordon on the first ballot. He was elected without opposition and was reelected in 1888.

With Brown and Colquitt in the United States Senate and Gordon serving as Georgia's chief executive, a political calm settled over the state. During Gordon's administration a favorable climate for business prevailed and few reforms were enacted. He continued the policy of reducing the state's debt and holding down taxes, and he ignored the agrarian distress that plagued the state. As a result some growth occurred in factories, railroads, and population, but little money was available for improving the public schools, colleges, or social services. During Gordon's tenure the popular Piedmont Exposition was held in Atlanta in

1887, and the new state capitol was completed in 1889. Gordon did publicize the abuses of the convict-lease system and recommended modest reforms, but the General Assembly failed to implement them. At the end of his four years in office, the brutal convict-lease system remained, as one historian described it, "the blackest chapter in the record of the Bourbon regime in Georgia." Gordon's latest biographer, Ralph Lowell Eckert, has concluded that his tenure as governor proved "rather ordinary" and that "little of importance occurred during his four-year tenure."

Upon the expiration of his term, the legislature again elected him to the United States Senate, where he served from 1891 to 1897. When the United Confederate Veterans was organized in June 1889, Gordon became the commander-in-chief, a position he retained until his death. He helped build the UCV into a powerful organization. As a popular speaker at Confederate reunions, a frequent dedicator of Civil War monuments, and the author in 1903 of *Reminiscences of the Civil War*, an account noted for its generosity to friend and foe alike, he became the embodiment of the Lost Cause.

Gordon died in Miami on 9 January 1904 and was buried in Oakland Cemetery in Atlanta. A large army base near Augusta commemorates his name. A statue of Gordon astride his favorite Civil War mount, Marye, was unveiled on the capitol grounds in 1907.

William Jonathan Northen
1890–1894

He was an accomplished scholar

William J. Northen, who achieved distinction as an officeholder, educator, farmer, author, and religious leader, was descended from a cultured and wealthy family who had lived in America since 1635. His father, a teacher at Mercer University, served two terms in the legislature and for many years was treasurer of the Georgia Baptist Convention. The son followed the father's footsteps. The ninth of Peter and Louise Davis Northen's eleven children, William was born on 9 July 1835, on the family plantation in Jones County, Georgia, but was reared in Penfield, in Greene County. After receiving a degree from Mercer University in 1853, he opened a school at Mount Zion, near Sparta, and soon became a noted educator. When the Civil War erupted, Northen enlisted, but poor health limited his activities mostly to hospital service in Atlanta and Milledgeville. After the war he resumed his teaching at Mount Zion, but failing health forced him out of the classroom in 1874.

Retiring to his 800-acre farm in Hancock County, Northen devoted himself to rigorous study of agriculture. Rather than raising cotton, he specialized in dairying and breeding horses and pigs and soon became recognized as an expert on agricultural matters. His success convinced him that diversification and scientific farming would solve the plight of Georgia's farmers. Active in numerous farm organizations, he served as president of the prestigious Georgia State Agricultural Society from 1886 to 1890. In the meantime Northen had gained a popular following in state politics, having served three terms in the Georgia General Assembly, first in the House in 1877–1878 and 1880–1881 and then in the Senate in 1884–1885. In the legislature he sought to improve education and secure statewide prohibition. Anxious for greater responsibilities, he became a candidate for governor in 1890. Regarded as "progressive but safe" by business interests, he gained the backing of the Georgia Farmers Alliance and the *Atlanta Constitution*. When his chief opponent, Leonidas F. Livingstone, withdrew from the gubernatorial contest to seek a seat in Congress, Northen was elected without opposition. Two years later he won a second term, defeating William L. Peek, the Populist candidate, 140,492 to 68,900.

Fig.42. William J. Northen

After a decade of Bourbon rule, in 1890 the farmers regained control of Georgia's government in dramatic fashion. In addition to endorsing the governor and the entire congressional delegation, the Farmers Alliance also had backed three-fourths of the senators and four-fifths of the representatives in the General Assembly. The "farmers'" assembly passed several significant bills under Northen's leadership. It extended the power of the Georgia Railroad Commission to cover telegraph and express companies, adopted the thirteen-hour day for railroad employees, declared Labor Day a holiday, and expanded the inspection of fertilizer and cottonseed meal. Quite naturally Northen stressed education, and his efforts bore fruit. His administration extended the school term, increased the number of schools, established an agricultural and mechanical college for black students at Savannah, and established a normal school for training white teachers.

Sympathetic to blacks, Northen strenuously opposed mob rule and repeatedly urged the legislature to construct a reformatory for youthful offenders and to enact a "lynch law," but neither was adopted. A believer in sound currency, low tariffs, and frugal government, Northen was a conservative Democrat of the Grover Cleveland type. When the Panic of 1893 struck, creating widespread unemployment and producing the first decline in the value of taxable property since the Civil War, Northen blamed the problems on the "dangerous and pernicious policy of the general government known as protection." The governor, as historian Barton Shaw has noted, "was as dumbfounded by the crisis as most Georgians." An honest and competent executive, his moderate reforms satisfied some but did not prevent the growth of the Populist party, which sought more drastic changes in government. Indeed, Populist leader Tom Watson described Northen as a "long-whiskered imbecile" whose "brains are chronically stagnant."

After leaving office, Northen continued to live in Atlanta and remained active with many civic, religious, and scholarly activities. As manager of the Georgia Immigration and Investment Bureau, he was instrumental in bringing settlers into the state, including a group of Union veterans from Indiana who founded the town of Fitzgerald. In 1911 he succeeded Allen D. Candler as compiler of state records and completed part of a volume of *The Colonial Records of Georgia*. He also edited an extensive collection of biographical sketches published in seven volumes from 1907 to 1912 under the title *Men of Mark in Georgia*. He wrote several of the sketches himself and contributed a steady stream of articles to religious, agricultural, and educational journals. In recognition of his scholarly accomplishments, Mercer University, Richmond College, and Baylor University awarded him LL.D. degrees.

Becoming a Christian in 1853, Northen worked earnestly in the Baptist faith for six decades. For many years he was one of the South's leading Baptist laymen, serving as president of the Georgia Baptist Convention, the Georgia Baptist Educational Society, the Southern Baptist Convention, the National Baptist Congress, and the Baptist Educational Society. He also served as vice president of the American Bible Society and the American Sunday School Union, and was a trustee for Mercer University, a Baptist institution, from 1869 until his death. In these endeavors, he was assisted by his wife, Martha Neal Northen of Walton County. They were married on 19 December 1860 and had two children, Thomas and Annie Belle.

On 25 March 1913, Northen, in his seventy-seventh year, died at his home, ending a life rich in accomplishment in many different fields. He was buried in Oakland Cemetery in Atlanta.

William Yates Atkinson
1894-1898

He died in the prime of life

In many respects the life of William Y. Atkinson could serve as a stereotype for Georgia governors in the modern era. Born in a large family in Georgia, he was reared in a rural environment, earned a degree from the University of Georgia, practiced law in a small town, served in the General Assembly, worshipped in a Protestant church, and married and had children. Atkinson was atypical only by his early death.

Born in Oakland, Meriwether County, on 11 November 1854, William was the third of five children born to John Pepper and Theodora Phelps Atkinson. His father, a farmer of moderate means, also had three children by a former marriage. William became accustomed to the hard manual labor required of rural youths in that era but had little interest in academic pursuits. Neighbors were convinced that he would make a good plowhand but would never accomplish anything with books. His parents, concerned about his poor study habits, sent him to W. T. Revill's school in Greenville, where he finally became a capable student. The death of his father in 1873 forced William to seek odd jobs to accumulate enough money to attend college. He entered the University of Georgia in 1874, enrolling in the regular literary course of study. After receiving his degree in 1877, he moved to Newnan and established a law practice. His practice flourished, and in 1885 he became a director of the newly formed Newnan National Bank.

In 1879 Governor Alfred Colquitt appointed Atkinson to a three-year term as solicitor of the Coweta county court. Although physically small and frail with curly raven hair and a dense mustache, Atkinson had political ambitions, and through diligent effort soon mastered the machine methods the Bourbons had perfected. In 1886 he was elected to the General Assembly, where he quickly assumed a position of leadership. Reelected three times, he was chosen speaker of the house in 1892. A strict party loyalist, he served as president of the state Democratic convention in 1890 and also successfully managed William Northen's campaign for governor. In the legislature he sponsored bills to make the office of the commissioner of agriculture elective, to limit the pay of oil inspectors, and to place telegraph and express companies under the

HON. WILLIAM YATES ATKINSON,

REPRESENTATIVE FROM THE COUNTY OF COWETA.

Fig.43. William Y. Atkinson

regulative control of the Railroad Commission. His most noteworthy contribution, however, was in the establishment of the Georgia Normal and Industrial College for Girls in Milledgeville (now Georgia College).

In 1894, though not yet forty years of age, Atkinson ran for governor against a sixty-eight-year-old Methodist minister and popular Confederate hero, General Clement A. Evans. Evans had announced his candidacy much earlier and had the support of the *Atlanta Journal and Constitution*, but Atkinson used his political experience and oratorical skills to good advantage. After a series of debates, Evans withdrew a month before the state convention, assuring Atkinson of the nomination. In a bitter campaign Atkinson then defeated the Populist candidate, Judge James K. Hines of Atlanta, by a vote of 121,625 to 96,819. The Populists won forty-eight seats in the legislature, three times their number in 1892, and complained that the Democrats had stolen the election from them. Two years later Atkinson again turned back a Populist challenge, defeating Seaborn Wright, a handsome attorney from Rome, by a wider margin. In both races issues were ignored in favor of name-calling, racism, and fraud. The going rate for buying votes, it seems, was one dollar apiece.

Atkinson was an energetic chief executive who supported several progressive issues. He was even more hostile to lynching than was his predecessor, Governor William J. Northen. He repeatedly condemned the practice and urged the legislature to enact laws against it, but to no avail. In employing Ellen Dortch as assistant state librarian, he brought in the first woman as a salaried employee at the state capitol. He deplored the abuses in the convict-lease system and was able to establish a prison commission to oversee state prisoners and eliminate some of the most flagrant abuses. He supported increased funding for education, called for stricter accounting of election-campaign spending, and tried to attract more investment capital into the state. In a moment of extreme foresight, as historian James Dorsey has pointed out, he vetoed a law in 1897 which would have outlawed football in the state, a measure which grew out of the death of a University of Georgia player in a game with Virginia.

In his excellent book *The Wool-Hat Boys*, Barton Shaw vividly depicted another aspect of Georgia politics in this era:

> Much of the business of government was carried on at the Kimball House, the Markham, and other Atlanta hotels. When the General Assembly was in session, hotel lobbies were thick with politicians, officeseekers, and those wanting advice or favors. Upstairs in private rooms, politicos made deals and discussed delicate matters. Indeed, in these rooms the judiciary of Georgia was bought and sold every few years. Because the legislature appointed state judges, those who seriously aspired to the superior court bench or to a solicitor-generalship usually rented suites, hired waiters, bought cases of whiskey, and invited legislators up for refreshment and conversation. With forty-six judgeships and solicitor-generalships to be had, and more than two hundred legislators to be influenced, the convening of the General Assembly frequently resembled a drunken auction.

On 23 February 1880, Atkinson married Susie Cobb Milton, a charming and intelligent woman of distinguished family, who aided him and encouraged his advancement. They had six children—John, Lucille, Wil-

Allen Daniel Candler
1898-1902

He compiled Georgia's records

Allen D. Candler, known as the "one-eyed plowboy of Pigeon Roost," was a rugged mountaineer who neither looked nor sounded like the typical governor. A small, grizzled man who chewed tobacco, wore old clothes, and on occasion used such spicy language that it would "tear the teeth out of a sausage grinder," he had a long and eminently successful public career, serving without defeat in the United States House of Representatives and in Georgia as representative, senator, secretary of state, governor, and compiler of records.

Born in Auraria, Lumpkin County, on 4 November 1834, he was the first of twelve children born to Daniel Gill and Nancy Caroline Matthews Candler. Growing up in a mountainous gold-mining community, he worked hard on his father's farm and developed an enduring sympathy for the toiling, unpolished, illiterate mountaineers. His parents inculcated the values of honesty, industry, and devotion to duty in Candler—traits he later displayed in his public service. After studying under a Presbyterian minister, he attended Mercer University, where he earned a bachelor's degree in 1859 and later received an honorary master's degree. He taught school briefly in Jonesboro before enlisting in the Confederate army as a private. He fought in almost every battle engaging the Army of Tennessee—Vicksburg, Missionary Ridge, Resaca, Kennesaw Mountain, Atlanta, and Jonesboro—and rose to the rank of colonel in December 1864.

On 12 January 1864, he married one of his former students, Eugenia T. Williams, daughter of a Jones County planter, and their marriage was blessed with eleven children—Eugenia, Florence, Marcus, Thomas, Hortense, William, Kate, John, Victor, Margaret, and Benjamin. In the fighting around Jonesboro, Candler suffered a severe head wound, resulting in the permanent loss of the sight of one eye. At the war's end he quipped that he was quite wealthy, being the possessor of "one wife, one baby, one eye, and one silver dollar."

After an itinerant postwar career in education, Candler settled in Gainesville in 1870, where he prospered in various business enterprises. Successfully blending politics with business, he served as mayor of Gainesville in 1872 and during the 1870s completed four terms in the state legislature. Candler advanced to the national level after Democratic leaders in the Ninth Congressional District drafted him in 1882 to oppose incumbent Emory Speer for a seat in the United States House of Representatives. He defeated Speer and won the next three elections without opposition. Voluntarily retiring from Congress, he was appointed secretary of state by Governor Northen in 1894 to succeed Phillip Cook, who had died. In 1898 he resigned from that position to become a candidate for governor. Projecting himself as an "old-fashioned Democrat" without ties to any "ring, clique, or faction" and as a man of the people, Candler defeated both Judge Spencer Atkinson of Brunswick, a grandson of Governor Charles J. McDonald, and Robert L. Berner, the president of the Senate, to secure the Democratic nomination. In the general election he trounced the Populist-Republican candidate, J. R. Hogan, a farmer from Lincoln County, by a two-to-one margin. His election as governor marked the failure of fusion among Republicans, black Democrats, and Populists. In 1900 Candler easily won reelection over Populist John H. Traylor of Troup County.

At the completion of his term, the *Atlanta Constitution*, a friendly newspaper, made the following evaluation of his administration: "Governor Candler has given to the state the most scrupulous service. The Constitution has been sustained, the laws have been enforced, the treasury has been safeguarded, the peace and good order of the commonwealth secured, her industries promoted, and her fame defended against disparagement." Writing in a more critical vein many years later, Hal Steed asserted that the governors of the 1890s carried on the traditions of the Bourbon triumvirate, were the tools of lobbyists, and "had no distinguishing qualities, good or bad." The few who did protest against the existing order, he continued, lacked the force and ability necessary to back their rebellion. Elizabeth Marshall, a contemporary historian, concluded that Candler had a "relatively bland" administration, "more notable for what it failed to achieve than for what it accomplished."

Despite their differences, all three assessments have merit. A staunch conservative, Candler urged retrenchment of appropriations for public schools and advocated white supremacy. In 1903 he claimed credit for having masterminded the Democratic white primary in Georgia. While stressing honesty and frugality, his administration shunned innovations and reforms, aside from eliminating black voters from the Democratic primary. The problems he encountered—corrupt elections, lynchings, mob violence, inadequate revenues, and deficient school funds—remained

Fig.44. Allen D. Candler

largely unsolved when he left office. With few exceptions, his legislative proposals were defeated in the General Assembly, which, as Professor Marshall pointed out, "was notable for little except flagrant absenteeism."

Candler's most important service to the state came after his governorship. For decades Georgia's official records had languished in the capitol and in private hands. As a result many priceless documents had been lost. But the state's political leaders had showed little concern about the matter until Governor Joseph Terrell appointed Candler compiler of records.

Despite advancing years and waning vision, Candler laboriously studied Georgia documents and edited a remarkable amount of material from 1903 until his death on 26 October 1910. It was said that he died with a "pen in his hand." By the time of his death he had supervised the publication of twenty-one volumes of *The Colonial Records of Georgia* (1904–1910), three volumes of *The Revolutionary Records of the State of Georgia* (1908), and five volumes of *The Confederate Records of the State of Georgia* (1909–1911). Material for twenty-four additional volumes was left in manuscript form. He also collaborated with Clement Evans on a three-volume encyclopedia of Georgia in 1906. By any standard of measurement, this was a prodigious scholarly achievement.

Candler died of Bright's disease at age seventy-five. After his body lay in state at the capitol, he was buried in Alta Vista Cemetery in Gainesville. His cousin, Bishop Warren A. Candler, conducted the funeral services. In 1914 a county in the southeastern part of the state was named for him.

Joseph Meriwether Terrell
1902-1907

He provided stable, effective leadership

Joseph M. Terrell—Georgia legislator, attorney general, governor, and United States senator—entered public service at an early age and maintained the trust of the people throughout his successful political career. Of English and Scottish ancestry, he was a native of Greenville, Georgia, one of eight children born to Dr. Joel E. G. Terrell, a Meriwether County physician, and Sarah Anthony Terrell. Born on 6 June 1861, at the outbreak of the Civil War, Joseph attended school in Greenville, worked on the family farm, and studied law under Major John W. Park. Admitted to the bar in 1882, he established a substantial practice in his hometown. On 19 October 1886, he married Jessie Lee Spivey, daughter of a prominent Harris County planter. Both Terrell and his wife were active members of the Baptist church. They enjoyed a happy marriage but had no children.

Perhaps the most amazing aspect of Terrell's political career is the rapidity of his advancement. At age twenty-three he was the youngest member elected to the General Assembly; at age twenty-nine he advanced to the Georgia Senate; at age thirty-one he became attorney general; and ten years later, on his forty-first birthday, he became governor. If not brilliant, Terrell certainly provided solid, conscientious, and effective leadership in each of the positions he held. His opinions as attorney general were noted for clarity and conciseness of expression, and he had phenomenal success in trying cases before the United States Supreme Court. In a hotly contested campaign for the Democratic nomination for governor in 1902 in which prohibition was the main issue, Terrell defeated Dupont Guerry, a Macon lawyer, and John H. Estill, a Savannah newspaper editor. Guerry was a bone-dry prohibitionist, while Terrell and Estill favored local option. Terrell gained the nomination with 196 county unit votes to Estill's 82 and Guerry's 66, and the state Democratic convention endorsed local option. In the general election Terrell defeated the Populist candidate, Judge J. K. Hines, 81,344 to 4,747. Numerous defeats and improving economic conditions destroyed the Populist party, and two years later Terrell was reelected without opposition.

Terrell's major achievement as governor came in the field of education. In his first address to the General Assembly, he explained that "the evils of illiteracy are recognized." To combat them he proposed several remedies. He called for the establishment of a loan fund of $500,000 so that teachers could be paid in accordance with their contracts, passage of an amendment "to exempt from taxation the endowment funds and investments of all educational institutions," generous support for the Normal School at Athens and the Girls Normal School at Milledgeville, and the establishment of an agricultural school in each congressional district. The latter, he argued, would train thousands, and they were needed because Georgia was "pre-eminently an agricultural State." The governor repeated this request the next year and continued to exert pressure on the conservative legislature. Finally, in 1906, the General Assembly appropriated $100,000 to develop the College of Agriculture and Mechanical Arts at Athens and authorized the establishment of an agricultural and mechanical school in each congressional district in the state. The response was so enthusiastic that by 1910 eleven such schools were in operation with fifteen hundred students.

Traditionally Terrell has been regarded as a conservative, but historian Alton D. Jones has asserted that "a very worthy amount of progressive legislation was enacted during Terrell's two terms as Governor of Georgia." The record seems to justify his conclusion. In addition to improvements in education, the Terrell administration established a court of appeals, regulated child labor, enacted a pure food and drug law, curbed speculation in agricultural futures, placed a new tax on businesses and corporations, and made buying and selling votes in a primary election a misdemeanor. During this prosperous period, which saw the value of taxable property increase $160 million during his term, Terrell provided reliable and competent leadership. His accomplishments have not been adequately publicized in part because he was overshadowed by his successor, Hoke Smith. A genial, friendly man, Terrell lacked the flamboyance and combativeness of Smith, preferring to work in harmony with party leaders rather than disrupting the state with reform crusades. He believed the governor should be "the servant of the people—and not a dictator or czar."

After concluding his popular tenure as governor, Terrell retired from public office and resumed his law practice. Retirement was short-lived, however, for late in 1910 Governor Joseph M. Brown appointed him to the United States Senate to fill the vacancy caused by the death of Sena-

Fig.45. Joseph M. Terrell

tor Alexander S. Clay. Three months after assuming his duties in Washington, Terrell suffered a stroke that forced him to resign on 14 July 1911. Never fully regaining his health, he died at his home in Atlanta of Bright's disease on 17 November 1912. He was only fifty-one. By order of the governor, flags flew at half-mast and his body lay in state in the rotunda of the state capitol. He was buried in the city cemetery in Greenville.

Hoke Smith
1907–1909, 1911

He was Georgia's outstanding Progressive

Hoke Smith, Georgia's most outstanding Progressive, was born in New-ton, North Carolina, on 2 September 1855. His father, Hildreth H. Smith, a graduate of Bowdoin College, was then president of Catawba College, and his mother, Mary Hoke Smith, was a cultivated woman from a distinguished family who had produced the first chief justice in North Carolina. In 1857, when Hildreth accepted a professorship of modern lan-guages at the University of North Carolina, the family moved to Chapel Hill. Hoke received no formal education, but his keen mind was devel-oped by the tutoring of his scholarly father. When Hoke was thirteen, his father lost his position at the university and subsequently took his family to Atlanta, where he became a principal in the public school system.

After studying law briefly with the Atlanta firm of Collier, Mynatt and Collier, Hoke Smith was admitted to the bar at the age of seventeen. He opened an office in the same building where Woodrow Wilson practiced. The future president failed as a lawyer and soon abandoned the profession, but Smith quickly rose to prominence. Hardworking and shrewd, he invested his fees in profitable business ventures and report-edly was worth $300,000 by the time he was thirty-five. In 1887 he and several partners purchased the *Atlanta Journal*; when it was sold in 1900, his share was $159,000. On 19 December 1883, he married Marion "Bir-die" Cobb, daughter of General Thomas R. R. Cobb, and they had five children—Marion, Hildreth, Mary, Lucy, and Callie.

Attracted to politics, Smith became active in the Democratic party organization many years before he held public office. As a reward for his staunch support of Grover Cleveland at the Democratic National Conven-tion and in the presidential campaign of 1892, he was appointed secretary of interior. In that multifaceted job he discharged his duties with distinc-tion. His term was notable for instituting savings in the pension office and for encouraging forest conservation. Resigning in 1896, he was out of public office for ten years, during which time he concentrated on his law practice and profitable investments.

In June 1905, fourteen months before the Democratic primary, Smith announced his candidacy for governor and began a vigorous campaign.

Fig.46. Hoke Smith

Already a popular figure, he offered a platform of reform that caught the progressive spirit of the day. The support of the politically powerful Tom Watson ensured his victory. He easily defeated Richard Russell, Sr., Clark Howell, John Estill, and James M. Smith, carrying 122 of the 145 counties and capturing 104,796 votes to the combined total of 79,477 for all his opponents.

Before Smith could implement his program, prohibition erupted as a divisive issue in the legislature. The governor cleverly took no stand on the liquor issue, letting the legislators fight it out. After they adopted a statewide prohibition law in August 1907, the way was clear to fight for other reforms. Smith pressured the legislature into adopting an impressive body of legislation. His first administration reorganized and strengthened the Railroad Commission, abolished the convict-lease system, established juvenile courts and a parole system, increased appropriations for public schools by 30 percent, and enacted a law which fixed the location and time of statewide primaries. The term also adopted an amendment curtailing blacks' right to vote. Typical of Southern progressives, Smith supported the "grandfather clause" in the belief that removing the remaining black voters would eliminate a major source of corruption in the political system. His stand on disfranchisement also was necessary to gain the support of Tom Watson, whose influence among rural voters was so powerful that few governors were elected in this era without his endorsement. The voters approved the "grandfather clause" amendment by a two-to-one margin. No administration in recent Georgia history had enacted such a wide-ranging program of reform legislation. But in doing so Smith had made enemies, including Joseph M. Brown, whom Smith had fired from the Railroad Commission.

Although it was traditional for governors to serve two terms, Brown, the son of Civil War governor Joseph E. Brown, challenged Smith in 1908. With the country in the throes of a depression (the Panic of 1907), Brown used the slogan "Hoke and Hunger, Brown and Bread" and, surprisingly, upset the incumbent governor. In a rematch two years later, Smith won, 98,048 to 93,717.

Smith's second administration was short and controversial. When Senator Alexander Clay died in the fall of 1910, Governor Brown appointed Joseph M. Terrell to succeed him until the legislature could elect a successor. Smith let it be known that he wanted the post, and in July 1911 the legislature named him senator. Terrell promptly resigned, and everyone expected Smith to relinquish the governorship and move to Washington, but he did not. Instead, he held both positions for four months while his angry opponents watched helplessly. Despite the controversy, Smith managed to get more reforms adopted. The legislature enacted an anti-lobbying measure, forcing lobbyists to list their expenses, salaries, and employers with the state; established a department of labor; shortened the maximum workweek for textile workers to sixty hours; and established a state board of education, which included the governor, state superintendent, and four educators appointed by the governor. His work completed, Smith resigned on 6 November and set out for Washington. In 1914 he was reelected to a full term, defeating Joseph M. Brown.

Throughout his career Smith had been a strong advocate of improving education. For many years he served on the Atlanta Board of Education (president 1896–1907) and as a trustee of the Peabody Educational Fund. Quite naturally, in the Senate his chief interest was in furthering education, especially vocational training. His efforts led to the passage of two important laws. The Smith-Lever Act provided for agricultural extension work, and the Smith-Hughes Act provided vocational education below the college level in agriculture, industrial arts, and domestic arts. He also secured passage of a bill setting up a division of markets in the Department of Agriculture. When war erupted in Europe, he attempted to force all belligerents to respect American rights in international trade. After the United States entered World War I, Smith supported the administration's war measures, but his support did not extend to Wilson's League of Nations. World War I brought an end to the Progressive era and to the political career of Georgia's leading Progressive. As the postwar era dawned, Smith had difficulty adjusting to the new conditions. His wife died in 1919, and his political career ended the following year when Tom Watson, his former ally, defeated him for the Senate seat.

Smith remained in Washington and practiced law there until 1924, when he returned to Atlanta and married Mazie Crawford of Cordele. In his last years he continued to practice law, remained active in numerous civic and community affairs, and served as an elder in the North Avenue Presbyterian Church. He died in Atlanta on 27 November 1931 and was buried in Oakland Cemetery there.

Over six feet tall, Smith was a commanding figure, a forceful speaker, and a dynamic leader. In seeking reforms he was undeterred by public apathy or by entrenched economic or political opposition. Able and courageous, he made positive contributions on the local, state, and national levels. Even those who disliked his policies recognized his abilities. In an editorial his old opponent, Clark Howell of the *Atlanta Constitution*, wrote: "In going Senator Smith leaves an indelible imprint upon the history of the state which he served long and well."

Joseph Mackey Brown
1909-1911, 1912-1913

One of Georgia's most cultured and learned governors

Joseph M. Brown, perhaps the shiest and most taciturn of Georgia's governors, claimed that, like Moses, he was unable to make a political speech. In three campaigns for governor he made only one brief speech, but still won two of the races.

Born on a farm in Cherokee County, Georgia, on 28 December 1851, he was one of eight children born to Georgia's Civil War governor, Joseph E. Brown, and his wife Elizabeth Grisham Brown. When "Little Joe," as the younger Brown was called, was six years old, the family moved into the governor's mansion in Milledgeville. After attending private schools in Milledgeville and Atlanta, he earned a bachelor's degree at Oglethorpe University, graduating first in his class in 1872 with an academic average of 99.5. Like his father, he attended law school after being admitted to the bar. Eyestrain caused by rigorous study, however, forced him to withdraw from Harvard Law School and abandon plans to practice law. While under the treatment of an eye specialist, he spent several months traveling on horseback over the mountains of Georgia and the Carolinas, resting his eyes. Deciding upon a career in business, he completed a course at Moore's Business College in Atlanta and in 1877 began a long career in railroading with the Western and Atlantic Railroad, which was under lease to a syndicate headed by his father. Starting as a clerk in the freight office at forty dollars a month, Brown advanced steadily through the ranks, serving as conductor, claims clerk, claims agent, timekeeper, accountant, freight agent, and traffic manager.

On 12 February 1889, Brown married Cora McCord, a member of a distinguished Augusta family. Settling in a house in Marietta once owned by Governor Charles J. McDonald, they soon became the parents of Joseph Emerson, Charles McDonald, and Cora McCord. After twenty-three years with the W & A Railroad, including several years as general traffic manager, Brown served four years as general freight and passenger agent for the Seaboard Airline Railroad in Atlanta and then retired to his Marietta home. He remained active, developing residential property in Marietta, managing a 1,000-acre farm in Cherokee County, traveling extensively, and researching and writing a long romantic novel.

In 1904 Governor Joseph Terrell appointed Brown to the Railroad Commission. In that position he came into conflict with Governor Hoke Smith, who was determined to restructure the Railroad Commission and restrict the power of the railroads. Brown, who was sympathetic to the railroads, objected to Smith's major reforms. Consequently, Governor Smith dismissed Brown in 1907, precipitating a bitter feud that dominated Georgia politics for nearly a decade. Although Brown had never held elective office, he challenged Smith for the governorship in 1908. In the bitter campaign, Brown was accused of being a drug addict, of being discharged for incompetency, of squandering his father's patrimony, and of being supported by the whiskey ring. Without making a speech in the campaign, he defeated Smith in the Democratic primary and overcame Yancey Carter, an Independent, in the general election.

Brown had promised that if elected he "would attend to the duties of his office" and "not be found running all over the state for weeks at a time and allowing the business of his office to take care of itself." As governor from 1909 to 1911 he fulfilled that pledge. A fiscal conservative, he sought no major legislative innovations; he worked for economy in government, strict enforcement of prohibition laws, lower taxes, and limitation on the powers of labor unions.

In 1910 Brown ran for reelection but suffered a narrow defeat by his old adversary Hoke Smith. When Smith became a United States senator, Brown announced his candidacy for governor, pledging to protect the Constitution, cooperate with the courts, enforce the laws, and balance the budget. Brown made one ten-minute speech in this special election, which he won easily. His second term lasted from 25 January 1912 to 28 June 1913. An earnest conservative, Brown rarely offered workable solutions to the problems he attacked. In twice following Hoke Smith, one of the state's most active reform governors in the twentieth century, his administrations provided a respite from the hectic pace of change. In 1914 he challenged Smith for the United States Senate seat but lost by a landslide.

A calm and unflappable man, Brown was one of Georgia's most cultured and learned governors. Small in stature and frail in body, he read voraciously and displayed keen intellectual strength and energy. Author of two books—*Mountain Campaigns in Georgia*, a history of military operations in north Georgia during the Civil War, and *Astyanax*, a romantic novel—he also wrote numerous articles on a variety of subjects, including women's suffrage, the Leo Frank case, and religious topics.

Fig.47. Joseph M. Brown

After retiring from politics, Brown remained active as an innovative farmer and prosperous businessman, serving as a director of the First National Bank of Marietta. In 1914 he purchased Cherokee Mills, a 450-acre tract, which included grain and feed mills, sawmills, cotton gins, and other industries. After 1928 Brown declined rapidly in body and mind. He died on 3 March 1932 at his home in Marietta and was buried in Oakland Cemetery in Atlanta.

An oddity in politics, Brown was a man of formidable intellectual endowments and strong convictions. His biographer, William Gabard, has stated that Brown's mode of life was simple: "He believed in hard work, frugality, and avoidance of the Devil's vices. He generally eschewed social affairs; instead he found pleasure in his family and in reading, writing, and farming." A devout life-long Baptist, he was a "kind, loving husband and father, and a public-spirited citizen."

John Marshall Slaton
1911-1912, 1913-1915

He put principle above ambition

John M. Slaton's political career demonstrates the fickleness of public opinion, for he was, at varying times, Georgia's most popular and most unpopular political leader. A capable and conservative executive, he won the governorship by a landslide in 1912, receiving 110,143 of the slightly more than 150,000 votes cast and carrying 136 of 146 counties. But two years later he had become an object of contempt, hated passionately by many Georgians. Indeed, Slaton had aroused such animosity that at the inauguration of his successor police and national guardsmen had to protect him from angry mobs shouting "Lynch him!"

John Slaton was born on Christmas Day 1866 to Major William Franklin and Nancy Martin Slaton. He spent his early childhood on the family's large farm in Meriwether County. In 1875 the family moved to Atlanta, where his father became superintendent of the city's public schools. Young Slaton was graduated from Boys' High School with highest honors and then worked as a railway clerk for three years to pay his way through the University of Georgia, where he was graduated with highest honors in 1886. After reading law with John T. Glenn, one of Atlanta's most respected attorneys, he passed the bar and opened a practice in Atlanta. Quickly earning a reputation as an intelligent and conscientious worker, he formed a partnership with his mentor, Benjamin Phillips, in 1894. On 12 July 1898, Slaton married Sally Francis Grant, a wealthy socialite from one of Atlanta's pioneer families and a direct descendant of Governor James Jackson. The Slatons, who never had children, were active in the Atlanta community and socialized with some of the nation's wealthiest and most prestigious families. Their eighteen-room Tudor mansion on Peachtree Street symbolized warm hospitality, and their annual gala barbecues for the legislature attracted much attention.

After achieving success in the legal profession, Slaton embarked on a political career and quickly rose to prominence. Having previously cultivated friendships within the Democratic power structure in Atlanta, he won a seat in the Georgia House of Representatives in 1896. He served several terms in the lower house, including two terms as speaker, and then advanced to the upper house in 1908, where he immediately was elected president of the Senate, a position he held for two terms. Although a conservative Democrat, he was responsible for strengthening numerous reforms during this progressive era. He supported child labor reform, prohibition, stricter regulation of the railroads, and abolition of the convict-lease system. When Hoke Smith finally relinquished the governorship on 16 November 1911 and departed for the United States Senate, Slaton, as president of the Senate, assumed the duties of acting governor until Joseph M. Brown was elected to the office in a special election on 10 January 1912.

With Brown choosing not to seek another term and Hoke Smith safely away in Washington, Slaton entered the gubernatorial race of 1912. Campaigning aggressively, he called for tax equalization, frugality in government, strict regulation of public utilities, and leasing the Western and Atlantic Railroad. He easily defeated Joseph Hill Hall and Hooper Alexander, capturing nearly 75 percent of the popular vote. An able executive, Slaton secured the passage of several important bills, including a tax-equalization measure, an inheritance tax, a stronger pure food and drug act, child labor legislation, the establishment of a home for wayward girls, and a voter registration bill. He considered tax equalization and refunding the state's bonded indebtedness the most significant accomplishments of his administration.

When United States Senator A. O. Bacon died in February 1914, Slaton appointed W. S. West of Valdosta to the position until it could be filled in the next general election. When West declined to run, Slaton announced his candidacy for the seat. He won a slight plurality of the popular vote but failed to capture a majority of the county unit vote. The race went to the state Democratic convention in Macon where, after a bitter confrontation, Slaton lost on the fourteenth ballot to Congressman Thomas Hardwick, who had the support of Hoke Smith. Slaton vowed to avenge his bitter defeat, probably by challenging for a Senate seat in 1919.

After nearly two decades of distinguished public service, Slaton's popularity ended abruptly on 21 June 1915, five days before the end of his term, when he commuted to life imprisonment the death sentence of Leo Frank, the convicted murderer of young Mary Phagan. His act took rare courage, for Slaton knew that his political career would be ruined if he denied the public the blood of the convicted Jew. He also realized that public opinion was so aroused against Frank that his own life would be placed in jeopardy. But, having made a thorough study of the trial, the

Fig.48. John M. Slaton

appeals, and all of the evidence he could uncover, he still had serious doubts about Frank's guilt. When Slaton informed his wife of his decision, as well as the danger involved, she reportedly replied: "I would rather be the widow of a brave and honorable man than the wife of a coward." Slaton's life indeed was threatened, and national guardsmen had to stand guard around his home in Buckhead as animalistic mobs demonstrated for a week, threatening to kill the governor and dynamite his home. Sixteen guardsmen were injured protecting Slaton from the crowd of over five thousand. Immediately after the inauguration of his successor, Nat Harris, Slaton went on an extended tour of the West and Europe, his political career at an end. Ironically, Slaton's "act of conscience" failed to save the life of Leo Frank, who was entirely innocent of the crime. On 16 August 1915, a mob overpowered prison officials, seized Frank, drove him to Marietta, Mary Phagan's hometown, and lynched him.

When the hysteria finally subsided, Slaton returned to Georgia and eventually regained the status and honor he deserved. He resumed his practice of law and participated in civic and political affairs long after most of his contemporaries had died. In 1928 he was elected president of the State Bar Association, and in 1935 he received an honorary doctorate from the University of Georgia. He taught a Sunday school class at Trinity Methodist Church in Atlanta for almost half a century and practiced law for sixty-eight years, until a week before his death at age eighty-eight. He died of a cerebral hemorrhage on 11 January 1955, almost forty years after sparing the life of Leo Frank. He was buried in Oakland Cemetery in Atlanta. In a tribute to him, the *Atlanta Constitution* wrote: "He was that rare independent man in modern politics—putting principle and integrity above gain and ambition."

Nathaniel Edwin Harris
1915–1917

He founded Georgia Tech

Nat Harris, the last Confederate veteran and the first citizen of Macon to be elected governor of Georgia, was born on 21 January 1846, in Jonesboro, Tennessee, the first of eleven children born to Alexander Nelson and Edna Haynes Harris. His family had deep roots in Tennessee and Virginia, and the plantation on which he was born had been in the family since the mid-1700s. His father, a physician and Methodist minister, instilled high moral principles and a deep respect for education in him, but his mother, a modest and retiring woman, seems to have exerted even more influence upon the children. In his autobiography Harris states that "there was not one of the eleven children who did not yield to her influence and acknowledge her sense of right and justice." The task of punishing the children fell mostly to Mrs. Harris, whose firm discipline made a lasting impression on Nat. Writing when he was nearly eighty, he remembered that she used the rod "according to the Scriptures."

An apt student of ancient history, Harris read Tacitus, Herodotus, Caesar, Xenophon, Socrates, and Virgil in an old field school and an academy, but cut short his education by joining the Confederate army in 1862 as a sixteen-year-old private. Before allowing him to enter the army, his mother made him promise that he would not swear, drink liquor, or play cards; though mightily tempted by cards, the popular pastime of soldiers, he kept his promise. He served honorably until his unit disbanded in April of 1865, having participated in thirteen pitched battles and sixty-three skirmishes. Shortly after the Civil War ended, Alexander Harris died, leaving young Nat a legacy of debts and the responsibility of supporting his large family. Since the family property had been destroyed by the war, the Harris family rented a small farm in Bartow County, Georgia, where they eked out an existence.

After being tutored in Latin and Greek by Dr. William H. Felton, a popular physician-minister-politician, Harris secured a loan from Alexander H. Stephens and entered the University of Georgia as a sophomore in 1867. Despite financial woes, he was graduated at the top of his class in 1870 and delivered the valedictory address. After graduation he taught school at Sparta, studied law under Linton Stephens, and was admitted to the bar in 1872. The next year he moved to Macon and established a law partnership with Walter B. Hill, a classmate at the University of Georgia. The partnership lasted until 1899 when Hill became the chancellor of the University of Georgia.

After holding several local political offices, Harris was elected to the Georgia General Assembly in 1882. He served until 1886 and was the driving force behind the establishment of the Georgia School of Technology in Atlanta. Convinced that Georgia needed a technical school, he chaired a legislative committee that visited the outstanding technical schools in the country. He drummed up support for the project by delivering speeches throughout the state, asserting that the creation of such a school in Georgia could move the "throne of commercial enterprise" from Bunker Hill, Lowell, and Pittsburgh to "the banks of the Ocmulgee, the Chattahoochee, and the Savannah." Final approval for establishing the new school as a branch of the University of Georgia came on 12 October 1885. Harris served on a five-man commission to select a location for the technical school. He supported Macon, but the commission chose Atlanta instead. The commission then became a local board of trustees, and Harris served on it faithfully as chairman until his death in 1929.

Although establishing Georgia Tech was his chief interest, he became actively involved in other issues in his two terms in the House of Representatives. Business oriented, he sided with the railroads in their attempts to dilute the power of the new Railroad Commission. In 1885 he sponsored a successful bill that granted a charter for constructing a railroad from Macon to Covington. He later became a member of the company's board of directors and served as its general counsel. As chairman of the Finance Committee during his second term, he supported Governor Henry McDaniel's program, especially refunding the state debt and constructing a new state capitol in Atlanta. The controversial issue of prohibition, however, convinced Harris to retire from politics.

Having many interests outside of politics, Harris concentrated on his lucrative law practice, his family, and his many civic, educational, and religious interests. He married Fannie Burke of Macon on 12 February 1873, and they had seven children—Carrie, Walter, Nat, Fannie, John, David, and Nora. In 1898 his wife of twenty-five years contracted typhoid and died. On 6 July 1899 he married Hattie Gibson Jobe of Elizabethton, Tennessee. Harris was a member of the Mulberry Street Methodist Church, where he taught an adult Sunday school class for many years. He served one uneventful term in the Georgia Senate from

Fig.49. Nathaniel E. Harris

1894 to 1896 and was offered many other political positions which he turned down. He rejected the chancellorship of the University of Georgia three times and declined Governor Terrell's offer to serve as a justice of the Georgia Supreme Court. At the insistence of Governor Joseph M. Brown, he did accept the judgeship of the Superior Court of the Macon Circuit in 1912 but resigned after serving only five months. In view of this reluctance to hold office, many were surprised when Harris announced his candidacy for governor in 1914. Despite advanced age, he waged a vigorous campaign, delivering 162 speeches promising tax reductions and a more economical administration. With the backing of Tom Watson and the state's Confederate veterans, he won an easy victory in the Democratic primary over J. Randolph Anderson of Savannah and Dr.

Lamartine G. Hardman, a physician from Commerce who later served as governor.

Harris took office on 26 June 1915, five days after Governor John Slaton had commuted the death sentence of Leo Frank. In response to the lynching of Frank, Harris offered a reward for the capture of those responsible and ordered a special session of the Cobb County Superior Court to investigate the crime. Although he outwardly deplored mob violence, he privately observed that Governor Slaton had made a grave "mistake in judgment" in handling the Frank case.

Demonstrating little executive leadership, Harris allowed the prohibition issue to dominate the 1915 legislative session. It took up so much time that the session ended without approving a general appropriations bill. In a special session, the legislature adopted four prohibition bills. After signing the first one, Harris said "he felt that he had performed the greatest duty of his life for the uplifting of the state." Despite this legislation, individuals still could possess large quantities of alcoholic beverages in their homes. Shortly before leaving office Harris eliminated this loophole with the "bone dry" law, which made Georgia "the dryest state in the country."

Upon leaving office Harris stated that the three greatest accomplishments of his administration were the prohibition law, prompt payment of teachers' salaries, and re-leasing the Western and Atlantic Railroad for fifty years at $45,000 per month. His administration also increased benefits to Confederate veterans, established a State Highway Commission, which allowed the state to receive federal funds to construct rural roads, and adopted a compulsory education law, which required children between eight and fourteen years of age to attend public schools four months a year. In addition, Harris proposed other moderate reforms which the legislature failed to adopt. Harris had few delusions about politics, and in his autobiography, a work of rare candor, he states that "my experience as Governor was in the main only a tragedy."

The voters of Georgia evidently agreed, for when he sought reelection he lost by 35,000 votes. Despite the support of prohibitionists, the seventy-year-old Harris was trounced by Hugh M. Dorsey, the popular prosecutor in the Leo Frank case who had the backing of Tom Watson. In the 1916 Democratic primary, Dorsey won 106,680 votes to Harris's 70,998. Harris accepted the defeat philosophically, remarking that "the people have given and the people have taken away; blest be the name of the people."

After leaving office Harris spent much of his time working for the development of Georgia Tech; he served as its interim president in 1918. He maintained a keen interest in politics and continued to attend every session of the General Assembly. Despite advancing age, he was a Democratic presidential elector in 1924 and served as state pension commissioner in 1924–1925. In poor health the last three years of his life, Harris died at his summer home in Hampton, Tennessee, on 21 September 1929, at the age of eighty-three. He was buried in Rose Hill Cemetery in Macon.

Nathaniel Harris rose from poverty to become a successful attorney and dabbled in politics as a gentlemanly practitioner. In spite of a distaste for politics, he served his state well as legislator, judge, governor, and patron of education. But only in his sponsorship of the Georgia Institute of Technology did he exhibit the skill and tenacity needed for a successful political career. Consequently, historian James Dorsey has ranked Harris as a minor force in Georgia's New South development. Dorsey stated, however, that Harris served the state honorably, "free from much of the acrimony and contentiousness that characterized the personality-laden politics of his day."

Hugh Manson Dorsey
1917–1921

He prosecuted Leo Frank

Hugh M. Dorsey, the son of Rufus Thomas and Matilda Bennett Dorsey, was born in Fayetteville, Georgia, on 10 July 1871. In 1879 the family moved to Atlanta, where his father became a leading member of the bar and later a judge in the city court. Young Dorsey attended the public schools of Fayetteville and Atlanta, as well as private schools in Atlanta and Hartwell. After earning a bachelor's degree at the University of Georgia in 1893, he studied law at the University of Virginia, gained admittance to the bar, and worked briefly with the Southern Railway before entering his father's firm of Dorsey, Brewster, Howell, and Heyman in 1895. A competent attorney, he soon became a partner in the firm. On 29 June 1911, he married Adair Wilkinson of Valdosta, and they had two sons, James Wilkinson and Hugh Manson, Jr.

In 1910 Governor Joseph M. Brown appointed Dorsey solicitor general of the Atlanta Judicial Circuit, a position he held until 1916. In that capacity he prosecuted several famous criminal cases, the most controversial of which was that of Leo Frank, convicted of murdering Mary Phagan. Dorsey, who had failed to gain convictions in two recent murder cases, prosecuted the Frank case with great determination. The highly charged case generated so much publicity that Dorsey became a popular figure throughout the state. His work in securing the guilty verdict and in defeating all appeals also endeared him to Tom Watson, the power behind the throne. Although Watson held no office from 1902 to 1920, he often determined the outcome of state elections. His influence among rural voters was so pervasive that it was nearly impossible to win the governorship without his support. A crusader for human rights in his early career, Watson, embittered by many defeats, became an outspoken racist and anti-Semite. Convinced that Frank had been found guilty in a fair trial, he demanded the execution of the "Jew pervert" in scores of articles in his publications. When Governor Slaton commuted Frank's sentence to life imprisonment, Watson exploded: "Our grand old Empire State HAS BEEN RAPED!" He urged mobs to do what the governor had been unwilling to do. Even after a mob lynched Frank and mutilated his body, Watson kept the case in the public eye until the next election,

Fig.50. Hugh M. Dorsey

nearly a year away. Watson's choice for governor in 1916 was Hugh Dorsey, "the fearless, incorruptible Solicitor General who won the great fight for LAW AND ORDER, and the PROTECTION OF WOMANHOOD in the Leo Frank Case."

In the Democratic primary Dorsey faced three other candidates: Nat Harris, the incumbent governor who stressed prohibition; Dr. L. G. Hardman, who contended that Georgia had had enough lawyers as governor and now needed a physician; and Joseph E. Pottle of Milledgeville, an ex-solicitor general of the Ocmulgee Circuit. Dorsey, who endorsed President Woodrow Wilson's program and pledged to uphold the verdicts of the courts, won an easy victory in the primary and was reelected in 1918 without opposition.

Although defense measures dominated the Dorsey administration as Georgia supplied over 85,000 troops for the armed services, twenty-seven amendments to the Georgia constitution also were adopted. They added eight new counties, raised salaries of state officials, and increased the size of both the House and the Senate. In addition, the Neill Primary Act, which Governor Harris previously had vetoed, became law in 1917. It legalized and broadened the application of the county unit system, which already had been used in several previous elections. Under this system, unique to Georgia, Democratic party candidates were nominated by county unit votes rather than by popular votes. Each county received a unit vote commensurate with its representation in the House of Representatives. Thus the state's eight most populous counties received six unit votes apiece, the thirty middle-sized counties received four, and the remaining counties got two. The candidate for state office who received the largest popular vote in a county received all of that county's unit votes. A plurality of unit votes was sufficient to nominate a candidate for any office other than governor or United States senator, which required a majority vote. This system practically ensured rural domination of Georgia's government by placing disproportionate power in the small rural counties and grossly discriminating against city residents, especially as the state became more urbanized. Under the county unit system, which remained in effect until 1962, the most successful politicians geared their campaigns to the rural elements and ignored the cities. However, candidates nominated by county unit votes almost always received the most popular votes too. In fact, during the entire period of the county unit system only one governor, Eugene Talmadge in 1946, failed to receive a popular victory as well as the majority of county unit votes.

Dorsey published a pamphlet during his second term which attacked the state's treatment of blacks. He expressed concern that peonage was a widespread problem in many rural areas of the state. His charges provoked heated discussion and alienated Tom Watson, who easily defeated Dorsey in a race for a United States Senate seat in 1920.

Upon leaving office on 25 June 1921, Dorsey resumed his law practice in Atlanta. From 1926 to 1935 he served as a judge of the Civil Division of the Atlanta Municipal Court, an office once held by his father. He then served as a judge of the Fulton Superior Court from 1935 until 4 March 1948. He died on 11 June 1948, at age seventy-six, and was buried in West View Cemetery in Atlanta.

Thomas William Hardwick
1921-1923

He opposed the Ku Klux Klan
and appointed the first female U.S. senator

A politician of recognized ability, independence, and courage, Tom Hardwick fought for honest and efficient government throughout a long and turbulent political career. Governor from 1921 to 1923, he maintained his principles even when they were unpopular with a majority of the voters. As his biographer Josephine Cummings pointed out, he "preferred defeat and political oblivion to compromising his convictions." Consequently, he suffered many defeats.

Born in Thomasville, Georgia, on 9 December 1872, he was the son of Robert William and Zemula Schley Matthews Hardwick. Reared in Washington County, he attended public schools and earned a bachelor of arts degree at Mercer University in 1892. Following his graduation from the law school of the University of Georgia, he was admitted to the bar and established a law practice in Sandersville, where he became county prosecuting attorney in 1895. On 25 April 1894, he married Maude Elizabeth Perkins of Burke County. In their forty-three years of marriage only one child, Mary, survived infancy. After Mrs. Hardwick's death in 1937, he married Sally Warren West.

A lifelong Democrat who feared the Populist doctrines, Hardwick served in the Georgia House of Representatives from 1898 to 1902 before advancing to Congress, where he served sixteen years, six terms in the House and one term in the Senate. His first speech in Congress was "The Disfranchisement of Negroes." Regarded as an expert constitutional lawyer, he sought the repeal of the Fourteenth and Fifteenth Amendments, arguing that both had been illegally ratified. During his tenure in the state house, Hardwick supported most of President Woodrow Wilson's domestic reforms, including the Underwood Tariff Act, the Federal Reserve Act, the Clayton Antitrust Act, and the Seaman's Act.

Following the death of Senator Augustus O. Bacon in 1914, Hardwick became a candidate for the unexpired Senate vacancy. He ran second to Governor John M. Slaton in a field of five candidates in the Democratic primary, but no candidate received a majority. At the state Democratic convention, Hardwick, with the support of Hoke Smith, won the Senate nomination on the fourteenth ballot. In the Senate he generally supported Wilson's congressional program, but opposed the Child Labor Act, the Eighteenth Amendment, the Espionage Act, and the Selective Service Act. Basically a Jeffersonian states' righter, he shuddered at the growth of Federal authority. Despite deep concerns over the extraordinary wartime powers granted to the president, he reluctantly voted to enter World War I on 2 April 1917. His isolationism angered Wilson who called Hardwick a "constant and active opponent of my administration." Hardwick sought reelection to the Senate in 1918, but with patriotism at its height and a popular president opposing him, he had little chance. William J. Harris of Cedartown, an ardent supporter of Wilson, won by a landslide; Hardwick ran third among five candidates for the office.

In 1920 Hardwick launched an aggressive campaign for the governorship. An opponent of the League of Nations and Wilson's "newfangled internationalism," he called for a return to the "old fashioned Americanism of George Washington and Thomas Jefferson," and promised a balanced budget, tax revision, the elimination of useless state offices, increased salaries for teachers, and adoption of the secret ballot. In the Democratic primary Hardwick carried 78 counties and 190 county unit votes, but fell four votes short of a majority. With the support of both Tom Watson and Hoke Smith, he easily defeated Attorney General Clifford Walker in the runoff election for the Democratic nomination, tantamount to election.

As governor, Hardwick faced many problems, especially a declining economy following the boll-weevil infestation of cotton. A crop that had yielded as much as 2 million bales a year produced only 600,000 bales in 1923, and, to compound the problem, the price of cotton dropped to about twenty cents a pound. To combat the economic distress Hardwick proposed numerous reforms, including the reorganization of the state-supported colleges and universities under a board of regents, the construction of a system of highways, and the development of a seaport. Unfortunately, the General Assembly adopted few of his proposals. It did enact the secret ballot, establish a state audit department, introduce the first tax on gasoline, and reorganize the Railroad Commission as the Georgia Utilities Commission; but it refused to institute the income tax and other economy measures, and, as a result, expenditures exceeded income. By executive order Hardwick abolished the flogging of prisoners, and he spoke out emphatically against the Ku Klux Klan, which had gained thousands of members in the postwar years. He demanded that the

Fig.51. Thomas W. Hardwick

Klan unmask and offered legal help to punish offenders and martial law to maintain order where Klan terrorism prevailed.

Hardwick's courageous stand against the Klan probably cost him reelection in 1922. Though supported by the business and professional community and by Hoke Smith, he lost to Clifford Walker, who enjoyed the support of the agrarian population, the Klan, and Tom Watson. Hardwick had alienated Watson by failing to appoint enough of his friends to office. The "Sage of Hickory Hill" grumbled that his men had been good enough to vote for Hardwick but were not good enough to receive appointments from him. In the Democratic primary Hardwick carried only 118 county unit votes to Walker's total of 294. He lost the popular vote by an equally lopsided margin—123,784 to 86,389.

When Senator Watson died on 26 September 1922, Hardwick first offered the seat to Watson's widow, who declined to serve. He then selected Mrs. Rebecca Latimer Felton, a popular reformer and eighty-seven-year-old widow of Dr. William H. Felton. Although Mrs. Felton attended only two sessions, she gained the distinction of being the first woman ever to serve in the United States Senate. In the special election to fill the remainder of Watson's term in the Senate Hardwick lost to Walter George. Two years later Hardwick made a final attempt to regain

Fig.52. Seven Georgia governors (lf. to rt.): Rivers,
E. Talmadge, Russell, Walker, Hardwick, Dorsey, and Slaton.

a Senate seat, but was trounced by the incumbent William J. Harris.
Hardwick carried only twelve counties to Harris's 148. In 1932 he made
a futile attempt to regain the governorship, but lost overwhelmingly in
the Democratic primary.

Between political campaigns Hardwick resumed the practice of law
in Washington, D.C., and Atlanta, and after 1927 in Sandersville, a practice which he continued until his death of a heart attack on 31 January
1944. He was buried in the Old City Cemetery in Sandersville. The
Macon Telegraph, an opposition newspaper, described him as "one of the
few Georgians whose public service in recent years has measured up to
the highest standard of statesmanship." Contemporary historian William
Gabard has observed that "dishonesty never tainted his character" and
that "his dynamic participation in the turbulent and tortuous Georgia politics of the twentieth century entitles him to a prominent place in Georgia
history."

Clifford Mitchell Walker
1923-1927

He was a member of the Ku Klux Klan

A cousin and neighbor of former governor Henry D. McDaniel, Clifford Walker was born in Monroe, Georgia, on 4 July 1877. One of seven children born to Billington Sanders and Alice Mitchell Walker, he attended Johnson Institute, the Georgia Military Institute in Marietta, and the University of Georgia, where he received a bachelor of arts degree in 1897. An outstanding student, at the university he established the college literary magazine and was elected to Phi Beta Kappa. After graduation he read law with Monroe attorney R. L. Cox and was admitted to the bar in 1898. On 29 April 1902, he married Rosa Carter Mathewson of Anderson County, South Carolina, and they had three sons: Clifford, Sanders, and Harold. He served as mayor of Monroe from 1902 to 1904 and was solicitor general of the Western Circuit from 1909 to 1913. In 1915 Walker was elected Georgia attorney general, a post he held until April of 1920, when he resigned to run for governor.

The Ku Klux Klan, dormant since Reconstruction, was revived in a ceremony atop Stone Mountain, Georgia, on Thanksgiving night 1915. In the ensuing years it gained millions of adherents throughout the country and became a formidable political force in many states, including Georgia. In the 1920 gubernatorial primary, Tom Hardwick, who had praised the Klan, easily defeated Clifford Walker. But when Governor Hardwick turned against the Klan and demanded that it unmask and cease its violence, the Klan rallied its legions in support of Walker. In the Democratic primary of 1922 Walker easily defeated Hardwick, carrying 294 county unit votes and 123,784 popular votes to Hardwick's 118 county unit votes and 86,389 popular votes. With Klan support, Walker won reelection in 1924 without opposition.

At the national convention of the Klan, Walker promised that if the organization got into any trouble he would not report it to the newspapers or the electorate. "I am not going to denounce anybody," he told the Klansmen. "I am coming right here to your leaders and talk to you." True to his promise, Governor Walker, along with Chief Justice Richard B. Russell, Sr., often conferred with Klan leaders on state policy. Nevertheless, when Klan beatings and floggings got out of hand in Macon and

Fig.53. Clifford M. Walker

Lyons, Walker threatened to declare martial law and offered a reward for the apprehension of the culprits. In September 1924 Julian Harris, editor of the *Columbus Enquirer-Sun*, reported that Walker had travelled secretly to Kansas City to address a closed meeting of Klan officials. Walker denied the charge, claiming he was in Philadelphia at the time. Relentless pressure, however, forced him to admit making the speech and joining the Klan, but he insisted that he had been an inactive member. The press then dubbed him "Kautious Kleagle Kliff." Harris, who later received a Pulitzer Prize for his work, continued to lambast the "disgraceful conduct" of Georgia's "sorry little governor" and called for Walker's impeachment.

In campaigning for governor, Walker had advocated revising the tax system completely, eliminating unnecessary offices, providing free textbooks, and increasing appropriations for pensions and roads. Despite Walker's calling of two special sessions of the legislature in 1923, the General Assembly refused to adopt much of his program. His adminis-

Fig.54. Clifford M. Walker

tration created the state forestry commission, increased the gasoline tax, adopted other minor tax reforms, and provided for biennial sixty-day legislative sessions, but it failed to provide free textbooks or enact an income tax. Compiling an undistinguished legislative record, he considered getting programs underway for better schools and roads his most successful accomplishment.

After leaving office, Walker moved from Monroe to Atlanta and opened a private law practice. In 1933, he and Joseph B. Kilbride founded the Woodrow Wilson College of Law in Atlanta, and he served as president of that institution until his death. Recognized as an expert on Georgia criminal law, he wrote a textbook, *Walker's Notes on Criminal Law*. From 1937 until his retirement in 1952, he also served as general counsel for the Georgia Department of Labor.

A lifetime member of First Baptist Church of Monroe where he was a deacon, Walker served for many years as a trustee for two Baptist colleges, Mercer University and Shorter College. He also was active in the Masons, Knights of Pythias, and Odd Fellows. He died on 9 November 1954 at his Monroe home and was buried a short distance away in the Old Baptist Cemetery.

Lamartine Griffin Hardman
1927–1931

He would run the state like a business

L. G. Hardman, doctor, businessman, farmer, and statesman, was born in Commerce, Georgia, on 14 April 1856. The son of William Benjamin Johnson and Susan Elizabeth Colquitt Hardman, he was reared in comfortable circumstances as his father, a physician and Baptist minister, had extensive business and farming interests. He was educated in the local public schools, studied medicine with his father, and was graduated from the medical department of the University of Georgia in 1876. He did postgraduate study at the University of Pennsylvania, the New York Polyclinic, and later at Guy Hospital in London. Hardman practiced medicine in Commerce with his brother, W. B. Hardman, and did innovative experiments in the developing field of anesthesiology. Like his father, he developed extensive business and farming interests. He founded the Harmony Grove Cotton Mill at Commerce and the Hardman Roller Mills, which processed grains. One of the largest farmers in the state, he owned 10,000 acres of peach and apple orchards. He organized the Northeastern Banking Company at Commerce, established the Hardman Drug Company, and founded the Commerce Telephone Company. He owned and operated the Hurricane Shoals Light and Power Company and the Nora Mills and was a director of the First National Bank of Commerce. A guiding force in developing Georgia Agriculture College, he served on its board of trustees for more than two decades. He also was a trustee for Shorter College, Mercer University, and the Southern Baptist Theological Seminary in Louisville, Kentucky. Like many Georgia governors, he was a Baptist and taught a Sunday school class. On 26 March 1907, he married Emma Wiley Griffin, a socially prominent woman from Valdosta. She was a member of the Daughters of the American Revolution, the United Daughters of the Confederacy, and was a trustee of Mercer University and the Tallulah Falls Industrial School. They had four children: Lamartine Griffin, Josephine Staten, Sue Colquitt, and Emma Griffin.

In addition to pursuing these varied interests, Hardman also was committed to a political career. In 1902 he was elected to the Georgia House of Representatives, where he served for eight years. He sponsored several agricultural bills and a measure that created the State Board of Health. In

Fig.55. Lamartine G. Hardman

1907–1908 he served in the Georgia Senate, where he coauthored the state's new prohibition law. During World War I he served as the state's fuel administrator. After two unsuccessful attempts, he was elected governor in 1926, defeating John Holder, controversial chairman of the Highway Board. Holder actually received more popular votes than Hardman in the Democratic primary, but in the runoff election Hardman won the county unit vote 276 to 138 and the popular vote 80,868 to 60,197. Following Nathan Brownson and Lyman Hall, Hardman became the third physician to serve as governor of Georgia.

Having promised to give the state a "business-like" administration and to eliminate waste and extravagance, Hardman proposed several reforms, including measures to revise the constitution, study the banking system, discontinue deficits, and increase the governor's term to four years. The General Assembly, however, rejected his measures. So little legislation was passed in the 1927 session that the *Macon Daily Telegraph* concluded that "the legislature might as well not have met." The General Assembly had neither balanced the budget nor reorganized the administrative or agricultural departments. Part of the failure must rest with Hardman who, though gifted in many ways, lacked political finesse and gave little direction to the legislature. On one occasion he appointed an enemy to a judgeship and then announced publicly that he had intended to appoint another man with the same last name. In response to charges of gross mismanagement in the Highway Department, he had promised to replace the chairman, John Holder, but he failed to do so. His first appointee, who had not been consulted, declined the offer, and his next two choices were rejected by the Senate. Consequently, Holder remained as chairman.

Despite Hardman's political inadequacies, he gained reelection in 1928 over E. D. Rivers, an aggressive young legislator who had Holder's backing and whose campaign was ably managed by Roy V. Harris of Augusta. Hardman, who was seventy-two years old and in failing health, delivered only two speeches in the campaign. He refused to debate Rivers and campaigned primarily through personal contacts and press releases. Rivers gained endorsements from the *Macon Telegraph* and the *Columbus Enquirer-Sun*, but Hardman won a decisive victory, carrying 117 counties and 310 county unit votes to Rivers's 44 counties and 104 county unit votes. Hardman also won the popular vote by a margin of 137,430 to 97,339.

Hardman's second term accomplished little more than his first term, as his relationship with the General Assembly became more antagonistic. Although the state faced serious economic problems and a growing indebtedness, few constructive measures were adopted. Indeed, even a sixty-day special session, called to deal with the deteriorating economy, failed to produce significant legislation because of the wide breach between governor and legislature. When the General Assembly finally adopted a revenue measure, Hardman vetoed it, bringing on himself an avalanche of abuse for wasting taxpayers' money in the futile special session. Minor accomplishments of his term include securing a plant to manufacture license tags, appropriating money to remodel the capitol, improving the experiment station at Griffin, and accepting the Rhodes home in Atlanta as a depository for the state archives. Hardman's major

Fig.56. Lamartine G. Hardman

achievement lay in the work of the Allen Commission on Simplification and Coordination. This commission, headed by Ivan Allen, Sr., was charged with seeking ways to streamline state government, a theme Hardman had stressed for four years. It laid the groundwork for the extensive reorganization achieved under Hardman's successor, Governor Richard B. Russell, Jr.

Hardman died on 18 February 1937 of a heart ailment and was buried in Gray Hill Cemetery in Commerce.

Richard Brevard Russell, Jr.
1931-1933

He was a "senator's senator"

In a political career that spanned half a century, Richard Russell never lost an election. After serving as Georgia's youngest popularly elected governor, he replaced Robert LaFollette as the youngest member of the United States Senate and remained there for thirty-eight years. One of three men to be elected to seven consecutive Senate terms, he was the first to serve more than half of his life in the Senate. His appeal to the Georgia electorate was so great that after defeating Eugene Talmadge for reelection to the Senate in 1936, he never again faced serious opposition. Known as a "senator's senator," he developed an intimate knowledge of the Senate rules and a clear understanding of how "the most deliberative body in the world" operated. A bachelor, some said he was married to the Senate. The Senate was his consuming interest, and few senators have ever exerted as much influence on national policies for such a long time as Russell. Respected for his judgment and integrity, he counseled six presidents, from Franklin Roosevelt to Richard Nixon. At the time of his death, Georgia's senior senator was president pro tempore of the Senate, chairman of the Senate Appropriations Committee, senior member of the Senate Democratic Policy and Steering Committees, ranking Democrat on the Senate Aeronautical and Space Science Committee, and ranking Democrat on the Joint Committee on Atomic Science. He was third in line for the presidency.

Born in Winder, Georgia, on 2 November 1897, he was the son of Richard Brevard and Ina Dillard Russell. He was the first of seven sons and the fourth child born in a family of fifteen children. His father, an unsuccessful candidate for governor and United States senator, served as chief justice of the Georgia Supreme Court for fifteen years. Russell attended public schools, graduating from the Seventh District Agricultural and Mechanical School in Powder Springs in 1914, from Gordon Institute in Barnesville in 1915, and from the University of Georgia in 1918 with an LL. B. degree. Admitted to the bar, he began practicing law in Winder in 1919 and was soon elected county attorney of Barrow County. In 1920 he won a seat in the Georgia House of Representatives, where he served ten consecutive years, the last four as speaker of the house. He rose to

Fig.57. Richard B. Russell, Jr.

a position of leadership by avoiding factionalism, emphasizing issues, and practicing the art of political compromise. His chief interests were public education and good roads.

In 1930, though only thirty-two years old, Russell announced his candidacy for governor. By campaigning aggressively he came in first in both popular and county unit votes in a five-man race, but had less than a majority. In the runoff election he trounced George Carswell, Hardman's secretary of state, by a popular vote of 99,505 to 47,157 and a county unit vote of 330 to 84.

In his inaugural address Russell urged the General Assembly to reorganize state government to eliminate waste and extravagance and achieve greater efficiency. Previous governors had obtained only meager results when they made similar pleas, but several factors now favored change. First, the legislature, with several new members, was more receptive to change; second, the governor, backed by a popular mandate, enjoyed a good relationship with the General Assembly and had campaigned as a reformer; third, the need for reform had been publicized by previous governors; fourth, the Ivan Allen Committee had presented a workable blueprint for simplifying the state bureaucracy; and fifth, the Great Depression, by worsening an already unhealthy situation, made some form of reorganization almost mandatory.

The Ivan Allen Committee accurately described the antiquated bureaucratic structure that Governor Russell inherited. "We now have in the administrative branch 29 departments, 21 boards, 24 educational institutions, 2 experiment stations, 3 educational and eleemosynary institutions, 3 corrective institutions, 321 trustees, and thousands of employees," it asserted. In addition, there were 161 county school systems, 34 independent systems, 161 tax collectors, plus various departments collecting fees. The Allen Committee could find "no central oversight" and concluded that "our past experience has been that we reward extravagance with deficiency appropriations and punish economy by failure to provide the necessary means of expansion."

Prodded by Governor Russell, the legislature passed the Reorganization Act of 1931, which reduced the number of state agencies and bureaus from 102 to 17. Probably the most important change was placing all of the state-supported colleges under one board of regents. Under the old system there was duplication of programs and an utter lack of coordination among the institutions since each one had a separate board of trustees and received a separate appropriation from the legislature. Under the new system, the Board of Regents, consisting of eleven members appointed by the governor and the governor ex officio, governed all of the public colleges and received one lump sum appropriation from the legislature. Other reforms of the Russell administration included reapportioning the state into ten congressional districts; giving the governor greater power over the budget process and state spending; and amending the constitution to inaugurate the governor in January instead of June. Russell also favored greater support for public education but could do little because of the Depression. Altogether, more substantive reforms were adopted during Russell's two-year administration than in any term since Hoke Smith—perhaps more than in any previous administration in the state's history.

When Senator William J. Harris died on 18 April 1932, Russell appointed *Atlanta Journal* editor John S. Cohen to succeed him. Rather than seek a second term as governor, Russell announced his candidacy for the unexpired Senate term. After a hard campaign he defeated Con-

Fig.58. E. D. Rivers and Richard B. Russell, Jr.

gressman Charles R. Crisp of Americus by a vote of 162,745 to 119,193. Arriving in Washington in January 1933, he supported Franklin Roosevelt's New Deal with enthusiasm. Since Georgia was heavily rural, Russell was especially anxious to pass federal farm relief. He supported soil-conservation legislation, rural electrification, commodity price supports, the Agricultural Adjustment Act, and the Farm Security Administration. He was the leading sponsor of the school lunch program, which he considered his proudest legislative achievement.

By the 1940s Russell had become one of the most respected and powerful leaders of the Senate, especially in the areas of the federal budget, defense, and farm policy. His influence came in part from key committee assignments. He was appointed to the Appropriations Committee in 1933 and served there until his death in 1971. He also was a member of the Armed Services Committee, chairman for sixteen years. Working with his counterpart in the House, fellow Georgian Carl Vinson, Russell made sure that Georgia received its share of military installations. From World War II onward, the Georgia economy has benefited significantly from military investments. Indeed, when Lockheed Georgia in Marietta was building the C5A, the world's largest airplane, it was the biggest single employer in the state.

Russell gained national visibility by serving on several special congressional committees. In 1943 he headed a special Senate committee that made a fact-finding tour of the world's battlefronts. In 1951 he chaired the committee that investigated the dismissal of General Douglas MacArthur. After the assassination of President John F. Kennedy, Russell was appointed to the Warren Commission, which investigated that tragedy. Russell also gained national attention by his staunch opposition to federal civil rights laws. By the late 1940s he had become the leader of a group of senators known as the Southern bloc, who opposed integration and social equality. He fought federal anti-lynching legislation, the Fair Employment Practices Commission, and school desegregation. Largely because of his racial views, he never secured the Democratic nomination for the presidency. His best chance came in 1952 when he received 294 votes at the convention. After that disappointing loss, he never sought the office again.

While Russell consistently supported a strong defense, he recognized the limits of American power. He opposed sending American troops to Vietnam, but once the nation was committed, he strongly supported a military solution there. He opposed liberalizing immigration restrictions after World War II and he sought reductions in foreign aid expenditures. He opposed the Civil Rights Acts of 1964 and 1965 and much of Lyndon Johnson's Great Society legislation. While still wielding great power, he gradually became more of a sectional than a national leader, observed Gilbert Fite in his excellent Russell biography: "His opposition to growing federal powers and functions, his devotion to states' rights, and his segregationist position alienated him from the nation's mainstream."

From the early 1960s onward Russell suffered from emphysema and later cancer. He died of respiratory difficulties in Walter Reed Army Medical Center in Washington on 21 January 1971. His body was returned to Georgia, where it lay in state in the capitol. Thousands paid respects, including most of the political leaders of the nation. President Richard Nixon placed a wreath on his casket. He was buried in the Russell family cemetery in Winder.

Fig.59. President Nixon at a reception
for Richard B. Russell, Jr. (1970)

The Russell name has been commemorated in many ways by a grateful state and nation. His vast collection of papers are housed in the Richard B. Russell Memorial Library at the University of Georgia. His statue stands on the capitol grounds in Atlanta. An elementary school in Cobb County bears his name, as does an agriculture research center in Athens, a scenic highway in north Georgia, a post office in Winder, an airport in Rome, a nuclear submarine, and a Senate office building in Washington.

Eugene Talmadge
1933–1937, 1941–1943

He was called "the Wild Man from Sugar Creek"

Described by liberal critics as "Georgia's demagogue," "a wool hat dictator," and "the wild man from Sugar Creek," Eugene Talmadge was the most dynamic force in Georgia politics since Tom Watson and one of the most popular politicians in the state's history. Rural Georgians identified with Talmadge, a "dirt farmer" who spoke their idiom, and they voted for him with unrestrained enthusiasm. He directed his campaigns almost exclusively to them. Ignoring the cities, Talmadge maintained that he did not campaign where the streetcars ran. Unsurpassed as a stump speaker at county political rallies, he interspersed flamboyant political rhetoric with barbecue, moonshine, and the hillbilly music of Fiddlin' John Carson and Moonshine Kate. Other colorful antics, such as wearing red suspenders, arriving at political rallies atop a bale of cotton in an oxen-drawn wagon, and grazing cattle on the grounds of the executive mansion enhanced his standing with the "wool hat boys." Like Watson, he could rely on thousands of rural votes in any campaign.

The scion of a conservative and respected family, Talmadge was born on the family plantation near Forsyth on 23 September 1884, the son of Thomas Remalgus and Carrie Roberts Talmadge. Following in the footsteps of his father and grandfather, he attended the University of Georgia, where he received an LL. B. degree in 1907. He began to practice law in Atlanta, but within a year he moved to Montgomery County. On 12 September 1909, he married Mattie Thurmond Peterson, a widow with a young son, John A. Peterson. Talmadge and "Miss Mitt" had three children: Margaret, Vera, and Herman, who later served as governor of Georgia. Three years after his marriage, Talmadge purchased a farm on Sugar Creek in Telfair County, adjoining property his wife owned. There he quietly farmed, practiced law, and operated a sawmill for the next fourteen years.

Bored with farm life and disappointed in his meager income, Talmadge entered the political arena. After serving as solicitor of the City Court of McRae and attorney for Telfair County, he ran unsuccessfully for state representative in 1920 and for state senator in 1922. Undeterred by successive defeats, he ran for commissioner of agriculture in 1926

Fig.60. Eugene Talmadge giving a fiery speech

against J. J. Brown, the powerful incumbent. Although Talmadge was virtually unknown, had little financial support, and practically no political organization, the time was ripe for a change. Capitalizing on his opportunities, he gained an early endorsement from the *Atlanta Constitution*, managed to get Brown's many enemies to unite behind his candidacy, and campaigned adeptly. His irreverent posture, earthy humor, and emotional rhetoric appealed to the rural Georgia voters, who flocked to the polls. Talmadge shocked Georgia politicos by trouncing Brown, carrying 139 counties to Brown's 22 and winning the popular vote 123,115 to 66,569.

Upon taking office, he cleaned house thoroughly, replacing Brown's appointees with his own cronies. He also displayed administrative ability by increasing the number of food and drug inspections, analyses of fertilizer samples, and marketing inspections at less cost to the taxpayer. He used the departmental newspaper, the *Market Bulletin,* to communicate his political and economic philosophy to Georgia's rural population. In addition to relating the latest agricultural information, he urged farmers to stay on the land, withhold their crops from the market in order to raise prices, diversify their operations, and develop processing industries. His remedy to the farmers' distress was hard manual labor, rugged individualism, honesty, and frugality. He may not have grasped the complexities of national economics, but his understanding of the Southern rural mind was exceptional. Georgia farmers, needing a spokesman, rallied behind Talmadge, and he championed their cause by railing against big business, unfair economic conditions, lobbyists, and railroads. His popular appeal was so great that he won easy reelections as commissioner of agriculture in 1928 and 1930.

In 1931 a Senate investigating committee disclosed that Talmadge had paid $40,000 in salaries to himself and other family members over a three-year period. State funds, it appeared, had financed Talmadge's annual trips to the Kentucky Derby and other personal matters. Talmadge defied the committee until it appeared that he might actually be impeached. Then he told the committee, "If I stole, it was for the farmers like yourselves!" He escaped impeachment, but the House insisted that he repay the state $14,136 he had spent on a harebrained scheme to raise the price of hogs. Talmadge refused to pay, and the attorney general refused to sue him. Thus he emerged from the sordid affair victorious and unscathed.

Talmadge ran for governor in 1932 on a platform calling for strict economy in government and low taxes. Taking full advantage of the county unit system, he won an impressive victory over seven other candidates in the Democratic primary. Although polling fewer than 117,000 popular votes—45,000 fewer than the total of his opponents—he received almost twice as many county unit votes as all of his opponents combined. Two years later he won reelection, carrying all but three of the state's 159 counties.

A powerful executive, Talmadge never hesitated to fire an opponent, rule by executive decree, or declare martial law. When the legislature adjourned in 1933 without lowering the price of license tags to three dollars as he had requested, he did it by executive decree. When the Public Service Commission refused to lower utility rates to his satisfac-

Fig.61. Eugene Talmadge among the voters

tion, he dismissed the entire commission and appointed a new one that reduced the rates. When a massive textile strike occurred in the fall of 1934, he responded by declaring martial law and sending troops to Cartersville, Rockmart, Columbus, Trion, Barnesville, Griffin, Macon, and Newnan. When the legislature adjourned in 1935 without passing an appropriations bill, he ran the state without a budget. When the state treasurer and comptroller general refused to countersign warrants, he forcibly removed them from office.

Talmadge, who thrived on controversy, frequently was at odds with the Roosevelt administration. While he welcomed the money the New Deal poured into Georgia, he balked at federal controls. Intellectually and temperamentally opposed to public welfare, government debt, and big government, he became a bitter critic of the New Deal. When President

Roosevelt came to Atlanta on a scheduled visit in 1935, Talmadge refused to greet him. The governor lamely explained that he had more pressing business to attend to on his farm. He publicly described Civilian Conservation Corps workers as "bums and loafers." Talmadge tried to supplant Roosevelt as the Democratic presidential nominee in 1936, but when his campaign fizzled he lowered his sights to the United States Senate seat held by Richard Russell. In a hard-fought contest Talmadge suffered his worst political defeat, carrying only 16 counties and 134,695 popular votes to Russell's total of 143 counties and 256,154 popular votes. Still ambitious for a Senate seat, he made a much better showing two years later but lost again to incumbent Senator Walter George.

Somewhat chastened by two successive defeats, Talmadge sought a third term as governor in 1940, promising low taxes, fiscal responsibility, and more restraint in running the affairs of the state. Opposed by Abit Nix and Columbus Roberts, he won a popular majority and carried 132 counties. Back in the governor's office, he was soon embroiled in controversy. Talmadge charged that certain educators—initially the president of Georgia Teachers College in Statesboro and the dean of the College of Education at the University of Georgia—should not be re-employed because they had advocated racially integrating Georgia's schools. When the Board of Regents refused to fire the distinguished scholars, he purged the board. The new Board of Regents, totally dominated by the governor, dismissed the two educators and ousted several others, including the vice chancellor, on trumped up charges. As a result of Talmadge's blatant political interference, all of Georgia's state-supported colleges for whites lost their national accreditation. A storm of protest then erupted against Talmadge, which kept the state in turmoil for months. Largely because of the education issue, Talmadge lost the 1942 gubernatorial election to young Ellis Arnall. It was Talmadge's only gubernatorial defeat and Arnall's only victory.

Talmadge resumed his law practice and supervised his extensive landholdings, but politics remained his chief interest. His editorials in *The Statesman*, the newspaper he had published since the mid-1930s, became more stridently anti-Roosevelt, anti-New Deal, anti-black, and isolationist. After being out of office for four years, Talmadge sought a fourth term as governor in 1946. Though Arnall had been an extremely capable and progressive governor, his faction was in disarray over the choice of a successor. After alienating Ed Rivers and Roy Harris, Arnall eventually endorsed James V. Carmichael. To further complicate matters, a federal

Fig.62. Eugene Talmadge, Mrs. Talmadge, and their daughter Margaret

court ruled early in 1946 that blacks must be allowed to vote in the Democratic primary. Talmadge promised a "Democratic white primary unfettered and unhampered by radical communist and alien influences." He also promised to raise teachers' salaries by 50 percent, provide a million dollars a year to the counties for rural medical facilities, pave every road over which a mail truck traveled, and give a lifetime driver's license and a five-year ad valorem exemption to veterans. In a bitterly fought contest, Carmichael won the popular vote, tallying 313,389 to Talmadge's 297,245 and Rivers's 69,489. But Talmadge won the election by amassing 242 county unit votes to Carmichael's 146 and Rivers's 22. In winning, Talmadge proved that in addition to being one of the state's most colorful governors, he also was one of the most resilient.

In declining health before the campaign began, he was physically exhausted when it ended. The 272 speeches he delivered in the grueling campaign had taken their toll. He attempted to recuperate by taking an extended vacation in Florida, but while there he collapsed with a bleeding vein in his stomach. While he was being treated at an Atlanta hospital, a friend remarked: "Governor, you are the first man in the history of Georgia to cause every single person in the state to pray at the same time—half of 'em praying for you to get well and half of 'em praying you won't." He died on 21 December 1946 and was buried in McRae.

By capitalizing on the rural poverty of the 1920s and 1930s, the white primary, the one-party tradition, and the county unit system, he rose to a dominant position in state affairs. From 1926 to 1946 he won seven out of ten statewide campaigns, including four elections as governor, a feat equalled only by Joseph E. Brown in the Civil War era. The spokesman for white rural Georgians, he bragged that "the poor dirt farmer ain't got but three friends on earth: God Almighty, Sears Roebuck, and Gene Talmadge." Ironically, his policies of limited government and low taxation benefited businessmen more than the dirt farmers he claimed to represent. Vehemently opposed to the New Deal, civil rights, and organized labor, his record as governor is largely negative. Moreover, his penchant for taking liberties with the law, his flamboyant behavior, and his instigation of the education crisis gave the state adverse national publicity. Essentially, he was attempting to maintain a traditional culture that was being eroded by modern forces. His political success resulted entirely from his personality. He was colorful, humorous, magnetic, and exasperating—but never dull. Thousands loved him and thousands hated him, but few could be indifferent to him.

Eurith Dickinson Rivers
1937-1941

He brought the New Deal to Georgia

Ed Rivers, who succeeded Talmadge as governor in 1937, was the anti-thesis of the "wild man from Sugar Creek." Taking office in the midst of the Great Depression, he supported President Franklin Roosevelt with unrestrained enthusiasm and is credited with bringing the New Deal to Georgia.

Born in Center Point, Arkansas, on 1 December 1895, he was the son of James Matthew and Millie Annie Wilkerson Rivers. In his youth he showed more interest in sports than in books. To get him away from sports, his parents sent him to Young Harris College, a small Methodist institution in the north Georgia mountains which had no intercollegiate sports program. A bright and gregarious lad, Rivers excelled as a debater, edited the school newspaper, and organized the college's first basketball team. On 7 June 1914, while still a student, he secretly married Mattie Lucile Lashley, the daughter of his science professor. They had two chil-dren, Eurith Dickerson, Jr. and Geraldine. After receiving his A.B. degree in 1915, he lived briefly in Arkansas before settling in Cairo, Georgia, where he and his wife taught school. After school Rivers studied law with a local attorney and earned a law degree from LaSalle Extension University in 1923.

Always friendly and outgoing, Rivers became interested in politics at an early age and even told classmates at Young Harris that one day he would be governor. He served as justice of the peace, city attorney for Cairo, and attorney for Grady County before moving to Lakeland to be-come editor of the *Lanier County News*. In 1924 he was elected to the Georgia House of Representatives, and two years later advanced to the Senate. After unsuccessful races for governor in 1928 and 1930, he re-turned to the House of Representatives, where he served as speaker from 1933 to 1937. Initially Rivers supported Governor Eugene Talmadge, but in 1935 he broke with Talmadge when the governor refused to cooperate with New Deal programs. In 1936 Rivers sought the governorship again, promising to bring to Georgia a "Little New Deal." His chief opponent was Talmadge stalwart Charles Redwine, who pledged to reduce taxes and state expenditures. Rivers won an overwhelming victory, capturing

60 percent of the popular vote and carrying 142 of the state's 159 counties.

Once in office, Rivers thoroughly purged Talmadge's supporters and promoted legislation, formerly blocked by Talmadge, which allowed Georgia to receive federal funds for a variety of programs. To assist the state in obtaining and utilizing federal funds, a State Planning Board was created. Rivers pushed through the General Assembly a bill reorganizing and strengthening the Department of Public Welfare. It made welfare departments mandatory in all counties and set standards for all local agencies. Soon Georgians began receiving old-age pensions, aid to the blind and disabled, aid to dependent children, and unemployment compensation. Upon Rivers's recommendation, the General Assembly created the State Housing Authority and the Rural Housing Authority to enable Georgia to receive federal funds for slum clearance and construction of new housing projects. By the end of Rivers's term, Georgia led the nation in the number of rural housing projects and in the amount of money per capita spent on urban housing. Under the supervision of the newly created Department of Natural Resources, the number of acres in state parks expanded from 5,000 to 17,000. Rivers secured legislation for Georgia to participate in the national rural electrification program. By the end of his administration Georgia had received $17 million in Rural Electrification Administration allotments and led the nation in the number of REA cooperatives.

Another major achievement of the Rivers administration was the expansion of the state's public health services. Professor Jane Herndon of DeKalb College, the most thorough student of the Rivers administration, has pointed out that expenditures increased from $100,000 in 1936 to $1,000,000 in his first term, enabling the state to expand the number of maternal health-care centers and county health departments and to increase the number of clinics for the treatment of venereal disease from 19 to 154.

Deeply concerned about the deplorable condition of the state institutions that cared for the mentally ill, tuberculosis patients, the handicapped, and juvenile delinquents, Rivers induced the legislature to create the State Hospital Authority, with power to issue self-liquidating bonds. Using this agency, he circumvented the constitutional limitation on borrowing and matched federal funds for public works projects. State bonds, combined with federal matching funds, raised $6 million, which was used to construct five new buildings at the huge mental institution at Mil-

Fig.63. Ellis Arnall and E. D. Rivers leaving the White House

ledgeville, build a new tuberculosis sanatorium, and make major repairs at five other state charitable institutions.

In campaigning for governor Rivers had promised major improvements in public education. He fulfilled that pledge by pressuring the legislature to reorganize the Department of Education, institute a program of free textbooks, and provide state funds for a seven-month school term. During his term, appropriations for education nearly doubled. Other significant reforms of the Rivers administration include major revisions in the tax system, legislation classifying prisoners according to their offense, abolishing the chain gang, and establishing the State Highway Patrol.

After a very productive two-year term, Rivers was reelected in 1938, easily defeating Hugh Howell, John H. Mangham, and Robert Wood in the Democratic primary. He carried 101 counties with 282 county unit votes and received 50.7 percent of the popular vote. In his second term

Rivers sought new taxes to finance his expensive programs, but despite his desperate pleas the General Assembly refused to enact them. Consequently Rivers was forced to implement rigid economies. He sliced the budgets of many state agencies, closed the school for the deaf, released 1,800 patients from the state mental hospital, and drastically cut state welfare rolls. He succeeded in keeping the public schools open by diverting funds from the Highway Department, but his action precipitated a bitter dispute with the Highway Department. Despite the governor's strenuous efforts, the financial crisis continued. When Rivers left office, the state had a deficit of $14.5 million and future maturing obligations of $38.5 million. Clearly Rivers had grossly overestimated the state's ability to finance his programs.

Rivers's second term also was marred by charges of corruption and mismanagement. During his final year in office a federal grand jury indicted four members of his administration for conspiracy to defraud the state, and after he left office a Fulton County grand jury indicted Rivers, his son, and seventeen other members of his administration. Although only two convictions resulted from the federal indictments and none from the Fulton County indictments, the impression remained that the Rivers administration was corrupt.

Even more damaging to Rivers were allegations that he sold pardons as governor. During his four years in office he granted a total of 1,897 pardons, fewer than Talmadge had granted in a two-year period. Rivers was perceived to be running a "pardons racket" because he granted 717 pardons during his last four months in office, 75 of them on his last day as governor, including 22 for convicted murderers.

The grand jury indictments and the suspicion that he sold pardons destroyed Rivers's reputation. His attempt to vindicate himself in the gubernatorial campaign of 1946 failed, as he came in a distant third, far behind Talmadge and James V. Carmichael. Although he continued to exercise political influence behind the scenes as the titular head of the anti-Talmadge faction, he never again held elective office. After leaving the governor's office his political fortunes suffered, but his finances prospered. Through investments in radio stations in Georgia and Florida, he became a millionaire. Although he spent most of last years in Miami, he died in Atlanta on 11 June 1967 and was buried in the family mausoleum in Lakeland, Georgia.

Despite his genuine concern for the less fortunate and the enactment of measures which brought material benefits to the poor and downtrodden, Rivers never won the allegiance of the masses. Georgia's yeomen farmers, it seems, could more readily identify with the red-gallused Talmadge than with the polished and urbane little Arkansan who spoke rapidly, fancied black suits, and was never seen without a black bow tie. Moreover, his failure to finance his programs, the allegations of a pardons racket, and corruption in the Highway Department, have obscured his many accomplishments. But, as Professor Herndon has noted, his administration began a trend toward the centralization of power in state government by creating a system of administration that met local needs and made possible cooperation with growing federal power.

Ellis Gibbs Arnall
1943-1947

Georgia's most progressive modern governor

When Ellis Arnall became governor of Georgia in 1943 in the midst of World War II, the state was rural, poor, provincial, undeveloped, and often ridiculed by Northern liberals and the national media. When he left office four years later, Georgia rivaled North Carolina as the South's most progressive state.

As governor, Arnall pressured the legislature to adopt a vast array of New South ideas of governmental reform, economic development, and biracial voting. His sweeping and far-reaching reforms largely erased Georgia's "Tobacco Road" image and earned plaudits from contemporaries as diverse as Senator Wayne Morse of Oregon, who praised Arnall for establishing "one of the greatest liberal records of any governor" in recent years, and columnist Drew Pearson, who called Arnall "the South's greatest leader since the Civil War."

Born into an affluent mercantile-textile family in Newnan on 20 March 1907, Arnall was the son of Joseph G. and Bessie Ellis Arnall. Reared in comfortable circumstances, he attended public schools and, after a brief stint at Mercer University, received a bachelor's degree from the University of the South in 1928 with a major in Greek. He then earned a law degree at the University of Georgia, where he compiled an exceptional academic and social record. Graduating first in his class, he served as president of his class as well as president of the Interfraternity Council, his legal fraternity, the Gridiron Club, and the student body. Personable, energetic, shrewd, and efficient, Arnall already displayed qualities that would carry him to success in politics, business, and law.

Arnall practiced law with an uncle in Newnan, but, even with family connections, clients were scarce in the early years of the Great Depression. Finding politics more appealing than law, he won a seat in the Georgia General Assembly in 1932, capturing 3,164 of the 3,510 votes cast in Coweta County. Before taking his seat in the House of Representatives, Arnall traveled throughout the state campaigning for the office of speaker pro tempore—the second highest position in the body. To the surprise of practically everyone, the brash young legislator, one year out of law school, was elected on the first ballot. Always a firm believer in

Fig.64. Ellis Arnall inauguration with Eugene Talmadge looking on

planning, Arnall set high goals for himself and often resorted to unorthodox means to achieve them. This would be the pattern of his political
career.

In many ways Arnall was a typical traditional, folksy, small-town
lawyer-politician, undistinguished from dozens of others operating in the
extremely conservative political environment of Georgia. But in other
ways he was exceptional. He possessed a keen intellect, a driving ambition, an abiding faith in democracy, a determination to improve the
shabby image of his state and region, and the courage to innovate and
use unorthodox methods.

In the legislature Arnall supported the flamboyant Governor Eugene
Talmadge. Since the governor then totally dominated the state, an
aspiring politician had little choice but to cooperate with him. In 1935,
Talmadge named Arnall special assistant attorney general. Talmadge's
successor, Governor E. D. Rivers, made Arnall assistant attorney general
and then attorney general. At age thirty-one Arnall was the youngest
attorney general in Georgia's history. He was elected attorney general
without opposition in 1940, the same year Talmadge was elected governor a third time.

The break between Arnall and Talmadge came when the governor attempted to purge the University System of Georgia of liberal professors, those he deemed "furriners" too favorable to blacks. By forceful, arbitrary means Talmadge succeeded in removing several distinguished professors and administrators, including the vice chancellor, as well as several members of the Board of Regents itself. This blatant racism and infringement of academic freedom was more than Arnall could tolerate.

Talmadge's political interference in the schools did great damage to the state's reputation and subsequently cost Georgia's state-supported colleges their accredited status. But it also gave Arnall a political issue he could exploit. As attorney general, he refused to condone Talmadge's action and thus was thrust into the midst of the controversy. Overnight Arnall became the champion of academic freedom.

On 1 November 1941, Arnall announced his candidacy for governor and presented a ten-point platform calling for substantial reform and promising to take politics out of education. Aided by ex-governor Rivers and Speaker of the House Roy Harris, Arnall waged an effective campaign, skillfully capitalizing on the idealistic, democratic sentiments of a nation at war by promising progressive reforms and depicting his opponent as another Hitler. In the Democratic primary Arnall captured more than 57 percent of the popular vote and 261 of the state's 410 county unit votes. It was Talmadge's first and only defeat in a gubernatorial race and Arnall's first and only victory. In upsetting the powerful Talmadge, Arnall, at age thirty-five, became the youngest governor in the country.

In his inaugural address Arnall emphasized lofty ideals. "Public officials are trustees and servants of the people, and, at all times, are amenable to them," he stated. Promising a "people's administration," he called for supporting the war effort, modernizing the prison system, removing the governor from membership on state boards and commissions, lowering the voting age to eighteen, limiting campaign expenses, and many other reforms. To a remarkable degree, Arnall succeeded in accomplishing his goals. Dominating the General Assembly completely, he skillfully pressured the legislature into adopting his entire program, most of which it did within a few weeks by unanimous vote. Politicos in Georgia were amazed by Arnall's extraordinary executive leadership, and the national media began to take notice of Georgia's "progressive" young governor.

By necessity as well as conviction, Arnall made education his first priority. "Education," he declared, "is the hope of the future. It is the salvation of our people. It is the cure for ignorance, poverty, prejudice,

Fig.65. Ellis Arnall

hatred and demagoguery." Working closely with the Southern Association of Colleges and Secondary Schools, he appointed a new Board of Regents and managed to have accreditation restored quickly to the State University System. Having promised to separate politics and education, he removed the governor from the Board of Regents so that future governors would not be able to control the state's colleges as Talmadge had done. To ensure the permanence of his educational reforms, he had both the Board of Regents and the State Board of Education changed from statutory to constitutional bodies.

When Arnall took office, Georgia's penal system may have been the worst in the country. Its grim record of cruelty, abuse, and political corruption had become a shameful tradition. Arnall began a vigorous program to change that tradition and modernize the system. With his prodding, the legislature abolished many longstanding abuses, such as whipping prisoners, leg irons, and the chain gang. The new law reorganized the whole system, placing state and county punishment under a corrections director responsible to the governor, and made rehabilitation of prisoners the chief aim.

Arnall hired the first trained criminologist for Georgia's penal system, and he employed a prison expert as warden of the Tattnall State Prison.

These penal reforms, like the educational reforms, contrasted sharply with the policies of his predecessor and received widespread coverage in the national media, including a lengthy article in *Life* magazine.

Convinced that industrial development in the South and West had been retarded by the discriminatory rates charged by the railroads, Arnall resolved to correct that abuse, and his efforts to secure more favorable railroad rates had a far-reaching impact upon the South. Rather than continue a fruitless appeal to the Interstate Commerce Commission, he adopted the startling legal device of suing twenty railroads for conspiracy against the state in violation of the Sherman Anti-Trust Act. Though ridiculed at first, he persevered and personally argued the case before the United States Supreme Court. The favorable verdict lowered freight rates in the South and contributed significantly to the subsequent industrial development of the region. Especially proud of this reform, Arnall frequently remarked that this change "brought about the readmission of the South into the Union on the basis of full fellowship and full equality."

Under Arnall's leadership the state received a new constitution to replace the Constitution of 1877, which had been amended more than 300 times. Arnall chaired the commission that wrote the document, and the voters approved it by a wide margin. Not only did the Constitution of 1945 make the system more understandable by incorporating the amendments into the document, it also created eight constitutional boards where none had existed previously. The existing Board of Regents, Board of Education, and Public Service Commission became constitutional bodies. In addition, five new agencies that had constitutional boards were created: the Game and Fish Commission, the Board of Pardons and Paroles, the Board of Corrections, the Veterans Service Board, and the Personnel Board. The Arnall administration also paid off the state's indebtedness and established the office of lieutenant governor, a merit system for state employees, a state board of workmen's compensation, the Teachers Retirement System, and the State Ports Authority. Little wonder that Professor Harold Henderson, Arnall's recent biographer, concluded that "to a large extent, the structure of Georgia's modern government came into existence in the Arnall administration."

Deeply committed to the principles of democracy, Arnall's motto as governor was: "There is nothing wrong with government that democracy won't cure." Consequently, he pursued several policies to incorporate more Georgians into the political process. Under his leadership, Georgia became the first state to pass a soldier voting law, the first state to lower

Fig. 66. Ellis Arnall

the voting age to eighteen, and the fourth Southern state to abolish the poll tax.

When the latter measure encountered strong opposition in the legislature, Arnall lobbied vigorously to get the poll tax repealed and threatened to abolish it by executive order if the legislature failed to act. His efforts were persuasive, and the Georgia House and Senate voted overwhelmingly to repeal the tax. Even more controversial than the poll tax was the white primary, which for many years had deterred blacks from participating in Southern politics. A United States Supreme Court decision in 1944 invalidated the white primary in Texas, and subsequent court rulings invalidated Georgia's white primary.

Former governor Talmadge and other staunch segregationists and white supremacists urged the state Democratic party and the legislature to take action to save the white primary. Although Arnall—like all Georgia politicians of that era—was a segregationist, he nevertheless recognized the injustice of the South's racial policies. Overcoming his prejudice and his heritage, he courageously resisted such pressures. He announced that he would abide by the decision of the federal courts and reminded Georgians that "it is our duty as good citizens to uphold the courts, the Constitution, and laws of our land." He refused to call a special session of the legislature, as Talmadge and others demanded, and threatened to veto any legislation repealing the state's primary laws. "The courts have spoken," Arnall said. "I will not be a party to any subterfuge or scheme to nullify the orders of the courts."

Northern liberals, accustomed to racism and demagoguery from Southern governors, were utterly astonished at such leadership. Clark Foreman, writing in *New Republic*, acknowledged that Arnall "has done more to extend the franchise than any other American since women were given the right to vote." Their astonishment increased when Arnall wholeheartedly endorsed the liberal Henry Wallace for vice president at the Democratic National Convention in 1944, spoke out against the Ku Klux Klan, and through his attorney general prosecuted the Klan for violating its corporate charter.

Unfortunately, as Arnall gained accolades throughout the nation from the liberal media, his popularity in Georgia declined. His enlightened racial views, support of Henry Wallace, and refusal to defend the white primary alienated many of his supporters. His unsuccessful attempt to amend the constitution so that he could serve a second term also proved divisive. Consequently, the anti-Talmadge coalition he had forged in 1942 fell apart by the end of his term. A political realist, Arnall understood the political consequences of his actions and expected to be vilified as a "traitor to the South." By deliberately defying Southern traditions, he became a pariah; by doing what he considered morally and legally right, he committed political suicide. Despite compiling a record of progressive reforms unsurpassed by any governor in Georgia's history, Arnall never again held public office in Georgia.

In view of his national popularity and friendship with Presidents Franklin Roosevelt and Harry Truman, Arnall frequently was rumored to be in line for a federal appointment as solicitor general, attorney general, or a federal judge, and he had some support for the vice presidency and even the presidency. But, surprisingly, none of these possibilities came to pass. At age thirty-nine, Arnall's political career virtually was over. Aside from a brief tenure as director of the Office of Price Stabilization in the Truman administration, he never again held public office. His only attempt came in 1966, twenty years after leaving office, when he ran for governor again. Although he won a plurality in a six-man race for the Democratic nomination, which included a young state senator named Jimmy Carter, he lost the runoff election to Lester Maddox. Failing in this comeback attempt, he never sought political office again.

Upon leaving office in 1947, Arnall embarked on an extensive and lucrative lecture tour which also advertised his best-selling books, *The Shore Dimly Seen* and *What the People Want*. He then concentrated on his law practice and made the firm of Arnall, Golden and Gregory one of Atlanta's most successful law firms. His other interests also flourished. He became president of the Columbus National Life Insurance Company, president of the Society of Independent Motion Picture Producers, president of the Independent Film Producers Export Corporation, and chairman of the board of Coastal States Life Insurance Company.

Arnall married Mildred Slemons of Orlando, Florida, on 6 April 1935, and they had two children, Alice and Alvan. In June of 1980, after forty-five years of marriage, Mrs. Arnall suffered a heart attack and died at age seventy-one. A year later, in July 1981, Arnall married Mrs. Ruby Hamilton McCord, a native of Kentucky. Arnall remained active and enjoyed good health until a series of strokes in 1990 left him incapacitated. He died on 13 December 1992 and was buried in Oak Hill Cemetery in Newnan.

The recipient of numerous honors and honorary doctorates, Arnall was the darling of the national media during his governorship and has received lavish praise from historians ever since. E. Merton Coulter, the dean of Georgia historians, praised Arnall as "the most dynamically constructive governor Georgia had within the memory of its oldest inhabitants." More recently, Professor Numan Bartley of the University of Georgia observed that Arnall's tenure as governor "was the most progressive and probably the most effective in modern Georgia history." In the first full biography of Arnall, Harold Henderson described Arnall's rise to power as "one of the most remarkable chapters in Georgia history" and concluded that he gave the state "four years of strong, exciting, and responsible progressive leadership as governor." A survey of Georgia historians conducted in 1985 ranked Arnall first among Georgia governors who served from 1943 to 1983 in the following categories: most positive national reputation, most effective political leadership, most liberal on social issues, best relationship with the press, most effective in recognizing and confronting historically significant issues, and most effective leadership as governor. Thus, a half-century after his election as governor, Arnall's reputation as a progressive reformer seems secure indeed.

Melvin Ernest Thompson
1947-1948

He purchased Jekyll Island for the state

The general election of 1946, the first under the new Constitution of 1945, provoked a storm of controversy that made Georgia the laughing-stock of the nation. Before it was finally resolved by the Georgia Supreme Court, three men—Ellis Arnall, Melvin Ernest Thompson, and Herman Talmadge—claimed to be governor at the same time. In disbelief the whole nation observed Georgia's political shenanigans, which included fistfights in the capitol, the seizure of the executive mansion, numerous protest rallies, court suits, and a report that tombstones had voted in Telfair County. *Newsweek* noted that Georgia politics had hit the front pages of every major newspaper in the country "as the state finds itself in a mixup so fantastic that it made the historic gyrations of the Balkans sound sedately sober in contrast."

Eugene Talmadge won the Democratic nomination for governor in 1946 by defeating James V. Carmichael of Marietta. Ironically, Carmichael won the popular vote, amassing more popular votes than any previous gubernatorial candidate in Georgia's history, but Talmadge gained the nomination by winning the county unit vote 242 to 146. In the entire history of the county unit system, this was the only time that the gubernatorial nominee failed to obtain a popular plurality. In the general election on 5 November, Georgians elected Talmadge to a fourth term as governor. His death on 21 December, three weeks before the inauguration, plunged the state into political chaos.

Thompson, a mild-mannered ex-school teacher, assumed that as the newly-elected lieutenant governor he should succeed the dead governor until the next general election. The Talmadge forces, however, seizing upon ambiguous language in the new constitution, claimed that the legislature had the right to pick the successor from among those who ran in the primary. When the General Assembly convened in January, it counted 675 write-in votes for Herman Talmadge, Eugene's son, and promptly named him governor on the basis of having the second highest vote total. Incumbent Governor Ellis Arnall, unwilling to vacate his office until his successor had been properly chosen, refused to recognize Herman Talmadge as governor and referred to him as "the pretender." Whereupon

Fig.67. Richard B. Russell, Jr., and M. E. Thompson

Herman Talmadge and his supporters stormed the capitol and the governor's mansion, literally throwing Arnall out of office and taking over the executive authority by force. When Thompson was sworn in as Georgia's first lieutenant governor on 18 January 1947, Arnall withdrew from the field in favor of Thompson.

While the courts decided whether Thompson or Talmadge should be governor, C. E. Gregory, political editor of the *Atlanta Journal*, acting on a tip from Thompson, checked the write-in votes for Talmadge from Telfair County. After studying the returns in the secretary of state's office, Gregory, white as a sheet, told Secretary of State Ben Fortson: "Do you know that they rose from the dead in Telfair County, marched in alphabetical order to the polls, cast their votes for Herman Talmadge and went back to their last repose?" That afternoon the front page of the *Atlanta*

Journal read: "TELFAIR DEAD WERE VOTED." This report aroused an already hostile electorate, and thousands of angry citizens marched in protest throughout the state, while the nation focused on Georgia's antics with bemused contempt. *Time* stated that the South historically loved "buffoons, corny oratory and the smell of violence" but this latest political escapade was "like something conceived late at night by three unemployed radio writers."

Quiet and unassuming Melvin Ernest Thompson, better known as M. E., was an unlikely candidate for high political office in a state noted for flamboyant politicians. Born on 1 May 1903, on a tenant farm in Jenkins County in southeast Georgia, he was the youngest of six children born to Henry J. and Eva Edenfield Thompson. Only two years old when his father died, Thompson spent his childhood struggling against abject poverty to get an education. While going to school, he supplemented the family income by working on a farm, in a grocery store, and in a restaurant. After high school, he attended Piedmont College for a year and then transferred to Emory University. Working as a dishwasher and brush salesman, he worked his way through Emory and received an A.B. degree in 1926. He did graduate work at Emory University, the University of Chicago, the University of Alabama, Peabody College, and the University of Georgia, where he received his master's degree in 1935. By 1941 he had completed all course work for a doctorate when his major professor, Dr. Walter Cocking, dean of the College of Education at the University of Georgia, was fired by Governor Talmadge. Because of problems in changing advisers, Thompson never completed the degree.

An educator by profession, Thompson began his career as the principal and coach of the Emanuel County Institute in 1926. He served as superintendent of the Hawkinsville public schools from 1927 to 1933, state school supervisor from 1933 to 1936, and assistant state superintendent of schools from 1937 to 1941. Attracted to Arnall because of the education controversy, Thompson served as one of his organizers in the gubernatorial campaign of 1942. For two years he served as Arnall's executive secretary and from 1945 to 1947 was state revenue commissioner. Knowing that he would lose his job if Eugene Talmadge became governor again, Thompson offered for the newly created job of lieutenant governor. Without making a speech he defeated Marvin Griffin by 30,000 popular votes and a county unit margin of 192 to 155. Thinking he was getting a part-time job that required only seventy days of work every other year presiding over the Senate, he bought an electrical appliance business in Valdosta.

In a five-to-two decision delivered on 19 March 1947, the Georgia Supreme Court ruled that the General Assembly had exceeded its authority in electing Talmadge. Arnall, the court asserted, was governor until he voluntarily resigned, at which point Thompson became governor. Thus, two days after being sworn in as the state's first lieutenant governor, Thompson became acting governor. The court decision was controversial, but Talmadge, who had held power for sixty-three days, accepted it and vacated the executive office immediately.

Few governors have ever taken office under such adverse conditions as Thompson did in March 1947. On the day he was inaugurated, Roy Harris of Augusta, a Talmadge stalwart, announced that Herman Talmadge would be elected governor in 1948 and that "we have already begun our campaign." The Talmadge-dominated legislature seemed determined to thwart anything the new governor proposed. Thompson sought to finance expanded state services through the adoption of a sales tax, but the General Assembly refused to pass it. The legislature also defeated two electoral reform bills the governor proposed and even refused to adopt an appropriations bill. Political factionalism, historian Harold Henderson has observed, brought legislative action to a standstill.

Although handicapped by the hostile legislature, Thompson succeeded in expanding state services because of unanticipated increases in state revenue collections. He raised teachers' salaries, extended the public school system to twelve grades, built a school of veterinary medicine at the University of Georgia and a textile engineering building at Georgia Tech, expanded the state's park system, and claimed to have built more roads and bridges than any other administration over a comparable period of time. Thompson's most important legacy was his decision in 1947 to purchase Jekyll Island for $675,000. Though ridiculed at the time as "Thompson's Folly," the purchase later was recognized as one of Georgia's wisest real estate transactions.

In the special election in the summer of 1948, Thompson stood on his record and tried to depict his opponent, Herman Talmadge, as a violent dictator. Talmadge promised to eliminate waste, maintain the county unit system, and uphold "our Southern way of life." He reminded voters that Thompson had vetoed the white primary bill and had close ties with the liberal Arnall administration. Thus Thompson, an opponent of the federal civil rights program, was portrayed as a racial liberal and kept on the defensive because of the race issue. Talmadge won the bitter campaign with a comfortable edge in county unit votes, 312 to 98, and with 357,865 popular votes to Thompson's 312,035. Talmadge called his election a "victory in the court of last resort." Two years later the vote was closer but the result was the same. In 1954 Thompson entered his last campaign for governor, coming in a distant second to Marvin Griffin. In 1956, after polling less than 20 percent of the popular vote in a race against Herman Talmadge for a seat in the United States Senate, he retired from politics.

On 3 February 1926, Thompson married Ann Newton of Millen, a graduate of Bessie Tift College and a teacher in the Jenkins County schools. They had one son, M. E. Thompson, Jr. In 1948 Thompson settled in Valdosta, where he established a prosperous real estate firm which developed numerous subdivisions in the Valdosta area. He died at his home in Valdosta on 3 October 1980 and was buried in Riverview Memorial Mausoleum. He was seventy-seven.

In an interview in 1963 Thompson looked back with pride on his two years as governor. "There was nothing I did as governor that today worries my conscience," he said. That same year the General Assembly placed a marker on Jekyll Island honoring him. The resolution, adopted on 2 April, reads: "Jekyll Island has become the best and soundest investment which the State has ever made, all of which is a result of Governor Thompson's keen foresight and acumen."

Herman Eugene Talmadge
1948-1955

He won six consecutive statewide elections

Who could have imagined that the brash young playboy who was entrusted with executive power by the General Assembly in 1947 on the basis of having fewer than 700 write-in votes would become, two decades later, the senior senator from Georgia, chairman of the Agriculture Committee, and one of the more powerful and respected statesmen in the nation? To say that Herman Talmadge matured in office is to understate the obvious, and for a generation he received phenomenal popular support from the voters of Georgia.

Born on the family farm in Telfair County on 9 August 1913, he is the son of Governor Eugene and Mattie Thurmond Talmadge. He attended public schools in McRae until 1930, when the Talmadges moved to Atlanta. After graduation from Druid Hills High School in DeKalb County, he became the fourth generation of Talmadges to enter the University of Georgia. Bright and well read in history and biography, he compiled a good academic record without much effort, served as president of his social fraternity, and excelled as a member of the debating team. After receiving his LL. B. degree in 1936, Talmadge practiced law with his father in Atlanta until 1941, when he enlisted in the United States Navy. Requesting combat duty, he served on the USS *Tryon* and the USS *Dauphin*. In November 1945, after fifty-two months of active duty mostly in the southwest Pacific, he was discharged with the rank of lieutenant commander.

Although Talmadge had actively campaigned for his father and had directed two successful campaigns for governor in 1940 and 1946, he had not decided upon a political career for himself until the death of his father on 21 December 1946 suddenly thrust him into the limelight. With pudgy Roy Harris of Augusta, the speaker of the Georgia House of Representatives and an excellent backroom political manipulator, lining up legislative support in his famed suite on the fourteenth floor of the Henry Grady Hotel in Atlanta, Herman assumed leadership of the Talmadge faction. The General Assembly elected him governor by the overwhelming vote of 161 to 87 abstentions. Talmadge later gave this explanation of his entry into politics:

Fig.68. Herman Talmadge addresses General Assembly (1947)

When I was in the Pacific [in World War II], I thought it was foolish to be in politics, and I thought I would never be active in that way again. But when I got back and my father launched his fourth campaign, I found it necessary to help him. After his death, circumstances forced me into the fight. Then when I was elected by the legislature and kicked out, of course, I felt I had to be vindicated. Too there was the pleasure of winning, and it's a great honor to be governor. Politics is a rough, hard, mean, vicious life.

When the Georgia Supreme Court ruled that Lieutenant Governor M. E. Thompson was the rightful governor, Talmadge relinquished the office after serving sixty-three days. In the special election on 8 September 1948, Talmadge was vindicated by the people. In a bitter campaign with racist overtones, he defeated the capable but colorless Thompson by 45,000 popular votes and by a county unit margin of 312 to 98. His inaugural address called for expanding state services. Taking a page from his father's book, he sought free lifetime driver's licenses for all veterans. He also sought—but failed to obtain—a constitutional amendment to extend the county unit system to general elections. To improve the state's highways, schools, hospitals, and forests, Talmadge needed additional revenue, but the voters, in a special referendum in April 1949, had expressed hearty disapproval of a tax increase by a whopping three-to-one margin. Despite the referendum, the fiscal situation became so acute that the governor called a special session of the General Assembly to increase taxes on cigarettes, gasoline, and hunting and fishing licenses.

The increased taxes hurt Talmadge's popularity, as did his inability to find a workable means to prevent or retard Negro voting, but he still managed to defeat Thompson in the 1950 Democratic primary. In that race former governor Rivers switched to Talmadge and former governor Arnall remained inactive, whereas both previously had supported Thompson. The popular vote was extremely close, 287,637 to 279,137, and years later Roy Harris implied that not all of Thompson's votes had been counted, but Talmadge won the county unit vote with ease, 295 to 115.

A forceful executive and a capable administrator, Talmadge made significant improvements in many areas of state government during his six years as governor. Like most recent Georgia governors, he placed particular emphasis on education. Appropriations to the common schools increased from $37 million in 1947–1948 to $99 million in 1953–1954. Average teacher salaries and allocations per pupil more than doubled during those six years. A School Building Authority was empowered to issue revenue certificates against future school construction appropriations to provide money for an immediate building program. Such a program was desperately needed to eliminate the remaining 1,758 one-room schools in the state and to bring the many dilapidated buildings up to modern standards. By 1954 over $168 million had been earmarked for new school construction.

Other accomplishments of the Talmadge administration include expanding the state network of farmers' markets, establishing the State Forestry Department and promoting forestry as a cash crop, expanding the State Ports Authority, launching a separate juvenile corrections system, and doubling state expenditures for mental health. Taking full advantage of the Hill-Burton Act, Talmadge constructed a network of hospitals and health centers throughout the state. He placed the Highway Department under a new State Highway Board and allocated all revenues derived from motor vehicle registration fees and motor fuel taxes directly to the Highway Department. With increased revenues, an unprecedented highway construction program was undertaken.

These improvements in state services were made possible by sound management, skillful utilization of federal aid, and, most importantly, the adoption of a 3 percent sales tax in 1951. With more revenue available, the governor dramatically increased funding for almost all state agencies. The people of Georgia clearly approved of his handling of state affairs, for when he left office in 1955 his popularity had reached a new high. Even the *Atlanta Constitution*—never a fan of his or his father's brand of politics—acknowledged that his administration had put Georgia on the path toward becoming a leading progressive state in the South.

Talmadge's popularity was so great that Georgia's senior senator, Walter George, decided to retire after thirty-four years of service rather than run against him. Thus in 1956 Talmadge advanced to the United States Senate, with only token opposition provided by M. E. Thompson. In gaining that seat, Talmadge attained a goal that had eluded his popular father, who twice failed to achieve it. Talmadge easily won renomination six years later by defeating Henry M. Henderson in the Democratic primary, 673,782 to 91,654, and was unopposed in the general election. In 1968 he won a third term, trouncing Maynard Jackson, an African-American attorney who later served as mayor of Atlanta, by a three-to-one margin in the Democratic primary. In the general election he crushed Earl Patton, a Republican from Atlanta, 885,093 to 256,796. In 1974 he had little difficulty winning a fourth term, defeating Carlton Myers in the primary and Jerry R. Johnson in the general election. For twenty-four years Talmadge remained a fixture in the United States Senate. Aside from Richard Russell, Talmadge is the only Georgia politician to win six consecutive statewide campaigns.

Much skepticism greeted Talmadge when he entered the Senate. The *Baltimore Evening Sun* stated, "Few men could step into Senator Walter George's shoes; Mr. Talmadge couldn't even shine them." *Time* magazine asserted that nearly every member of the U.S. Senate agreed with that observation. But Talmadge confounded his critics by displaying unexpected poise, restraint, and political acumen. Speaker of the House Sam Rayburn said, "Herman Talmadge fooled a lot of people by turning out to be a student of government, a convincing speaker and not a hell-raiser as some of his critics had billed him. I don't know of a freshman Senator who ever got off to a finer start." Georgia's senior senator, Richard Russell, who worked closely with Talmadge, stated that "in my time no man has ever come into the Senate, taken over and handled so ably such difficult assignments normally given to veterans as has Herman Talmadge."

Fig.69. Herman Talmadge, his mother
"Miss Mitt," and Richard B. Russell, Jr.

In 1955 Talmadge, then a defiant segregationist, published a seventy-nine page book, *You and Segregation*. In the Senate he consistently opposed civil rights legislation and forced busing. But as public opinion changed and more black Georgians registered to vote, he moderated his racial views to such an extent that predominately black Morris Brown College in Atlanta awarded him an honorary doctorate in 1975. With equal vigor he opposed "wasteful" spending in both domestic and foreign programs and called for frugality, fiscal responsibility, and balanced budgets. Though favoring a strong military posture, he recognized that there are limits to America's military power and that the United States cannot police the whole world. He often disagreed with the positions of the national Democratic party, which he laments has moved since 1948 "to the left politically and to the north geographically."

As chairman of the Agriculture Committee, he worked diligently for the passage of the Rural Development Act of 1972. He also played a prominent role in the passage of the Trade Expansion Act of 1962 and legislation in 1970 expanding the National School Lunch Program. As a man of the soil, he applauded President Richard Nixon's decision to sell wheat to the Russians and condemned President Jimmy Carter's grain embargo. In May 1973 Talmadge was appointed to the Select Committee on Presidential Campaign Activities, which investigated the Watergate affair. One of the most effective members of that prestigious committee, his penetrating questioning of witnesses and logical analyses, viewed by a national television audience, enhanced his national prestige.

Possessing remarkable stamina, Talmadge put in some of the longest work days on Capitol Hill, usually beginning by 4 A.M. and often lasting eighteen hours. His normal routine consisted of reading newspapers, studying committee reports, and perusing his mail before breakfast, followed by a two-and-a-half-mile jog around his neighborhood. By 7:30 he was usually at his desk in the Russell Senate Office Building. Shunning the formal Washington social circuit, he normally retired by 9:00 or 9:30 P.M. Such work habits were considered "oddball by most standards," as Talmadge admitted, but he came by them naturally growing up on a farm, studying in law school, and serving in the navy in World War II. In the governor's office he found that "the only time I had to think—make decisions, make inquiry without interruption—was before other people got up. I frequently went to the governor's office as early at 7 o'clock. When I came to the Senate, that habit was so firmly entrenched until I found it virtually impossible to break."

Unlike most Georgia governors, Talmadge has been married three times. His first marriage to Kathryn Williams, a New York model, lasted from April 1937 to January 1941. He then married Betty Shingler of Ashburn, Georgia, on 24 December 1941, and they had two sons, Herman Eugene and Robert Shingler. When young Robert drowned in Lake Lanier on 26 May 1975, Talmadge's life fell apart. Depressed, he began drinking excessively. He and Betty drifted apart, and on 19 October 1977 their thirty-five-year union was dissolved in a highly-publicized divorce. Finally realizing he had become an alcoholic, Talmadge, in January 1979, checked into Bethesda Naval Hospital and agreed to enter the alcohol treatment program at the naval hospital in Long Beach, California. That program, Talmadge admits in his autobiography, probably saved his life. It did not, however, save his political career. A few months after getting out of the program, the Senate Ethics Committee "denounced" him for mismanagement of his office finances. Politically vulnerable for the first time, Talmadge faced formidable opposition from Zell Miller, Dawson Mathis, and Norman Underwood in the 1980 Democratic primary. Although Talmadge came in first with 42 percent of the vote, he then had

Fig.70. Herman Talmadge

to face Lieutenant Governor Miller in a bitterly contested runoff. He trounced Miller, carrying 58.5 percent of the vote and 140 of the state's 159 counties, in what he regarded as "one of the sweetest" victories of his career. But it was his last victory. Opposed by Republicans, disgruntled Millerites, the Atlanta newspapers, and voters wanting a new face in Washington, Talmadge lost the general election to Mack Mattingly, the little-known chairman of the state Republican party. Thus, on 4 November 1980, Georgia, by electing its first Republican senator since Reconstruction, ended the Talmadge dynasty that had lasted for fifty-four years. In this century only a few families have dominated the politics of their states for more than a generation: the Byrds of Virginia, the Tafts of Ohio, the LaFollettes of Wisconsin, the Kennedys of Massachusetts, the Longs of Louisiana, and the Talmadges of Georgia.

Since his first and only defeat, Talmadge has lived quietly on his farm in Lovejoy with his young wife, Lynda Cowart Pierce. A graduate of the University of Georgia and a home economist, she and Talmadge were married in September 1984. He spends his time reading, smoking his ever-present cigar, and running his hound dogs. Happier than he has ever been in his life, he says he doesn't miss politics at all.

Samuel Marvin Griffin
1955–1959

The last of the rural, folksy governors

Having served a six-year apprenticeship as lieutenant governor under Herman Talmadge, Marvin Griffin seemed to be the heir apparent to the popular Talmadge. But to secure the gubernatorial nomination in the Democratic primary in 1954, he had to defeat stiff challenges from two Talmadgites and two Talmadge opponents. Commissioner of Agriculture Tom Linder and Speaker of the House Fred Hand, both loyal supporters of Eugene and Herman Talmadge, sought the nomination, as did former governor M. E. Thompson and Representative Charlie Gowen. Griffin announced that he stood for "Georgia's two greatest traditions—segregation and the county unit system." He also gave unqualified support to the "private school amendment," a measure Governor Herman Talmadge had endorsed, which, anticipating the *Brown* decision of 1954, would preserve segregated schools by allowing the state to make tuition payments to fulfill its educational obligations. Having to make a choice between three loyal supporters placed Governor Talmadge in an awkward position. He was "up a stump," as Griffin later observed. Eventually, however, he backed Griffin, who won easily. Although Griffin's popular vote of 234,690 was only 36 percent of the total, he carried 115 counties and 302 county unit votes.

In defending segregation, low taxes, states' rights, and the county unit system, the new governor espoused the typical political doctrine of that era, but his background was unusual for a Georgia politician. Unlike his immediate predecessors and successors, he was neither a lawyer, a graduate of the University of Georgia, nor a Baptist; instead, he was a newspaper publisher, a graduate of The Citadel in South Carolina, and a Presbyterian. He was born in Bainbridge, Georgia, on 4 September 1907, to, as he styled it, "a family of moderate means." Marvin was the fourth of six children born to Ernest H. "Pat" and Josie Butler Griffin. After attending the public schools in Bainbridge, he enrolled in The Citadel, where he exhibited considerable athletic ability as a pitcher on the baseball team and aptitude for military life. He was graduated in 1929 with an A.B. in history and political science and the cadet rank of major, commanding the 1st Battalion of the Corps of Cadets, the highest military

Fig.71. Marvin Griffin

achievement possible. He secured a teaching position at Randolph Macon Academy in Front Royal, Virginia, and taught history, Spanish, and military science there for four years. During this time he met Mary Elizabeth Smith of Winchester, Virginia, who became his wife on 11 July 1931. Their first child, Patricia Ann, was born on 10 July 1932, and their second child, Samuel Marvin, Jr., arrived on 12 February 1936.

His father's declining health forced Griffin to return to Bainbridge in 1933 to help run the family newspaper, the *Post-Searchlight*. His father, who was also a state legislator, died the following year. Marvin then entered the political arena and won election to the seat in the General Assembly previously held by his father. Two years later he attempted to unseat six-term incumbent Congressman Edward Cox and was soundly defeated. Cox, a gifted orator called "The Judge," administered such a tongue-lashing to his young opponent that years later Griffin recalled that "when The Judge got through flaying me from Dan to Beersheba, there wasn't enough political hide left on me to cover a postage stamp."

Utilizing the contacts he had made during his legislative term, Griffin found employment with the State Revenue Department and a state-owned radio station until late 1939, when he became an aide and then executive secretary to Governor Ed Rivers. The Rivers administration (and Griffin) received severe criticism for granting an abnormally high number of pardons and paroles, but preparations for World War II precluded a thorough probe. At the outbreak of the war Griffin resigned his reserve commission and enlisted in the Georgia National Guard as a private. Soon he was appointed captain and placed in charge of an all-Georgia antiaircraft battalion which was stationed in New Guinea throughout the war. His outfit, which bore the official code name "One Corrupt Group," returned to Georgia in July 1944 after thirty months of active duty. Griffin, who had contracted malaria, then held the rank of lieutenant colonel. His arrival in Georgia happened to coincide with the resignation of the state adjutant general. Governor Ellis Arnall, who had served with Griffin in the legislature, offered him the post and Griffin accepted it. He served as adjutant general from 1944 until the end of the Arnall administration and backed Herman Talmadge in the three-governors controversy. A few months after losing the lieutenant governorship to M. E. Thompson, he suffered a great personal tragedy when his daughter Patsy perished in the famous Winecoff Hotel fire in Atlanta on 7 December 1946. In the special election of 1948 Griffin easily won the lieutenant governorship and two years later gained reelection, receiving 57 percent of the popular vote and carrying 156 of the 159 counties.

With firm control over the legislature, Griffin had little difficulty implementing much progressive legislation during his four years as governor. Fortunately for Griffin, the ample revenues provided by the 3 percent sales tax enabled Governor Talmadge to leave a surplus in the treasury and provided sufficient funds to continue the expansion of state services. Like his predecessor, Griffin placed much emphasis on improving education. State appropriations for the common schools increased from $104 million in 1954–1955 to $145 million in 1958–1959. The increased appropriations enabled the state to hire more than 3,000 additional teachers, raise teachers' salaries each year of his administration, expand the curriculum, build 8,000 new classrooms, purchase 664 new buses, and expand library and vocational facilities. The University System

Fig. 72. Marvin Griffin in a relaxed mood

also made substantial progress during Griffin's term. State appropriations to the eighteen institutions nearly doubled during his term. A massive $13 million science complex at the University of Georgia and a $5 million nuclear reactor at Georgia Tech enabled those institutions to offer graduate training and do advanced research.

During the campaign Griffin had pledged to pave rural roads. He fulfilled that promise with the establishment of the Rural Roads Authority, which obtained $100 million from bond sales for the construction of roads in rural areas. Other major advances during the Griffin administration include purchasing Stone Mountain near Atlanta for development as a state park; constructing dock facilities at Brunswick and Bainbridge; constructing a $10 million farmers' market near Atlanta; building more parks than any previous administration; refurbishing the governor's mansion and state capitol; establishing the state's first alcohol-abuse clinic; and opening twenty-seven new public health centers.

In his inaugural address Griffin asserted that "so long as Marvin Griffin is your governor there will be no mixing of the races in the classrooms of our schools and colleges of Georgia." He also promised an administration that would practice "rigid economy," would "live within our income and available resources," and "would make certain that those who do business with the state do so legitimately." He carried out the former pledge but not the latter. Although he had promised not to raise taxes, when it became apparent that his program could not be financed with available revenue, he convened a special session of the legislature in June 1955 to enact multiple tax increases. To secure passage of the revenue bills, Griffin emphasized the need to upgrade black education to preserve racially segregated schools. After the taxes were adopted, more than half of the capital outlays and new school plants went to black facilities.

Despite the progress achieved in many areas, the Griffin administration was marred by corruption, especially in the Highway Department and the Purchasing Department. A grand jury found "perfidious conduct of state officials" in his administration "heretofore inconceivable in the minds of citizens." The investigations and charges made the national media, and an article in *Reader's Digest* asserted that "never in Georgia history had so many stolen so much." In a way Griffin was a victim of changing moral and ethical standards. The last of the rural, folksy governors who entertained voters with barbecues, fish fries, country music, fiery rhetoric, and bizarre antics, he rewarded his friends, punished his political opponents, and provided lax control over his subordinates. With uncommon candor he declared, "I plan to fire the hell out of my enemies and take care of my friends." And he did. In running the state government in a time-honored tradition, he was not the first governor to misuse public funds. Indeed, shortly after the inauguration his brother, Robert A. "Cheney" Griffin, his chief of staff, accidentally stumbled onto an odd payroll item. He discovered the existence of a "secretarial pool" in nearby East Point. "I went out there and found about fifty women and only one typewriter," he remembered. He fired the women and then sat back and waited. The next day many highly agitated senators and representatives complained that their mistresses had been sacked. The Griffin brothers quickly rehired the women, but only after extracting promises of political loyalty from the legislators. Aggressive young investigative reporters began to attack many of the old traditions, and the public demanded a higher level of accountability during the Griffin years. With allowances for its many achievements, Robert W. Dubay, the most careful student of the Griffin administration, has concluded that "the Griffin regime is fully deserving of its reputation as one of the most corrupt, amoral, mismanaged, and inefficient administrations in Georgia history."

In 1962, when eligible to run for governor again, Griffin sought reelection but lost to Carl Sanders, a clean-cut young state senator from Augusta and a proponent of the New South. Able to find humor in practically any situation, he remarked, "A lot of people ate my barbecue that didn't vote for me." Aside from serving briefly as George Wallace's vice presidential running mate in 1968, that was his last political race. According to Griffin, he retired from politics for reasons of health—"the voters were sick and tired of me."

In retirement Griffin maintained a keen interest in political developments. Though nominally a Democrat, he campaigned for Gerald Ford in 1976 and accompanied the president on his steamboat campaign trip down the Mississippi River. Active in community affairs, Griffin served as president of the Bainbridge Lions Club, the Bainbridge-Decatur County Chamber of Commerce, and the Decatur County Historical Society, and was general chairman of the Decatur County Sesquicentennial Celebration. With a love for people and a storehouse of humorous anecdotes, Griffin remained a popular public speaker.

In 1971, a year after the death of his first wife, Griffin married Mrs. Laura Jane "Lollie" Gibson, an attractive widow from Dublin, Georgia. She died of cancer in June 1982 at age fifty-seven. In 1981 Griffin was diagnosed with lung cancer. The disease gradually wore him down, but even in the most adverse circumstances he maintained his sense of humor. Commenting on his weight loss, he noted that "two pairs of my pants have been taken up in the waist so many times that I notice the two back pockets are touching in the seat." He died on 13 June 1982, at age seventy-four, a week after his wife died. Both are buried in the Oak City Cemetery in Bainbridge.

Samuel Ernest Vandiver, Jr. 1959-1963

He kept the public schools open

After a four-year apprenticeship as lieutenant governor, Ernest Vandiver, a soft-spoken young lawyer from Lavonia, was the overwhelming choice of the people to succeed Marvin Griffin as governor. In the most lopsided gubernatorial election in recent Georgia history, Vandiver won the Democratic primary on 10 September 1958, carrying 156 counties, 400 county unit votes, and 499,477 popular votes to William Bodenhamer's 87,830 votes and Lee Roy Abernathy's 33,099 votes. Several factors account for his impressive victory. Though only forty when elected governor, Vandiver already had considerable experience in the executive branch of government. Mild-mannered and serious, he had few political enemies and faced unusually weak opposition. Moreover, he was intelligent, conscientious, and honest, and had close ties to the most popular political factions in Georgia. A protege of Senator Herman Talmadge, Vandiver had served as his adjutant general for six years, and his wife was the niece of Senator Richard Russell.

A native of Franklin County, Georgia, Vandiver was born in Canon on 3 July 1918, the son of Samuel Ernest and Vanna Osborne Vandiver. He attended public schools in Lavonia, Darlington Preparatory School in Rome, and the University of Georgia, where he received an A.B. and an LL.B. degree. After serving as a pilot in the Army Air Corps during World War II, he joined the law firm of Joseph D. Quillian in Winder. Quillian, who later served as associate justice of the Georgia Supreme Court, described his young associate as "an excellent student," an "indefatigable worker," a "forceful and gifted orator," and "a skilled practitioner," but his most outstanding traits were his "integrity and fairness." As Quillian put it: "He is a person who has never learned to lie."

Attracted to politics at an early age, Vandiver was elected mayor of Lavonia in 1946. Since his father was a close friend of Governor Eugene Talmadge, Vandiver became an aide to the governor. After his death, Vandiver served as an aide to Herman Talmadge, supported him during the three-governors controversy, and managed his successful gubernatorial campaign in 1948, after which Talmadge named him adjutant general. Only thirty years old when appointed, Vandiver was the young-

Fig. 73. Ernest Vandiver at his inauguration

est adjutant general in the country. A capable administrator, he also served as state director of selective service and after 1951 as state director
of civil defense. In 1952 he was promoted to the rank of major general
in the United States Air National Guard. Although a political opponent
of Governor Marvin Griffin, Vandiver served as his lieutenant governor,
an office that seemed to be a stepping stone to the governorship.

Prior to Vandiver's inauguration as governor, the issue of honesty
and integrity erupted, creating a crisis of confidence. Governor Griffin's
revenue commissioner was indicted, and a judge demanded the purchasing records of seven state departments for presentment to a grand jury.
Irregularities were uncovered in the Education and Highway Departments,
and the state treasurer disclosed that state spending was exceeding
income by $12 million a year. It was in this troubled environment that
Vandiver took office.

Determined to eliminate waste and corruption and straighten out the
state's fiscal affairs, Vandiver pursued economy with a vengeance. He
appointed competent administrators to the most troubled departments
—purchasing, revenue, parks, and forestry—and gave them strict instructions to "clean up the mess." To a large extent they succeeded by in-

stituting competitive bidding and implementing more efficient business practices. Upon taking office, Vandiver immediately ordered most of the state departments and agencies to reduce their expenditures by 10 percent. Revenue Commissioner Dixon Oxford, on his first day in office, removed 216 employees from the departmental payroll. By such forceful actions, the new administration demonstrated emphatically that it meant business. Economy and frugality characterized the Vandiver administration, and there was no hint of scandal.

Even more troubling to Vandiver than the fiscal crisis was the issue of racial integration, which the governor described as "the most overriding internal problem ever to confront the people of Georgia in our lifetime." Vandiver, like practically all of Georgia's politicians, held conservative political views. He believed in states' rights and segregation. In campaigning for governor he had promised that Georgia's schools would not be integrated while he was governor. His popular slogan, which he later regretted using, was "No, not one will enter." Even though the United States Supreme Court had ruled in 1954 that racial segregation in public schools was illegal, Georgia had made no effort to begin integration when Vandiver became governor. Indeed, in 1955, the legislature adopted a measure that required that state funds be cut off to any college or school that admitted a black student, and in Vandiver's first legislative session additional school-closing laws were passed. Both the governor and the legislature seemed to believe that the federal courts would allow Georgia's public schools to be operated on a segregated basis.

A federal court order directing Atlanta to desegregate its public schools by September 1961 provoked widespread debate throughout the state. A few educators, businessmen, ministers, and civic leaders argued that closing the schools would be a tragedy, and former governor Ellis Arnall courageously called for token integration, but most politicians either remained silent or demanded "massive resistance." To ascertain public opinion, Vandiver and the legislature established a prestigious study commission and instructed it to hold hearings throughout the state. Headed by respected banker and civic leader John A. Sibley, it ultimately recommended that each local school district be allowed to determine for itself whether to accept integration or close its schools.

The integration issue suddenly shifted to Athens on 7 January 1961, when a federal judge ordered the University of Georgia to enroll immediately Charlayne Hunter and Hamilton Holmes, both highly qualified black students. Their admission, amid threats of violence and mob action, ended 175 years of segregated education at the University of Georgia and precipitated the most serious crisis in Georgia education since the loss of accreditation twenty years before. On January 9 Governor Vandiver, obeying state law as he understood it, closed the university, stating, "It is the saddest duty of my life." With Athens in chaos, Vandiver assembled over fifty of his top officials at the governor's mansion to discuss the issue. All of his advisors except legislators Carl Sanders and Frank Twitty recommended unyielding resistance to the federal courts. After much soul-searching, Vandiver accepted the Sanders-Twitty view that the public schools must remain open. On 19 January, Vandiver delivered the most courageous speech of his career to a joint session of the legislature. Reversing his previous position, he stated firmly: "We meet together to proclaim to the whole world that public education will be preserved." Calling for compliance with federal court orders, he asked the General Assembly to repeal the cutoff-funds laws and to enact local-option laws, as the Sibley Commission had recommended. With few dissenting votes, the legislature adopted his proposals. In the fall of 1961 nine black students entered formerly all-white high schools in Atlanta. By accepting a court ruling he disagreed with and urging the people of Georgia to obey the law, Vandiver displayed responsible leadership in a time of crisis. Limited integration of Georgia's public schools became a reality, and the state avoided the violence and embarrassment that Alabama, Mississippi, Arkansas, and other Southern states experienced.

Vandiver had barely recovered from the schools crisis when he was at loggerheads with the federal courts over the county unit system. Georgia's unique county unit system, used to nominate candidates for governor and other state offices in every statewide Democratic primary from 1898 to 1960, with the exception of 1908, was in jeopardy as a result of the 1962 *Baker v. Carr* ruling by the United States Supreme Court. Georgia's system, which may have been equitable in the nineteenth century, had become grossly unfair as the state became more urbanized. Urban voters were virtually disfranchised by 1960 by a system that granted two unit votes to the 1,876 residents of Echols County and only six unit votes to the 556,326 residents of Fulton County. Realizing the vulnerability of the county unit system, Vandiver called the General Assembly into special session to revise the laws relating to primary elections. After much bickering, the legislature adopted a new law which substantially reduced the disparities between rural and urban counties. On 28 April 1962, one day after Vandiver signed the new law, a United States district court rendered its decision in a suit challenging the county unit system. In the case of *Sanders v. Gray*, the court declared the new statute an improvement, but still short of constitutional standards. That historic decision ended the county unit system and ensured that candidates for statewide office in Georgia henceforth would be chosen by popular votes.

While these significant developments were imposed on the state by outside forces, the Vandiver administration made commendable progress in developing tourism, expanding foreign trade through improved port facilities, increasing appropriations for education, and expanding welfare benefits. Vandiver also made substantial improvements in two fields virtually ignored by previous governors. For many years Georgia's historical records had been woefully neglected, but in Vandiver's term a new seventeen-story building was constructed in Atlanta to house the state archives. Prior to Vandiver, Georgia's mentally ill had received even less attention than the state's historical documents. A tour of the overcrowded facility at Milledgeville, where twelve doctors were responsible for twelve thousand patients, appalled Governor and Mrs. Vandiver. Vandiver made the public aware of the horrible conditions at Milledgeville and began a complete reorganization of the mental health program. With increased appropriations from the General Assembly and federal assistance, new facilities, personnel, and programs were added. Mrs. Vandiver worked for the establishment of the chaplaincy program at the hospital and sought funding for a Chapel of All Faiths on the hospital grounds. Vandiver considered the improvements in mental health his "most gratifying achievement" as governor.

When Vandiver relinquished the office of governor to Carl Sanders, he remarked that he felt like "a fellow who has just finished his final exam and felt like he passed." Both his political colleagues and the press agreed that Vandiver had given Georgia four years of honest, competent leadership. By any standard of measurement, he left Georgia's government in a much better condition than he had found it four years earlier. The Vandiver administration had restored confidence in state government, weathered reforms in education and primary elections, expanded state services, reapportioned the Senate, and left $22 million in the treasury without increasing taxes. The *Atlanta Constitution* editorialized that he did "a great job" and left office "with the overwhelming respect and affection of the people." From a historical perspective, Vandiver was a transitional governor, following the "good-old-boy" system of Marvin Griffin and preparing the way for the urban-oriented and progressive

Fig.74. Ernest Vandiver congratulates
Carl Sanders as next Georgia governor

administration of Carl Sanders who followed.

After concluding his term as governor, Vandiver resumed his law practice. In 1966 he announced his candidacy for governor and appeared to be the front-runner when a heart attack forced him to withdraw from the race. He served as Governor Jimmy Carter's adjutant general from 13 January to 1 November 1971. Angered by Carter's failure to honor his promise to appoint him to succeed Senator Richard Russell, he waged a vigorous campaign to unseat Carter's appointee, Senator David Gambrell. Calling for strengthening America's military, balancing the budget, reforming the welfare system, and opposing forced busing of school children, Vandiver received 20 percent of the vote in a fifteen-man race, but came in third behind Gambrell and Sam Nunn, the eventual winner. That was his last political campaign.

Vandiver married Sybil Elizabeth "Betty" Russell of Winder on 3 September 1947. She shared her husband's concern for the mentally ill and worked untiringly for the patients at Milledgeville hospital. In 1963 she was named Atlanta's Woman of the Year for Civic Service. The Vandivers have three children: Samuel Ernest III, Vanna Elizabeth, and Jane Brevard. Since 1952 the Vandivers have lived in a beautiful white-columned mansion in Lavonia. In political retirement Vandiver has remained active in business and civic endeavors, serving as chairman of the board of directors of the Northeast Georgia Bank of Lavonia, president of the Georgia Association of Independent Bankers, president of the board of directors of the Lavonia Development Corporation, deacon in the First Baptist Church, and member of the "President's Club" of the University of Georgia.

Carl Edward Sanders
1963–1967

A calm voice making sense

Carl Edward Sanders, who succeeded Ernest Vandiver as governor on 15 January 1963, was perhaps the most handsome of Georgia's governors and certainly was the most athletic of the state's chief executives. He was also Georgia's first "New South" governor and gave the state four years of exceptional executive leadership. A moderate reformer, Sanders approached the future with optimism and a firm determination to modernize the state, but he did not sever all ties with the past. Indeed, he worked harmoniously with the conservative rural-dominated General Assembly and maintained close ties with traditional politicians, such as Jim Gillis, chairman of the State Highway Board, and George T. Smith, speaker of the house. Like the Bourbons of the late nineteenth century, he looked forward and backward at the same time. As Sanders stated, "I tipped my hat to the past, but took off my coat to the future."

Born in Augusta on 15 May 1925, he was the eldest of Carl T. and Roberta Alley Sanders's two sons. Reared in a happy and secure middle-class environment, he delivered newspapers and bagged groceries to earn money during his school years and excelled in athletics, participating in all major sports. A fierce competitor, he compiled such an outstanding record at the Academy of Richmond County that he earned an alternate appointment to the Military Academy at West Point. When the primary appointee accepted the position, a disappointed young Sanders then accepted a football scholarship to the University of Georgia.

World War II disrupted his studies, and he enlisted in the U.S. Air Force in 1943. At age nineteen, he was a lieutenant commissioned to pilot B-17 heavy bombers. After the war he returned to the University of Georgia, where he was active in campus programs and played quarterback on the football team that went to the Oil Bowl. After receiving his bachelor's degree, he entered the University of Georgia Law School and completed the three-year program in two years. In 1947 he received his LL.B. degree, was admitted to the bar, and on 6 September married Betty Bird Foy, a pretty and talented art student from Statesboro. They settled in his hometown of Augusta, where their two children, Betty Foy and Carl Edward, Jr., were born.

After practicing law for two years with the firm Hammond and Kennedy, the young Sanders, always eager to accept new challenges, started his own firm. He brought other young attorneys into the firm, and by 1952 he was the senior partner in the firm of Sanders, Thurmond, Hester, and Jolles. While establishing his law firm, Sanders provided leadership in civic affairs by serving on the local boards of numerous state and national organizations. He also served as deacon at Hill Baptist Church and taught an adult Sunday School class for many years. In 1955 the Augusta Chamber of Commerce elected him Young Man of the Year; in 1959 the Georgia Jaycees named him one of the five Outstanding Young Georgians.

Sanders's political career began in 1954 when a local delegation convinced him to seek a seat in the Georgia House of Representatives. Local sports hero, veteran, and rising attorney, he presented an all-American boy image and won the race easily. Two years later he advanced to the Senate, where he quickly emerged as a leader. His drive, ability, and political skill impressed Governor Ernest Vandiver, who made him floor leader in 1959. From 1960 to 1962, Sanders served as president pro tempore of the Senate, the highest office open to a member of that body.

Ambitious for higher office, Sanders contemplated running for lieutenant governor in 1962, but, throwing caution to the wind, decided to seek the governorship instead. He faced a formidable opponent in Marvin Griffin, a former governor with strong ties to the Talmadge faction and few peers as a stump speaker. Campaigning aggressively, as he did in all his campaigns, the clean-cut young attorney, untainted by scandal, kept Griffin on the defensive by repeatedly reminding voters of Griffin's record. The Griffin administration, Sanders cried, had made Georgia "the laughing stock of the nation." He accused Griffin of "favoritism, nepotism, rigged bidding, kick-backs and cronyism."

In contrast to Griffin's blatant racism, Sanders, seeing the futility of the diehard segregationist approach, took a more moderate position. While pledging to maintain "Georgia's traditional separation," he made it clear that "violence in any form will not be tolerated." By downplaying the race issue, he emerged as a voice of reason to many Georgians. Despite his strong criticism of the Griffin record, the Sanders campaign was, on the whole, positive in tone. He stressed the "new politics," which shunned old political warhorses and used the media effectively.

When Georgians voted in the Democratic primary in September 1962, they had a clear choice between a traditional rural-oriented, race-baiting

Fig.75. Carl Sanders

former governor and an urbane young attorney and proponent of the New South. By an overwhelming margin, Georgia voters chose the latter, as Sanders captured 494,978 votes to Griffin's 332,746. Griffin's strength was confined to the rural counties, especially the southwestern area near his home of Bainbridge, whereas Sanders ran strongest in the more populous counties and north Georgia. Indeed, over half of Sanders's statewide vote came from the eleven largest counties. His victory over Griffin marked a turning point in Georgia's political history. Following the demise of the county unit system, Sanders was the first Georgia governor chosen by popular vote, the first man from an urban area to be elected since 1916, and, at age thirty-seven, the youngest governor in the country.

Throughout the campaign and especially in his platform, which he called "a program of progress," Sanders had set forth clearly identifiable goals that he hoped to accomplish as governor. Promising an administration that would be both morally and fiscally sound, he made education his top priority. In addition, he intended to reorganize the Highway Department, attract new industry, improve mental health and correctional facilities, reapportion the General Assembly, and pursue research "to build constructively for the future." His inaugural address set the tone of his administration: "This is a new Georgia. This is a new day. This is a new era. A Georgia on the threshold of new greatness." Calling for teamwork, cooperation, and hard work to solve Georgia's problems, he sought better roads, a higher quality of education, more hospitals, more recreational facilities, better airports, new and expanded industries, and "greater opportunities for all." It was an ambitious program, but to a surprising extent, Sanders accomplished exactly what he set out to do.

Utilizing the findings of the Bowdoin Commission and other study commissions, the Sanders administration modernized many aspects of Georgia's government. It reorganized the Highway Department, the Welfare Department, and the Health Department; it brought greater efficiency to the Revenue Department, strengthened the mental health program, built a police academy and a new governor's mansion, made tourism a billion-dollar industry, expanded the merit system, and established the Water Quality Control Board. Working with the Department of Industry and Trade, the Sanders administration brought a billion dollars' worth of new and expanded industries to Georgia, creating thousands of new jobs.

Unlike most Southern governors of the 1960s, Sanders was a "national" Democrat who worked cooperatively with the administrations of Presidents John Kennedy and Lyndon Johnson; unlike most Georgia governors, he also worked harmoniously with Mayor Ivan Allen of Atlanta to secure funding for the city and build a new stadium, which became the home of major league baseball and football teams during Sanders's term. He also helped Atlanta get legalized mixed drinks, which cleared the way for a boom in luxury hotels and the emergence of Atlanta as one of the most popular convention cities in the nation.

At the end of the Vandiver administration, a federal court ordered Georgia to reapportion one house of its malapportioned legislature. As president pro tem of the Senate, Sanders pushed the controversial measure through a reluctant legislature. As governor, he successfully reapportioned both the House of Representatives and the congressional

Fig.76. Carl Sanders

districts despite strong opposition from rural members of the General Assembly. The federal courts accepted Georgia's reapportionment plans, which gave urban areas more representation and eliminated the worst abuses in the system. They also accepted a new election code adopted in a special session in 1964. But, surprisingly, the federal district court refused to allow Georgians to vote on a new constitution approved by the same legislature because it was "malapportioned." An angry Sanders appealed the verdict to the United States Supreme Court, which reversed the ruling of the lower court, but by then it was too late to place the constitution on the November ballot. Interest in constitutional revision waned, and Georgia remained under the often-amended Constitution of 1945 until the administration of Governor George Busbee. Constitutional revision was the most conspicuous failure of the Sanders administration.

By contrast, the most outstanding achievements of the Sanders administration came in the field of education. As Georgia shifted from an agrarian economy to a more complex urban and industrial economy,

Sanders realized that for the state to attract new high technology industries and federal research grants, it had to transform its educational system quickly or lag behind other states in economic growth. Thus, for Sanders, education was the key that unlocked the door to future growth and prosperity. Consequently, he made education his first priority and directed nearly sixty cents of every tax dollar into education. His administration added 10,000 new teachers and built more schools and classrooms than any previous administration. It established a Master Plan for Education, set minimum standards, and increased local support for education. In addition, it began the Governor's Honors program for exceptional students, developed an extensive educational television network, encouraged school consolidation, and greatly expanded vocational training.

Even more impressive improvements were made in the University System, where enrollments doubled. Under the leadership of Chancellor George Simpson, a network of junior colleges was begun; four junior colleges were elevated to four-year status; a new dental school was established at the Medical College; and $176.5 million was appropriated for building construction—more than the University System had received in the previous thirty years. Moreover, average faculty salaries increased 32.5 percent, moving Georgia from tenth to fourth place among the Southern states. No previous governor in Georgia's history had ever achieved so much for higher education. And despite such expenditures, Sanders left $140 million in the treasury—the largest amount ever left to a succeeding governor up to that time.

While the mid-1960s enjoyed booming prosperity and nearly full employment, there also was much turmoil and racial unrest, leading to numerous marches, protests, and emotional confrontations. Although reared in a rigidly segregated society, Sanders developed a moderate position on race matters. He befriended Leroy Johnson, the first black to serve in the Georgia Senate, and faced numerous racial disturbances in Savannah, Americus, Atlanta, and elsewhere with a combination of firmness and compassion. In contrast to many Southern leaders, Governor Sanders insisted that everyone must obey the law and that disputes should be settled in the courts, not in the streets. Because of his leadership Georgia avoided the kind of tragedies that occurred in Selma and Birmingham. By providing a voice of reason, moderation, and common sense in this turbulent and chaotic period, Sanders emerged as a leader of the New South.

In Georgia's long history, no governor had ever worked harder at the job, traveled to more places, given more speeches, or performed more ceremonial duties than Sanders. By training, experience, and temperament, he was ideally suited to lead Georgia during a period of turmoil and growth. A combination of visionary, planner, and practical politician, he was above all a leader—confident, capable, and tough. Acknowledging that his four years as governor had been "the most satisfying years of my life," he left office at the height of his popularity, basking in almost universal praise from the media. Typical of the press assessments was that of the *Rome News-Tribune*, which editorialized that the Sanders record "consists of definite progress in every field of state responsibilities—public health, education, welfare, trade and industry." More importantly, it continued, in addition to providing dedicated, honest government, he "projected for Georgia a national image of responsibility, integrity and vision." That Sanders was a successful governor is beyond dispute, and most scholars rate his administration as the only one that seriously challenges Ellis Arnall's for the title "Georgia's most progressive modern administration."

The success of the Sanders administration resulted from a happy conjunction of factors that seldom occur at the same time. First, Sanders provided strong executive leadership. Having served in both houses of the legislature, he understood the legislative process and was familiar with the state's most pressing needs. Already an acknowledged leader, he chose capable assistants, such as Doug Barnard, Hiram Undercofler, and Arthur Bolton; set the legislative agenda; delegated power effectively; used the media skillfully to publicize his program; and thoroughly enjoyed being chief executive. Second, the legislatures Sanders worked with included many competent members, as he frequently pointed out, and the General Assemblies, having confidence in the governor, willingly adopted his legislative program. Sanders was the last governor who totally dominated the legislature. He picked the speaker of the house (George T. Smith), named the committee chairmen, wrote the budget, and as one young legislator put it, "ran the state from his hip pocket." After his term, the General Assembly became more independent and assertive and forced all subsequent governors to make concessions to get their programs adopted.

Third, federal courts, by applying increasing pressure on the state to reapportion its legislature and congressional districts on the basis of "one man one vote" and allow blacks to serve in the legislature and exercise other constitutional rights, served as a catalyst for reform. Fourth, the public in the mid-1960s was receptive to moderate political reform and often demanded it. Fifth, state revenues increased by 42 percent during the Sanders administration, providing the funds needed to improve state services. Finally, there was continuity with the Vandiver administration, which prepared the way for Sanders by strengthening the state's finances and beginning the integration of Georgia's public schools. Rarely have the talents of a dynamic governor and the needs of a state blended together so effectively as they did in the administration of Carl Sanders.

At the conclusion of his term as governor, Sanders seemed poised for national leadership, especially since he had cultivated close ties with President Johnson and the national Democratic party. Rejecting several federal positions offered by President Johnson, Sanders instead started a new law practice in Atlanta. In 1970, when again eligible to serve, he sought a second term as governor and appeared to be a prohibitive favorite. In an unusually bitter campaign, however, state senator Jimmy Carter, who had run third in the 1966 Democratic primary, upset the former governor. Embittered by his first political defeat, Sanders never sought public office again.

After 1970, Sanders's political activity consisted primarily in working behind the scenes for candidates he favored. An adept fund-raiser, he drummed up support for George Busbee's two campaigns for governor, for his law partner Norman Underwood's unsuccessful gubernatorial race in 1982, for Zell Miller's gubernatorial campaigns in 1990 and 1994, and for many others. Continuing to reside in Atlanta, he directed his talents and energies to the practice of law, numerous business investments, and civic activities. Starting from scratch, he built a law firm that grew steadily until it became one of Atlanta's largest and most prestigious firms, employing two hundred attorneys. Sanders continues to serve as the chief partner of Troutman Sanders Inc., which currently occupies seven floors of the new NationsBank Plaza on Peachtree Street and recently opened a branch office in Washington, D.C. Long associated with Augusta businessman J. B. Fuqua, Sanders expanded his business investments after leaving the political arena. Achieving extraordinary success in real estate and banking, he continues to serve on the boards of several companies, including First Union Bank, Fuqua Industries, Healthdyne Inc., Learning Technologies, Ltd., and Carmike Cinemas.

An active member of the Atlanta Chamber of Commerce, he has given generously of his time and resources to many civic and charitable

Fig.77. Governor and Mrs. Sanders with President Johnson (1965)

causes. Deeply committed to improving education, for many years he has supported Augusta College, Clayton State College, the United Negro College Fund, and especially the University of Georgia. He served as president of the University of Georgia Alumni Association in 1969–1970, and for many years he has been a key fund-raiser for his alma mater. At a special ceremony on 2 October 1993, Sanders and developer Tom Cousins received the prestigious Bill Hartman Award, the highest honor a former student-athlete can receive from the University Athletic Association. He is also active at Second Ponce de Leon Baptist Church and with the YMCA, the Boy Scouts, the United Fund, and the Democratic party.

Having achieved conspicuous success in three fields—politics, law, and business—Sanders is now a wealthy and respected member of the Atlanta elite. His legendary clout, however, extends beyond Georgia's capital, for his business interests have an international flavor and his name consistently appears on *Georgia Trend's* list of "The 100 Most Powerful People in Georgia."

Lester Garfield Maddox
1967-1971

An anomaly as governor

Georgia has produced more than its share of flamboyant and bizarre politicians, but none in the state's long history was more colorful—or controversial—than Lester Maddox. Completely uninhibited and without guile, he lambasted with unrelenting fervor all who disagreed with his deeply-held beliefs in states' rights, segregation, private property, Christianity, and "Americanism." Nothing in his career seemed to fit the pattern of twentieth-century governors. Neither a lawyer nor a graduate of the University of Georgia, Maddox was the only modern Georgia governor who did not attend college. Totally inexperienced, he had never served in the legislature nor held any elective office when he became governor. He lacked family prominence, professional distinction, financial backing, and military service—traits common to governors of this era—and he was physically unimpressive. Yet, though unaffiliated with any political faction and considered a "loner" and a "loser," having lost his first three political campaigns, he became Georgia's chief executive. In short, Maddox was an anomaly, a unique character who broke all the rules but managed to get elected governor in 1966 in what *Atlanta Constitution* reporter Sam Hopkins called "the most hectic, confusing, complex election in the history of the state."

Born in Atlanta on 30 September 1915, Maddox was the second of Dean and Flonnie Castleberry Maddox's seven children. He grew up in a working-class area of Atlanta near Georgia Tech. His father, a rollturner at Atlantic Steel, managed to keep his family slightly above the poverty level until the onset of the Depression and alcoholism became burdens too great for him to bear. To help support the family, Maddox dropped out of school in the tenth grade. After holding several menial jobs, he gained steady employment with Atlantic Steel. During World War II he briefly held a civilian job with the U.S. Navy and then worked for the Bell Bomber plant in Marietta. As a father in a war-related job, Maddox was not subject to the draft. Longing to be his own boss, he quit the B-29 factory and, with $400 capital, opened a small short-order grill in his old neighborhood near Atlantic Steel. Less than a year later he sold Lester's Grill for $4,000.

Fig.78. Lester Maddox

Late in 1947 he opened the Pickrick Restaurant which specialized in fried chicken and low-cost food. Located near Georgia Tech, it earned only $1,719 the first year, but business increased steadily thereafter, bolstered by clever advertisements in the Atlanta newspapers. Expanded many times, by 1956 the Pickrick had a seating capacity of four hundred and an acre of parking. Showing great entrepreneurial skill, Maddox, starting from scratch, had within a decade made the Pickrick one of Atlanta's largest restaurants, serving half a million customers annually.

An avid believer in states' rights and segregation, Maddox refused to serve Negroes at his restaurant. Whenever any black customers appeared, he personally drove them away. On 3 July 1964, the day after President Lyndon Johnson signed the Civil Rights Act, three blacks tried to enter his establishment to test the new law. In a dramatic encounter that received national publicity, Maddox met them with a pistol in hand and drove them off his property. When the courts found his refusal to serve blacks a violation of the Civil Rights Act, he closed the Pickrick rather than allow it to be integrated, claiming that "my President, my Congress and the Communists have closed my business and ended a childhood dream." By losing his business, Maddox suddenly became a martyr to the cause of private property rights, a folk hero to white segregationists, and a defiant symbol of reactionary racism to the national media.

After the *Brown v. Board of Education* decision of 1954, Maddox became increasingly interested in politics. In 1957 he ran for mayor of Atlanta against longtime incumbent William B. Hartsfield. Charging that school integration would lead to "widespread racial amalgamation," Maddox made a respectable showing but lost. Four years later he ran for mayor again, this time against moderate businessman Ivan Allen, Jr. The race issue dominated the campaign, and once again the moderate coalition prevailed, and Allen won in a runoff. Encouraged by his strong showing among white voters, Maddox ran for lieutenant governor in 1962. In an eight-man race, he lost a runoff election to Peter Zack Geer, a south Georgia lawyer and protege of Governor Ernest Vandiver and Senator Herman Talmadge.

The publicity generated by the closing of the Pickrick and other events in 1964 and 1965 made the obscure Georgian a national symbol of defiance and energized his lagging political career. Basking in media attention, he announced his candidacy for governor in 1966. In the Democratic primary Maddox faced five other candidates: Ellis Arnall, former governor staging a political comeback after twenty years; Garland T. Byrd, former lieutenant governor; Jimmy Carter, young state senator from Plains; James Gray, newspaperman from Albany and former chairman of the State Democratic Executive Committee; and Hoke O'Kelley, a perennial candidate from Lawrenceville. In addition, Herman Talmadge considered entering the race but decided to remain in the United States Senate, and former governor Ernest Vandiver did become a candidate but had to withdraw for health reasons. Maddox branded his opposition as "cowardly political leaders who ask you to follow their programs of cowardice into the pits of hell and destruction—integration and amalgamation." In a spirited campaign, Arnall came in first as expected with 231,480 votes. Maddox, who promised to chase Martin Luther King, Jr. out of the state and invite Alabama Governor George Wallace in, surprised the experts by placing second with 185,672 votes. Carter, taking a middle position between Arnall on the left and the Maddox-Gray-Byrd position on the right, came in third with 165,562 votes. Since no candidate had secured a majority, Arnall faced Maddox in a runoff two weeks later. An overconfident Arnall, who could not imagine losing to Maddox, did no campaigning during the runoff. Maddox, by contrast, continued to campaign throughout the state, tirelessly shaking hands and tacking up MADDOX COUNTRY posters. His indefatigable campaigning paid immediate dividends, for the underdog Maddox pulled a major upset, winning the nomination with 54 percent of the vote by carrying the rural small-town areas and the non-affluent city precincts.

Ordinarily winning the Democratic nomination was tantamount to election, but conditions had changed. The Republican party, dormant since Reconstruction, had nominated a strong candidate in Howard "Bo" Callaway, West Point graduate, wealthy heir to a textile fortune, and extremely conservative congressman from the Sixth District. The polls consistently indicated that he had an excellent chance of defeating any of the Democrats and becoming Georgia's first Republican governor since Reconstruction. Democrats could no longer count on the "solid South," for in 1964 Georgia, for the first time in history, had cast its electoral votes for the Republican presidential candidate. The Callaway forces were delighted that Maddox, Georgia's most fanatical defender of racial segregation, had won the nomination, and many Republicans probably voted for him in the runoff, assuming that he would be easier to defeat than Arnall. Benefiting from a lavishly financed and meticulously organized campaign, Callaway won the popular vote, although his total of 453,665 was only slightly more than Maddox's 450,626. More than 50,000 voters, unwilling to support Maddox or Callaway, had written in the name of Ellis Arnall, thus denying either candidate a majority and forcing the General Assembly to choose the governor. In a chaotic situation, reminiscent of the three-governors controversy twenty years before, the heavily Democratic General Assembly, after the last legal challenges had been dismissed, dutifully elected Maddox governor by vote of 182 to 66 with 11 abstentions.

Until Maddox became governor, neither the news media nor the other candidates had taken him seriously. He seemed to be a comical little fellow with a flair for publicity who, without any noticeable army of followers, was waging a one-man war on communists, socialists, integrationists, the Supreme Court, the Atlanta newspapers ("fishwrappers," he called them), Presidents Kennedy and Johnson, and Martin Luther King, Jr. In commenting on the odds against him in 1966, Maddox did not exaggerate much when he remarked, "All that was necessary was to defeat the Democrats, the Republicans—on the state and national level—159 courthouses, more than 400 city halls, the railroads, the utility companies, major industry, and all the daily papers and TV stations in Georgia."

That Maddox genuinely tried to be a good governor cannot be denied, but he was severely handicapped by the peculiar circumstances of his election, his lack of education and political experience, and his reputation for bizarre behavior and extremism. Following the example of Governor Carl Sanders, he provided healthy raises for teachers and substantial increases in funding for the University System. He also retained several of Sanders's appointees and relied heavily on such Sanders stalwarts as Gene Holley in the Senate and Zell Miller as his executive secretary. In general, Maddox made competent appointments and received much praise for naming Peyton Hawes revenue commissioner and General Louis Truman director of the Department of Industry and Trade. To the surprise of practically everyone, he put more blacks on advisory boards and into white-collar jobs than any previous governor. Despite having future speaker of the house Tom Murphy as his floor leader, he could not control the increasingly independent legislature. During the power vacuum following the controversial 1966 election, the House of Representatives independently chose George L. Smith as its speaker, and Smith made committee assignments without gubernatorial input. Maddox, who believed in legislative independence, showed little interest in mastering the legislative process or in influencing legislative deliberations. Lacking influence in the General Assembly, he failed to secure funding for all of his proposals for education, mental health, and welfare. Much of his program languished, as historian Bradley Rice has pointed out, but in 1970, having learned by experience, he effectively used the threat of a veto to get funding for a women's prison and a work release center, and for the first time the state budget broke the $1 billion barrier. A man of the people, Maddox instituted "People's Day," a specific time set aside each month when anyone who wished to see the governor personally could do so. People by the hundreds, from all walks of life, queued up in his office to tell him their woes and ask for his help. A battery of bureaucrats, from corrections, welfare, and other departments, was stationed at the governor's elbow to get to the bottom of every problem.

At the beginning of Maddox's term, liberals, aghast at his election, predicted catastrophe. Expecting severe persecution of blacks, race riots, bitter confrontations with the federal government, and possibly the collapse of state government, they were dismayed when none of these things occurred. Indeed the most remarkable feature of the Maddox administra-

Fig. 79. Lester Maddox pickets White House (1965)

tion, aside from his occasional red-faced temper tantrum and backward bicycle riding antics, may have been how little it differed from those that preceded it. His segregationist philosophy, extreme rhetoric, and pious self-righteousness brought scorn and derision to Georgia, but his personal integrity, zeal for honesty in government, and sympathy for the downtrodden served the state well. By the end of his term many critics reluctantly admitted that he had done a better job than they had expected. His performance even earned lavish praise from Charles Weltner, who in 1966 abandoned a promising congressional career rather than appear on a Democratic ticket with Maddox, and from Atlanta journalist Bill Shipp, one of the most astute observers of Georgia's political scene. Both concluded that Maddox had served the state well as governor. "Oh, he may have made us seem foolish up there in Yankeeland," wrote Shipp in 1985. "But, in fact, he made excellent judicial appointments, instituted the most far-reaching prison reforms ever tried in Georgia, brought black officials into government for the first time and generally showed himself to be a compassionate governor with a certain amount of wisdom concealed just below that zany veneer."

After concluding his term as governor, Maddox became the first governor to seek the office of lieutenant governor. Garnering 51 percent of the vote, he easily defeated three capable opponents to secure the Democratic nomination and then soundly trounced the Republican candidate, Frank Miller, in the general election. As lieutenant governor and presiding officer of the Senate, Maddox was a constant thorn in the side of Governor Jimmy Carter. In 1974 he sought the governorship again. He came in first in the Democratic primary, but that was his last electoral victory. He lost the runoff election to George Busbee and lost several subsequent campaigns as well. Though heavily in debt from the 1974 campaign, Maddox refused to allow his old antagonist Jimmy Carter to capture the presidency without a direct challenge. As the nominee of the American Independent party, Maddox lashed out at Carter, claiming he was an inept governor, an ultraliberal, and a liar. His campaign had a negligible impact on the outcome, and some observers suggest that it may have increased Carter's total. His last gubernatorial campaign came in 1990, when most voters considered him a relic of a bygone era.

Maddox faced much physical and financial adversity after leaving office in 1975. He published his autobiography, *Speaking Out*, and opened another restaurant called Lester Maddox's Pickrick, but subsequently sold it and embarked on numerous business ventures in a valiant effort of pay off his campaign debts of nearly $300,000. Financial solvency seemed within reach until he suffered a massive heart attack in September 1977, which severely restricted his activities. In 1978 a group of the state's leading politicians—including George Busbee, Sam Nunn, Herman Talmadge, Zell Miller, and Tom Murphy—established a "Get Well Lester Maddox" committee to help pay off his debts. Three years later they proudly announced that the last of Maddox's debts had been paid in full. In 1982 Maddox underwent surgery for prostate cancer. Showing remarkable resilience, he recovered quickly and resumed his active schedule.

In May of 1986 Maddox and his wife, the former Hattie Virginia Cox, celebrated their fiftieth wedding anniversary. They have four children, Linda, Virginia, Lester Jr., and Larry, and they continue to reside in Marietta. Despite advancing age and physical problems, Maddox remains as ebullient as ever and as committed to his beliefs, which he frequently expresses to civic and religious groups. In his speeches, in addition to assailing his liberal opponents and defending traditional values as he has done for many years, Maddox invariably thanks God for his family, his country, and "for every breath and heartbeat he gives me."

James Earl Carter, Jr.
1971-1975

From Plains to the Presidency

James Earl Carter, Jr., Georgia's most complex and contradictory governor, was born on 1 October 1924 in the small farming community of
Plains in the southwestern part of the state. The Carters, who had resided
in Sumter County for many generations, could trace their ancestry in
America back to Thomas Carter, a poor English immigrant farmer who
arrived in Virginia in 1637. Jimmy learned the satisfactions of hard work
and public service from his father, Earl Carter, a successful businessman
who owned considerable real estate and operated a warehouse and
brokerage in peanuts. He inherited the dreams of a visionary from his
free-spirited mother, Lillian Gordy Carter, a nurse who served in India
with the Peace Corps after she was widowed. Jimmy, the first born, had
two sisters, Gloria and Ruth, and a much younger brother, Billy, born in
1937.

Reared in an environment reminiscent of the one described so vividly
by Harper Lee in *To Kill a Mockingbird*, Carter, intense, studious, and
somewhat of a loner, was graduated from high school in 1941. He then
spent two years boning up on science courses at Georgia Southwestern
College and then the Georgia Institute of Technology before receiving a
congressional appointment to the United States Naval Academy, which
had been his goal since he was six years old. Taking accelerated wartime
courses, he thrived in the academic environment, made good grades, and
fondly remembered this period as a time of "challenge, excitement, and
learning." Graduating sixtieth in a class of 822, he subsequently did
graduate work in nuclear physics at Union College and worked under
Captain (later Admiral) Hyman Rickover on the development of the
world's first atomic submarine. The brilliant captain, a demanding task-
master, made a profound and lasting impact upon the young officer. After
receiving his commission at Annapolis, Carter married Rosalyn Smith,
who was also from Plains, and they soon had three sons, Jack, Chip, and
Jeff, and daughter, Amy, who arrived fifteen years later in 1967. Selected
to be the chief engineer on the nuclear submarine *Seawolf* when it put to
sea, Carter seemed destined for a successful career in the navy, but the
death of his father in 1953 suddenly altered his plans. After much soul-

searching and against the wishes of his wife, he abandoned his naval career and returned to Plains.

The first years back in Plains were difficult for Carter as he readjusted to rural living and tried to rebuild his father's faltering warehouse peanut business during one of Georgia's worst droughts. But conditions soon improved. Carter became skilled at raising peanuts and his business prospered. Within a few years he expanded his small business to include a cotton gin, a peanut-shelling plant, and warehouses. Active in local affairs, he served as district governor of the Lions International, chairman of the local planning commission, president of the Georgia Planning Association, chairman of the Sumter County Board of Education, and deacon and Sunday school teacher in the Plains Baptist Church. By 1960 Carter had become one of Plains's most respected business and civic leaders.

Although Carter had shown little interest in politics, he came from a politically active family. His father, a staunch Talmadge supporter, had served on the county school board and had been elected to the state legislature the year before he died. In 1962 Carter won a seat in the Georgia Senate in a bitterly contested race involving fraud, illegal voting, and other irregularities, which he later described in his book *Turning Point*. Reelected two years later, he generally supported the policies of the Sanders administration, looked out for his constituents, showed particular interest in improving education, lashed out at lobbyists for special interests, and expressed concern for the poor and underprivileged. Perhaps the best informed member of the Senate, he took pride in reading every bill introduced in the General Assembly—a practice many legislators considered a waste of time. According to Speaker of the House George T. Smith, many legislators regarded Carter as an "intellectual fool" because he had no common sense. Secretary of State Ben Fortson described him as "stubborn as a South Georgia turtle." But a newspaper poll in 1965 named him one of the state's most influential legislators.

Ambitious for higher office, Carter announced his candidacy for Congress in 1966, but at the last minute decided to run for governor instead. Virtually unknown outside his district, he waged a grueling campaign and came in third behind Ellis Arnall and Lester Maddox, the eventual winner. For a political novice to get 19.4 percent of the vote in a crowded race was a formidable accomplishment, but Carter was devastated by the defeat. He fell into a deep depression, which was lifted only by the solace he found as a born-again Christian. Convinced that his calling was

Fig.80. Jimmy Carter inspects his peanut crop

to serve mankind, he became committed to a career in public service.

At peace with himself, he decided to run for governor in 1970 and win whatever the cost. Though successful, his campaign was not, as his recent biographer Burton Kaufman quaintly put it, "one of Carter's finest moments." He acted, according to Kaufman, "with a ruthlessness and disregard of principle that was difficult to excuse even on grounds of the ends justifying the means." To defeat former Governor Carl Sanders, his chief opponent in the Democratic primary, he resorted to negative and racist campaigning. Methodically charting the voting patterns in each of the state's 159 counties, he campaigned relentlessly for four years, shaking hands with citizens at factories, service stations, sporting events, and on street corners. By his own estimate he made 1,800 speeches and shook 600,000 hands. Taking a stance to the right of Sanders, he depicted "Cufflinks Carl" as the liberal tool of the Atlanta Establishment, a wealthy elitist out of touch with ordinary people. Moreover, he charged that Sanders had misused the office of governor to enrich himself and his friends. Though never supplying credible evidence that Sanders had stolen or misappropriated state funds, he nonetheless created the suspicion that some wrongdoing had taken place. In his brochures, billboards, and television ads, Carter projected himself as a man of the soil, a hardworking peanut farmer who understood the problems of ordinary Georgians. Assuring Georgians that he was "basically a redneck," he visited a segregationist academy, cozied up to George Wallace and Lester Maddox, spoke out against busing, and injected profanity into his speeches. By using racist code words and symbols throughout the campaign, he attracted the segregationist vote and even gained strong endorsements from archsegregationists Marvin Griffin and Roy Harris. Such tactics enabled Carter to overcome Sanders's advantages of name recognition, an excellent record as governor, unlimited financial resources, and endorsements from most of the state's political leaders and practically all of the state's newspapers. There was nothing "highminded" about the Carter campaign, observed Gary Fink, Carter's sympathetic biographer, but it produced the desired results. Carter won the primary with 48.6 percent of the vote to Sanders's 37.7 percent. He then crushed Sanders in a runoff and easily defeated the Republican candidate, Hal Suit, in the general election.

After being sworn in as Georgia's chief executive on 12 January 1971, Carter delivered one of the most memorable inaugural addresses in the state's history. Surveying the large gathering before him, Carter informed the assemblage that the time for racial discrimination had passed. "No poor, rural, weak, or black person," he declared, "should ever have to bear the additional burden of being deprived of the opportunity of an education, a job, or simple justice." Having stirred up racial and class prejudices for months in an unusually nasty campaign, Carter shocked almost everyone with those words. Conservatives were dismayed, liberals were elated, Lester Maddox called him "a hypocrite," and the national media labeled him a New South governor. In May 1971 he appeared on the cover of *Time* magazine. "Soft-voiced, assured, looking eerily like John Kennedy from certain angles," *Time* reported, "Carter is a man as contradictory as Georgia itself, but determined to resolve some of its paradoxes."

Carter backed up his words with action. During his tenure as governor, the number of blacks on state boards and commissions increased from three to fifty-three and the number of black state employees increased from 4,850 to 6,684. He appointed the first black ever to serve

Fig.81. Jimmy Carter reads from the Carter family Bible
used in his inauguration as Georgia governor and later as president.

on the Board of Regents of the University System. He also was the first
governor to allow portraits of black Georgians to be displayed in the state
capitol. On 17 February 1974, portraits of Martin Luther King, Jr., Lucy
Laney, and Bishop Henry McNeal Turner were unveiled despite the
angry protests of Lieutenant Governor Lester Maddox and a small band
of Ku Klux Klansmen.

Shortly after becoming governor, Carter launched "Goals for Georgia," a program designed to facilitate citizen participation in the determination of public policy. Fifty-one public meetings were held throughout
the state, enabling participants to establish goals in education, prison
reform, industrial development, and many other areas. Ideas generated in
these meetings formed the basis of much of the legislative package Carter
presented to the General Assembly.

Carter's top priority as governor was to reorganize the executive branch of government to improve its operation and cost effectiveness. Since no systematic reorganization had been attempted since Richard Russell's administration in the 1930s, one was long overdue. Despite intense opposition from Maddox and his cohorts in the Senate and entrenched bureaucrats, Carter eventually succeeded in getting practically all of his program adopted. The reforms did not save the state $50 million, as Carter later claimed, nor did they reduce to any appreciable extent the number of state employees. But by eliminating and consolidating three hundred agencies into twenty-two, they made the system more efficient and responsive, with the one glaring exception of the unwieldy Department of Human Resources. Carter also instituted the practice of "zero-base budgeting," a system requiring an annual review of budgetary priorities as a means of promoting and measuring efficiency.

To a greater extent than any previous governor, Carter was committed to preserving Georgia's natural resources. Aside from reorganization, he spent more time on this issue than any other. A charter member of the Georgia Conservancy, he realized the importance of preserving historical sites and the natural environment for future generations. Under his leadership the Georgia Heritage Trust program was established, which enabled the state to acquire sites valued for historic, recreational, archaeological, or geological purposes. Two of the first acquisitions were Wormsloe, a tract near Savannah granted to Noble Jones by King George II, and the Jarrell Plantation in Jones County, which was donated to the state. By the end of his term, 20,000 acres of historic and scenic land had been acquired. Carter also struck a blow for ecology when he blocked efforts by the Army Corps of Engineers to construct the Sprewell Bluff Dam on the Flint River. Carter also achieved substantial improvement in the merit selection of judges, the mental health program, the prison system headed by Ellis MacDougall, and the Highway Department under Bert Lance. Although Carter accomplished most of his objectives, he expressed disappointment in failing to secure meaningful property tax relief and consumer protection legislation.

Despite a commendable record of legislative accomplishment, the Carter administration was controversial, aggressive, and combative. An observer at the time quipped that his victories and defeats as governor were forged in the teeth of "The Three L's—Lester, the Legislature and the Lobbyists." Consequently, Carter was not a popular governor. When a group of Georgia historians surveyed the effectiveness of the post-

World War II governors, they ranked Carter as an average governor, at best. They ranked him above Herman Talmadge, Lester Maddox, Ernest Vandiver, and Marvin Griffin, but substantially below Ellis Arnall, Carl Sanders, and George Busbee. His popularity suffered from the constant verbal warfare with Maddox and conflicts with others. In addition, as Gary Fink has pointed out, Carter claimed the moral and ethical high ground, but he "sometimes practiced a style of politics based on exaggeration, disingenuousness, and at times outright deception."

Midway through his governorship, Carter began a serious evaluation of his chances of winning the presidency. His political advisor Hamilton Jordan, encouraging him to run, presented him a seventy-two-page memorandum brilliantly outlining a strategy for victory in 1976. "Perhaps the strongest feeling in this country today," he told Carter, "is the general distrust of government and politicians at all levels." The Jordan brief became the blueprint for the Carter campaign. When Carter announced to his mother that he was going to run for president, she responded, "President of what?" The Atlanta press ridiculed his chances and the rest of the nation ignored him—at first. Undaunted by the odds against him, Carter entered the contest with the same intensity that had marked his previous campaigns. For two years he traveled throughout the country, meeting people, shaking hands, appearing on television, and holding news conferences. Remaining deliberately vague on issues, he stressed values instead. Capitalizing on the anti-Washington sentiment following the Watergate scandal, he gradually accumulated a national following. He entered all of the presidential primaries and systematically eliminated all of his better-known opponents—Edward Kennedy, George Wallace, Morris Udall, Fred Harris, Birch Bayh, and others. The longest of longshots, Carter secured the Democratic nomination on the first ballot. In achieving this political miracle, Carter used many of the techniques he had employed in the 1970 gubernatorial campaign. The first candidate in the field, he campaigned harder and longer than his opponents, took his message directly to the people, staked out a position to the right of his major opponents, and stressed values and image more than issues. With Walter Mondale as his running mate, he held together the Democratic coalition and defeated the Republican team of Gerald Ford and Robert Dole. The thirty-ninth President, Carter was the first Georgian ever elected to that office.

An ineffectual President, he lost his reelection bid to Ronald Reagan in 1980, and for several years appeared as a discredited symbol of well-

Fig.82. Jimmy Carter

intentioned ineptitude. Ignored by the media and the Democratic party, Carter retired to Plains, where he devoted himself to research and writing. A prolific writer, by 1994 he had published ten books, mostly on political and diplomatic topics, and most recently a book of poetry entitled *Always a Reckoning*. In addition, he publicized Habitat for Humanity and performed manual labor constructing housing for the poor. His most important post-presidential work, however, has involved the Carter Center, a non-profit think tank which he started in 1982. Located in Atlanta adjacent to the Carter Presidential Library, the Carter Center attempts to "wage peace" around the world. Utilizing the expertise of Emory University faculty, Carter has become extremely knowledgeable about world affairs. Acting in the belief that one person can make a difference, he has traveled as "a representative of the Carter Center" to trouble spots throughout the world. As a freelance peacemaker, he monitored elections in Nicaragua, Panama, Haiti, Guyana, and Paraguay in the late 1980s and early 1990s. In 1994 alone he participated in high-profile peacemaking missions in Haiti, North Korea, and Bosnia. Going where others are reluctant to go, Carter says, "is my life's work." In toiling for peace, human rights, and democracy around the world, Carter has redefined the post-presidency, gained the admiration of millions throughout the world, and received numerous prestigious awards, including the Martin Luther King, Jr. Nonviolent Peace Prize, the J. William Fulbright Prize for International Understanding, and the Albert Schweitzer Prize for Humanitarianism. Committed to serving mankind since 1966, he at last has found his niche.

George Dekle Busbee
1975–1983

"A workhorse, not a showhorse"

George Busbee, a problem-solver rather than a headline-seeker, was the first Georgia governor to serve two consecutive four-year terms. He gave the state eight years of effective, low-keyed leadership—a welcome relief after the tumultuous administrations of Lester Maddox and Jimmy Carter —and ranks among the most popular and least controversial of modern Georgia governors.

Born in Vienna, Dooly County, on 7 August 1927, he was the second of Perry and Nell Busbee's five children. His mother was a teacher and his father was a farmer, mule trader, and house builder. Following the death of his mother, Busbee left home at age fifteen. He completed high school at Georgia Military College and attended Abraham Baldwin College briefly before joining the United States Navy when he was seventeen. Trained as a pilot, he took courses at Duke University, and after his discharge from the U.S. Navy continued his education at the University of Georgia, where he received a bachelor's degree in 1949 and a law degree in 1952. While studying at Athens, he met Mary Elizabeth Talbot, a medical technologist from Ruston, Louisiana. They were married on 5 September 1949 and have two sons, Buz and Jeff, and two daughters, Beth and Jan.

In 1952 Busbee began to practice law in Albany with his closest friend from law school, Bill Divine. The new firm of Divine and Busbee struggled at first, but after a few years it began to prosper. Busbee's political career began in 1956 when a group of local leaders urged him to run for a seat in the state legislature. Only four years out of law school and having no particular interest in politics, the twenty-nine-year-old attorney was less than enthusiastic about seeking elective office. But, after consulting his wife and law partner, he agreed to run, primarily to gain name recognition to benefit his law practice. Intending to serve only two years, he wound up serving eighteen years in the Georgia House of Representatives and eight years as governor before retiring from politics.

Never flamboyant, Busbee shunned publicity while working quietly and methodically in the House. His first headline came in January 1960 when, at the suggestion of Griffin Bell, Governor Ernest Vandiver's chief

Fig.83. George D. Busbee

of staff, he proposed the creation of a commission to study the tense question of racial integration. The famous John Sibley Commission resulted, and it took the position that racial integration was preferable to closing Georgia's schools. In 1962 Busbee sponsored a bill that gave an income tax break to purchasers of new industrial machinery. With the backing of House leaders and Governor Vandiver, it became law. Steady and reliable, Busbee's "common sense" approach to issues and his willingness to spend long hours at the job made a favorable impression on his colleagues and enabled him to advance to positions of leadership. Appointed assistant floor leader and then floor leader by Governor Carl Sanders, Busbee helped secure legislative approval of the Sanders program and played a pivotal role in reapportioning the House in 1964.

At the same time the General Assembly was being reapportioned on the basis of "one man one vote," it also was becoming more independent of the governor. The decisive event occurred during the controversial gubernatorial election of 1966. While the courts were deciding whether

Lester Maddox or Howard "Bo" Callaway should become governor, Busbee and other leaders took advantage of the chaotic situation to organize the House independent of the governor. The representatives chose George L. Smith as speaker and Busbee as majority leader, a position he held continuously until his election as governor. Working closely with Speaker Smith, Busbee supported Governor Jimmy Carter's reorganization plan, wrote the 1974 Campaign Financing Disclosure Act, and initiated legislation to correct abuses in the welfare program. In view of his leadership and popularity in the House, he could have succeeded Smith, who died suddenly in 1973. But Busbee had no desire to serve as speaker. He had higher ambitions.

Despite Busbee's accomplishments in the House, he faced an uphill battle to secure the Democratic nomination for governor in 1974. Outside of Atlanta and Albany he had little name recognition, certainly less than Lester Maddox, the nationally known, colorful lieutenant governor, or Bert Lance, Carter's highway director, or former United States Senator David Gambrell. In addition, several other candidates, including Harry Jackson, Bobby Rowan, and George T. Smith, had substantial support. Stressing the slogan, "A workhorse, not a showhorse," Busbee gradually increased his following and forged ahead of Lance to place second with 20.8 percent of the vote, behind Maddox with 36.3 percent. Gaining momentum, he easily defeated Maddox in the runoff, capturing nearly 60 percent of the vote. In the general election he trounced Republican Ronnie Thompson of Macon, 646,777 to 289,113.

Breaking the tradition of having the inauguration on the steps of the state capitol, Busbee saved the taxpayers thousands of dollars by holding his inaugural ceremony in the Atlanta Civic Center. His inaugural address stressed the need for cooperation among the state's elected officials. "The people are tired of personal bickering, petty infighting and political clatter," he said, in an obvious reference to the stormy Maddox and Carter administrations. Lieutenant Governor Zell Miller echoed the call for harmony, stating that "teamwork is not only needed but is absolutely necessary." A consistent supporter of education throughout his legislative career, Busbee made education his top priority as governor. Economic development, prison reform, constitutional revision, and restructuring the Department of Human Resources were other priorities. Working cooperatively with Miller and the General Assembly, he made noteworthy progress in each of these areas during his eight years, despite a recession, soaring inflation, and an economic slowdown.

Establishing a statewide kindergarten program was Busbee's chief educational reform. Despite the lukewarm support of teachers' organizations and the opposition of House Speaker Tom Murphy, he secured funding in his initial legislative session. The governor's victory was short-lived, however, as a national recession plunged the state into what Busbee characterized as the state's worst financial crisis in forty years. With an estimated deficit of $108 million, he had little choice but to call a special session that eliminated property tax relief, state pay raises, and funding for kindergartens. Forced into a policy of retrenchment, he sought economies in all areas of state government and reduced the 1976 budget by $176 million. Later, when the economy improved, he obtained full funding for kindergartens and provided substantial raises for public school teachers and college professors.

When Busbee took office, the Georgia Constitution, with 831 amendments, was the longest in the nation. The need for revision had been apparent for many years. Both Governors Sanders and Maddox had attempted to revise the Constitution, but without success. Having participated in both failed efforts, Busbee had gained valuable experience. Determined to produce a new document with the advantages of clarity, brevity, and flexibility, he incorporated existing amendments into a re-edited version, which the voters approved in 1976. He planned to revise the Constitution a few articles at a time, but when voters defeated the first two revised articles in 1978, that plan was scrapped. The governor persevered, however, and finally obtained legislative approval of a new constitution in a special session in 1981. Voters endorsed it the next year.

Recognizing that Georgia could no longer depend on agriculture and textiles as its major industries, Busbee sought to attract high technology companies and disperse new industries throughout the state. For Busbee, economic development was a major priority, surpassed in importance only by improving education. Working closely with the Department of Industry and Trade, his administration established a favorable business climate in Georgia and improved the infrastructure by rapidly completing the original interstate highway system, investing more than $100 million in the ports at Savannah and Brunswick, and expanding efforts to provide sufficient water and sewage. New emphasis was placed on agribusiness, tourism, and films. Under Busbee, Georgia became a popular site for movies and television productions as a total of 160 feature films, television movies, and specials were produced on location in the state.

Fig.84. George D. Busbee

Busbee's 1976 legislative package included a statute to allow international banks to operate within Georgia, and by the end of his term sixteen international banks had offices in the state. The World Congress Center in Atlanta, which hosted international trade shows and conventions, doubled in size, bringing in $12 million a year in state taxes and employing 7,500 persons. Finally, Busbee's travels throughout the United States, Mexico, Central America, Canada, the Far East, and Europe advertised Georgia and encouraged investment in the state. These efforts produced impressive results. International companies in the state increased from 150 in 1975 to 680 in 1982, over $1 billion in investment was attracted each year of his administration and per capita income rose from $4,753 to $9,350 during his two terms. Georgia also received additional exposure when Busbee was unanimously elected by his fellow governors to serve as chairman of the National Governors Association in 1980–1981.

Genuinely modest and unpretentious, Busbee provided sensible and competent leadership to a state experiencing rapid population, economic, and urban growth. With more legislative experience than the eight previous governors combined, he had mastered the political process and understood the details of government. He made several excellent appointments, including Norman Underwood, Thomas Marshall, Tom Moreland, Joe Tanner, Nick Chilivis, David Poythress, and James McIntyre. Applying business practices to many agencies, he streamlined the processing of Medicaid payments and removed that program from the Department of Human Resources. Ranked by a 1985 poll of Georgia historians as the most fiscally conservative of the post-World War II governors, he avoided major tax increases and raised the bonded indebtedness only slightly while state appropriations jumped 118 percent. More inclined toward compromise than conflict, he worked harmoniously with the bureaucracy and the General Assembly. Indeed, he was so popular with the legislators that he managed to get the state constitution amended so that the governor could serve two successive terms. In 1978 he won a second term, easily defeating Republican Rodney Cook of Atlanta, 534,572 to 128,139.

Busbee's non-confrontational style of leadership was popular with the public and the press, until an ill-advised attempt to secure a pension under the state's "involuntary separation" clause ended his term on a sour note. The first elected governor of Georgia to serve eight years, he led the state skillfully through a difficult period. His administration produced tangible results and earned lavish praise from the media. In a typical commentary, the *Atlanta Constitution* editorialized in 1983 that Busbee was leaving office "with an enviable record of progress and stability" and that his "legacy of achievement and sound government should serve as a model for future state executives."

After leaving office, Busbee served on the board of directors of Union Camp Corporation and Delta Airlines and became a partner in King & Spalding, a prestigious law firm with offices in Atlanta and Washington, D.C. Having served on the Export Council for both Presidents Jimmy Carter and Ronald Reagan, Busbee possessed considerable expertise on foreign trade which he continued to use to develop Georgia's economy. An active member of the Atlanta Chamber of Commerce, he headed the international division and frequently traveled abroad with business leaders from Georgia. He also chaired for three years the Metropolitan Atlanta Council for Economic Development, a joint effort of the six metropolitan chambers of commerce.

When Busbee lived in Albany, he was a leader in local civic and religious activities, serving as a charter member of Sherwood Baptist Church. After leaving office, he continued such activities and recently helped establish another new church, Parkway Baptist Church. He now resides on an estate in Gwinnett County overlooking the Chattahoochee River. Though still busy with professional work and foreign travel, he now has more time for wife, children, and grandchildren.

Joe Frank Harris
1983-1991

He refused to change

Joe Frank Harris, who succeeded George Busbee as governor on 11 January 1983, bore striking similarities to his predecessor. Like Busbee, he surprised the political experts by winning an upset victory in the Democratic primary, advanced to the governorship after a lengthy career in the Georgia House of Representatives, and brought substantial progress to the state during two four-year terms as governor. Also like Busbee, he was tall, handsome, modest, and totally without charisma.

Born on 16 February 1936 in Bartow County, Joe Frank was the second of Franklin and Frances Morrow Harris's three children. His father, a native of Gilmer County who dropped out of school at age thirteen, worked in a textile mill. Since the family struggled to make ends meet, Joe Frank learned the value of hard work at an early age. In his early youth he delivered newspapers and sold chickens and vegetables from the garden to supplement the family income. During his high school years he abandoned his afternoon and weekend job as a gas station attendant in order to deliver milk before school. Though it paid better, the new job required getting up at 3:30 in the morning and walking a mile to meet the milk truck. After delivering the milk, he had just enough time to change clothes, grab a bite to eat, and walk—or run—another mile to school. Despite working such hours, Harris made good grades and served as president of the Key Club and HI-Y Club, vice president of the senior class, and participated in athletics, including quarterbacking the football team.

Reared in a deeply Christian home, Harris made a profession of faith at age twelve. His conversion was profound. He acknowledges that accepting Jesus Christ as personal savior was "the greatest event" and "the most lasting and dramatic experience in my whole life." After completing high school, Harris, still unsure of his calling, considered going into Christian work or teaching school. While still seeking the Lord's will in his life, he entered Asbury, a small Methodist liberal arts college in Kentucky. After one year at Asbury, he decided to pursue a business career. Since Asbury did not offer a degree in business, he transferred to the University of Georgia, where he earned a B.B.A. in 1958. Immediately after graduating, he served six months in the United States Army to fulfill his military obligation.

Returning to Cartersville, Harris went into the concrete products business with his father and brother. While working at Goodyear, his father dreamed of getting into the concrete business. He realized that as Atlanta sprawled northward many new houses, with concrete foundations and driveways, would be needed in Bartow County, an area that had no concrete supplier. Shortly after World War II ended, he and a partner entered the concrete business on a part-time basis. Soon he abandoned the security of his job at Goodyear to devote full time to it. After struggling for the first few years, his dream became a reality as his business prospered. When Joe Frank joined Harris Cement Products, Incorporated, in September 1958, it was still a relatively small firm with fewer than fifteen employees, but it grew rapidly thereafter. Expanding into Cobb County, it produced concrete products and precast concrete. It also engaged in subcontracting and construction. As comptroller of the company, Joe Frank's primary responsibilities were in the financial area, but he also supervised subcontract work, such as pouring concrete floors and installing septic systems. When the Harris family sold the business in 1981, it had grown to ninety employees and was then operating nearly seventy trucks.

Harris's political career began in May 1964 in a manner reminiscent of George Busbee's experience, when a delegation of Bartow Countians urged him to seek a seat in the Georgia legislature. The request came at a most inopportune time for the busy Harris, who, besides developing the cement business, had built a new house and moved into it in February. In addition, his wife, the former Elizabeth Carlock, daughter of the local Methodist minister and graduate of LaGrange College, delivered their only child, Joe Frank Jr., on 22 March, only two months before the delegation arrived. Aside from putting up a few posters for Carl Sanders in 1962, Harris had no political experience. But after praying about the matter, he decided to run for office and immediately began to campaign door-to-door. In defeating a popular incumbent, Harris carried all but two of the county's fourteen precincts. Never defeated in a political campaign, he served nine consecutive terms in the House, a total of eighteen years, and rarely had opposition.

Arriving in the House in the middle of the Sanders administration, he quietly mastered the rules of the House as he looked out for the interests of his constituents. Keenly interested in budgetary matters, Harris secured

Fig.85. James F. Cook interviewing Joe Frank Harris (1987)

appointment to the Appropriations Committee and gradually gained influence in writing the state budget. When Representative Tom Murphy became speaker of the house following the death of George L. Smith, Harris succeeded him as one of the three House members on the Conference Committee, a powerful committee which reconciled differences between the state budgets passed by the House and Senate. Harris was vice chairman of the Appropriations Committee when James "Sloppy" Floyd of Trion, long-time chairman of the committee, died suddenly in 1974. Speaker Murphy, wondering if the soft-spoken Harris was tough enough to chair that important committee, hesitated before naming a successor to Floyd. "I know you want the job," Murphy explained, "but you're too good a fellow, you're too mild mannered to be chairman of the committee. You've got to be a tough son of a bitch." Harris assured the speaker that he could do the job. The next day, after Floyd's funeral, Murphy announced that Harris was the new chairman of the Appropriations Committee. By serving capably in that key position throughout the eight years of the Busbee administration, Harris proved his toughness and earned the speaker's respect. Indeed when Harris announced his candidacy for governor, one of his strongest supporters in the House was Tom Murphy.

In the Democratic primary of August 1982 Harris faced strong opposition from Congressman Bo Ginn, the early favorite, as well as Norman Underwood, Jack Watson, and Billy Lovett. An ineffective public speaker with little name recognition, Harris seemed to have almost no chance of winning. Few political observers expected him to make the runoff. Early in the campaign Atlanta journalist Durwood McAlister dismissed Harris as a dull candidate with "the charisma of a bowl of cold grits." Taking exception to his remarks, Elizabeth Harris cornered McAlister and lectured him about her husband. "You just don't know Joe Frank," she said. "He is a warm, loving man who really cares about this state. He believes —really believes—in the programs he advocates and he believes in the people of Georgia. When they get to know him, when they understand what he is saying, they'll vote for him. He won't change himself to win votes. He won't have to. Joe Frank is going to win."

Mrs. Harris, it turns out, was an astute political prophet, as her husband placed second in the primary with nearly 25 percent of the vote to Ginn, who came in first with 35 percent. Without obtaining the endorsements of any of the defeated candidates or the Georgia Association of Educators, Harris trounced Ginn in the runoff, 500,765 to 419,259. In the general election he easily disposed of Republican Bob Bell, carrying 62.8 percent of the vote. Harris won, as his wife predicted, without changing his position. During the campaign, advisors urged him to downplay his religious beliefs and disavow his friendship with controversial Speaker of the House Tom Murphy, but he refused. When Bob Bell insisted that he make a complete disclosure of his personal finances, Harris declined, even though trusted advisors urged him to do so. Having decided against campaign disclosure early in the campaign, he resisted such pressure. He did promise, however, to place his holdings in a blind trust, if elected. Unlike many politicians, Harris refused to base his policies on shifts in public opinion polls. Staking out positions he truly believed in, he adhered to them consistently. His conservative platform, promising no tax increase, improvement in education, enforcement of capital punishment, industrial growth, and opposition to the proposed Equal Rights Amendment, had greater appeal in this conservative era than the promises of his flashier opponents. His low-keyed, businesslike style of campaigning generated little excitement, but it conveyed sincerity and credibility. Consistently gaining momentum throughout the campaign, he received overwhelming support from the rural areas and the northwest part of the state and proved the experts wrong.

Taking the oath of office in a simple ceremony on the steps of the capitol before 10,000 well-wishers, Harris delivered a short inaugural address reiterating his promises to operate the state government without a tax increase while making progress in education, transportation, and industrial development through the use of businesslike management techniques. "I am a dreamer," he said, "but I want the history books to reflect that the state of Georgia was a better place to live because of the dreams and the efforts of the Harris administration. I want my administration to be characterized by openness, honesty, fairness and, above all, a burning commitment to excellence." Following the tradition of Governors Maddox and Carter, he served no alcohol at the inaugural ball at the Civic Center. The non-smoking, non-drinking Methodist then went them one better by keeping alcohol out of the governor's mansion, too.

The least assertive and dynamic of modern Georgia governors, Harris achieved his goals during his first term and maintained such a high approval rating that he won easy reelection to a second term. Benefiting from an expanding economy which brought vast increases in revenues to the state treasury, Harris was able to expand state services in many areas and provide major investments in education. Implementing the findings of the Governor's Education Review Commission, he secured legislative support for a comprehensive reform of public education. Known as Quality Based Education, the plan was designed to improve the quality of education throughout the state by providing a new formula for funding public education, extensive testing of students, additional training of teachers, and numerous pilot programs for handicapped and gifted students. An expensive and far-reaching program that would require much fine-tuning in the years ahead, QBE was the most important reform of the Harris administration. To begin to implement QBE in 1985, Harris sought $231 million to pay for the sweeping reforms, including $135 million for teacher pay raises. Although never completely funded, it marked an unprecedented commitment of state resources to education.

Next to education, the most important reforms of the Harris administration were the adoption of a one-cent increase in the sales tax and the establishment of the Georgia Growth Strategies Commission to provide statewide land-use planning. Both came during his second term. Other achievements were securing federal approval of a college desegregation plan after months of negotiation, making Martin Luther King, Jr.'s birthday a holiday, building a domed stadium in Atlanta, adopting a package of child welfare reforms, passing a mandatory seat belt law, and establishing a Research Consortium that matched state money with private funds to provide an impetus for economic growth in technology. Harris also helped lure the Democratic National Convention to Atlanta in 1988. Atlanta's growing importance also was evident in two decisions made in 1990: the selection of the Georgia Dome as the site for the 1994 Super Bowl and the choice of Atlanta to host the 1996 Olympic games. During his eight years, the state budget more than doubled, rising from $3.6 billion in fiscal 1983 to $7.7 billion in fiscal 1991. Despite the growing revenues and Harris's reputation of fiscal conservatism, excessive spending at the end of his term, coupled with a slowdown in the economy in 1990, forced the state to deplete its reserve funds to meet its record expenditures. Governor Harris appointed the first black to the Georgia Supreme Court (Robert Bentham in 1989), four blacks to head state agencies, and numerous blacks and women to state boards. Indeed, during his term 27 percent of all appointments to boards were black and 31 percent were women—the highest totals ever named by a Georgia governor.

Despite this commendable record of accomplishment, Harris received but scant praise from the media. Writers complained that his agenda was "skimpy" and that he avoided difficult issues. Others claimed that he lacked political skill. Bill Shipp described him as "politically impotent" and wondered why he vested so much of the power of his office in Tom Perdue, an aide who has "gone about creating brouhahas and turning Harris' administration into a laughing stock." Assessing the 1987 legislative session, *Rome News-Tribune* editor John Perry asserted that Governor Harris had "lapsed into a catatonic state." After the 1988 legislative session, Tom Teepen of the *Atlanta Constitution* observed, "We've got positive leadership in the Senate, negative leadership in the House, and little leadership in the governor's office."

In an age of slick professional politicians, Joe Frank Harris was, as Jim Wooten observed, a "political dinosaur." Preferring a more aggressive and articulate chief executive who would reform the political system and provide inspiring rhetoric, the media found his methodical leadership lacking. Conservative by nature, he was comfortable with the structure of government he inherited and saw no reason to tamper with it. His refusal to engage in public battles with his opponents and pressure legislators to adopt all of his proposals dismayed his critics who yearned for more dynamic leadership. They argued that his failure to lead created a

Fig.86. Joe Frank Harris

power vacuum, which Zell Miller, Tom Murphy, and other more dominant personalities filled. Writing in 1986, Frederick Allen of the *Atlanta
Constitution* complained that the governor's presence "is hardly felt." He
wondered why Harris refused to wield the immense power he possessed.
More adept at conciliation than confrontation, the governor rarely got
involved in disputes until opposing sides had reached an impasse and
then worked quietly behind the scenes to negotiate a compromise. When
proposals generated little public support, such as his attempts to increase
the gasoline tax by six cents and provide aid for the homeless, he quietly
dropped them rather than fight what he perceived as hopeless battles.
Comfortable with his style and pleased with the progress of his administration, Harris simply ignored his critics.

Much of the criticism was unwarranted, but certainly the governor's
presence was not felt when the 1986 legislature adjourned prematurely.

Normally, much legislation results from last-minute compromises on the last day of the session, as both houses frantically adopt measures until the mandatory ending at midnight (and sometimes even beyond it). But in 1986, thirty-four disgruntled senators, in a fit of pique, ended the session at 6 P.M., killing action on tort-law reform, abortion notification, a crackdown on uninsured motorists, and other measures. This embarrassment resulted largely from the feud between Speaker Murphy and Lieutenant Governor Miller, but, as many observers noted, a stronger governor would have prevented it.

At the end of his term, Harris proudly claimed that Georgia had achieved national leadership in economic growth during his two terms, and he could cite impressive statistics to prove it. The state added 947,000 new citizens, created almost 850,000 new jobs, enjoyed record capital investment of $14 billion in new and expanded industries, increased annual spending for education by $2.1 billion, built 140 new libraries, doubled the number of correctional facilities, and more than doubled spending for health, social services, and Medicaid payments. Even his critics admitted that the state had experienced noteworthy progress under his leadership. In acknowledging his accomplishments, commentators invariably praised his character. "He departs as he came," wrote Jim Wooten, "a principled man of conscience with ego and reputation intact." And Durwood McAlister, who earlier had found Harris so lacking in charisma, stated that "he has set a standard of personal integrity that will never be surpassed in state government."

Just before his term ended, a Joe Frank Harris Appreciation Celebration at the Georgia World Congress Center raised $128,000—enough to pay for the governor's portrait to be placed in the state capitol, publish all of his speeches and distribute them to libraries throughout the state, buy him an expensive Mercedes Benz, and send him and Elizabeth on a European vacation.

Since leaving the executive mansion, Harris has resided in Cartersville and engaged in business pursuits, serving as an advisor to an engineering and environmental firm, chairman of the board of Harris Georgia Corporation of Cartersville, and as a member of the board of directors of American Family Corporation, an insurance company based in Columbus. In the spring of 1994 he became a public affairs professor at Georgia State University and in December became that university's first distinguished executive fellow.

Zell Miller
1991–

An enigma from the mountains

Zell Miller, who succeeded Joe Frank Harris as governor on 14 January 1991, is one of the few governors from the mountainous northeastern section of the state. The great-great-grandson of one of the first white men to push across the Appalachian mountains and settle in picturesque Brasstown Valley, he was born in the scenic but impoverished village of Young Harris on 24 February 1932. Both his parents were employed by Young Harris College, a small Methodist-affiliated liberal arts institution established in 1886. His mother, Birdie Bryan, a native of South Carolina, came to the isolated college to teach art. There she fell in love with Stephen Grady Miller, a history teacher at the college, married him in 1921, and had two children, Jane and Zell. Seventeen days after Zell's birth, his father, then dean of the college, died of mastoiditis at age forty, leaving Birdie a widow with two small children, no home, and practically no money.

Zell's mother, an unusually strong and resourceful woman, eked out an existence during the Depression years by working at the post office. The Millers lived in a two-room house built of stones she dug out of a nearby creek. It had neither an indoor bathroom nor running water. A single fireplace provided the only heat until Zell was almost out of grammar school. Reared without a father, Zell's life reflects the powerful influence of his mother. "She taught me by example the importance of perseverance, hard work, initiative and family loyalty, and of recognizing that there are many things more important than material goods," he wrote many years later.

Shy and insecure, Zell entered the academy of Young Harris College as an eighth grader in 1945. Aided by caring faculty members, especially English teacher Edna Herren, he gradually overcame his timidity and flourished in the academic environment. When he was graduated from Young Harris College with an associate degree in 1951, he had held practically every office on campus, had been a winning champion debater four times, and had captained the intramural football, baseball, softball, and basketball teams.

Transferring to Emory University in Atlanta, he lasted only two quarters before dropping out of school, overwhelmed by the sophistication of the students there. Returning to Young Harris, he moped around for a year, experimented with alcohol, and joined the Marine Corps, where he experienced strict male discipline for the first time. At Parris Island and Camp LeJeune the young mountaineer matured rapidly. When his three-year enlistment ended in August 1956, he had gained confidence, a wife, Shirley Carver of Andrews, North Carolina, and a son, Murphy, born in July 1955. With a second son, Matthew, on the way, the Miller family moved to Athens, where Zell completed his bachelor's degree. To supplement the income from the G.I. Bill, Miller worked as a waiter and hamburger cook. Influenced by an outstanding history professor, E. Merton Coulter, he earned a master's in history, writing a thesis on Georgia governor and Young Harris alumnus E. D. Rivers. He had completed most of the work on a doctorate when, in the fall of 1959, he accepted a position at Young Harris College to teach history and political science. Earning $400 a month, he lived in a house owned by the college, as his parents had done thirty-seven years earlier. In addition to his teaching duties, he served as faculty advisor to the college newspaper and coached the college baseball team.

Miller's political career began in 1958 when he became mayor of Young Harris. His interest in politics came naturally, for his father had served one term in the Georgia Senate, and his mother had served on the Young Harris City Council for more than twenty-five years, including two terms as mayor. In 1960 the twenty-seven year-old crewcut history professor received permission from the college president to run for the Georgia Senate. Campaigning relentlessly door-to-door, he won by 151 votes. Two years later, despite reapportionment which created a new district of eight counties, he gained reelection. One of only five senators to be returned to the legislature, he carried every county except Habersham, the home county of his chief opponent. He won his home county, Towns, by the lopsided margin of 1,235 to 17.

Despite his youth and inexperience, Miller did not defer to his elders in the Senate. He kept his name in the news by forthrightly expressing his views and introducing bills on a wide variety of subjects. He proposed permanent "split sessions" for the General Assembly, the establishment of a committee to study the health code, and a plan for redrawing congressional districts. He also attempted to change the designation of Georgia from the "Peach State" to the "Poultry State," an idea that

Fig.87. James F. Cook, Carl Sanders, and Zell Miller (1994)

evoked derision in the legislature. "Who wants to be from the Chicken State," a critic grumbled. Always seeking ways to foster education, he advocated state grants for dental students, a program of state grants to qualified youths of low-income families to attend private colleges in the state, and an exemption for private colleges and universities from the 3 percent sales tax.

Ambitious for higher office, he resigned his teaching job in 1964 to challenge six-term incumbent Phil Landrum to represent Georgia's Ninth Congressional District. Campaigning as a liberal, Miller attempted to depict his opponent as an archconservative who opposed organized labor. His efforts were thwarted by President Lyndon Johnson, who not only endorsed Miller's opponent in a speech to an audience of 50,000 in Gainesville, but also urged the people to erect a statue of Landrum on the square in Gainesville because of his great work in Washington. With Johnson's enthusiastic support, Landrum won, as expected, but Miller made a respectable showing, losing by 5,000 votes. Two years later,

Miller staked out a position slightly to the right of Landrum, but lost again, this time by 9,000 votes.

After leaving the classroom and the Georgia Senate, Miller held numerous appointed positions in state government from 1964 to 1974. After serving on the State Board for Children and Youth, he became director of the State Board of Probation. He then served the Board of Corrections, first as personnel officer and later as assistant director. He became an aide to Governor Lester Maddox, and, when Maddox became lieutenant governor, he continued to serve as his executive secretary. Governor Jimmy Carter lured him away from Maddox in June 1971, by making him executive director of the Georgia Democratic party. On 2 April 1973, Governor Carter named Miller to the Board of Pardons and Paroles, an appointment that received widespread praise from the media. "The governor is to be congratulated for his choice," observed Reg Murphy in the *Atlanta Constitution*. "He could hardly have made a better selection." Eight months later, however, Miller gave up the security of the seven-year term as well as a salary of $30,000 to run for the office of lieutenant governor.

Recognized as a competent, intelligent, and honest public servant, Miller entered the race as the frontrunner. Assembling an effective state-wide organization, he appealed to a broad coalition of voters ranging from county courthouse crowds and Maddox backers to organized labor and black and white liberals. In a crowded field of ten candidates in the Democratic primary, he came in first, polling 31 percent of the vote. He then trounced Mary Hitt, a former mayor of Jesup, in the runoff and crushed Dr. John Savage of Atlanta, the Republican nominee, in the general election by nearly a two-to-one margin. Four years later he won an easy reelection against token opposition.

Despite these impressive victories, Miller had not yet abandoned his desire to serve in Washington, D.C. He seriously considered running for Congress when Representative Landrum announced his retirement in 1976. His mother dissuaded him, however, by bluntly stating that since the people had elected him to a four-year term as lieutenant governor, he ought to serve it. In 1980 he launched an aggressive campaign to unseat Senator Herman Talmadge, who appeared vulnerable for the first time. Campaigning as "The Best Senator Money Can't Buy," he lambasted Talmadge unmercifully. Although he managed to eliminate Norman Underwood and Dawson Mathis in the Democratic primary, he lost badly to Talmadge in the runoff. In carrying 58.5 percent of the vote and 140 of the state's 159 counties, Talmadge "left Zell sucking air," as he later described the outcome. The campaign left bitter scars, and Talmadge refused to speak to Miller thereafter. Miller not only suffered an embarrassing defeat, he also got stuck with the alliterative nickname "Zig Zag Zell." Norman Underwood first used that unflattering term in the campaign, and Miller's opponents have used it ever since. It seemed to fit Miller, since he had staked out positions all across the political spectrum during his twenty years in politics and had worked closely with governors Sanders, Maddox, and Carter. Miller, like Gene Talmadge in an earlier period, failed to win election to Congress, but he consistently won races for positions in state government. Convinced by the defeat in 1980 to concentrate on public service in Georgia, Miller won easy reelections as lieutenant governor in 1982 and 1986.

During his sixteen years as lieutenant governor, Miller became a mature and responsible statesman who sponsored numerous progressive reforms as the presiding officer of the Senate. Aware that the public was disgusted with the constant bickering between the governor and lieutenant governor in the previous administration, he pledged to improve the image of the Senate and to work cooperatively with the governor. Aside from a brief spat over the passage of the amendment allowing the governor to serve two consecutive terms, he worked harmoniously with Governor George Busbee and his successor, Governor Joe Frank Harris. He supported Busbee's efforts to provide kindergartens and lower the pupil-teacher ratio, and he backed Harris's Quality-Based Education program. A consistent supporter of private educational institutions, Miller sponsored tuition equalization grants which assisted students attending private colleges and universities in the state. Despite opposition from the old guard, he made the rules of the Senate more democratic and required open meetings. Occasionally his reforms were so far ahead of public opinion that they failed to get the support of the governor and the legislature. At various times he called for strict registration of lobbyists, passage of the Equal Rights Amendment, complete revision of state tax laws, campaign expense limits of $450,000 for governor and $300,000 for lieutenant governor, mandatory schooling for able-bodied welfare recipients, and voter registration by mail. "Voting," he argued, "should be as easy as breathing."

Never one to avoid controversial subjects, he told the Peace Officers Association the state needed gun control. He told big business it had itself to blame for meddlesome government regulations. Advising educators to go to work, he called for the creation of a new professional body to certify teachers. In 1976 he expressed the belief that government employees in non-critical areas, including teachers, should have the right to strike when they are not under contract. Such outspokenness early in his tenure as lieutenant governor dismayed observers. David Nordan of the *Atlanta Constitution* speculated that Miller was "either a far-seeing politician able to anticipate future public opinion to a surprising degree or one of the most adventuresome public officials in the recent history of the state." Miller, who was both adventuresome and politically astute, offered a simpler explanation. "People tell me the things I say are stupid," he mused. "But I believe they ought to be said anyway—so I say them." While claiming to practice the art of "conscience over politics," he admitted to having a "political suicide complex."

While Miller worked harmoniously with both Governor Busbee and Governor Harris, he feuded constantly with Speaker of the House Tom Murphy. The feud, which continued for sixteen years, was essentially a power struggle between the two headstrong presiding officers of the rival houses. Besides clashing personalities, political differences separated them too. Miller often favored more liberal or progressive measures, while Murphy, less willing to change, adhered to a more conservative philosophy. They battled furiously over open meetings, increased welfare benefits, and mountain protection legislation, all of which Miller favored and Murphy opposed. Early in Busbee's administration, Murphy sponsored a $35 million tax relief measure that Miller opposed. In 1982, when Miller obviously planned to run for governor, Murphy backed Joe Frank Harris with such enthusiasm that Miller decided against the race. He bided his time and waited eight more years before seeking the office.

Utilizing the talents of Washington consultant James Carville as his campaign manager, Miller waged a modern media campaign for governor in 1990. Abandoning the traditional grassroots organization, he erected few signs, shook few hands, rarely appeared with his rivals, and had no phone bank. Instead, he concentrated on fund-raising early in the campaign and presented a disciplined message on television ads. Spending $5 million on television ads, he called for a state lottery to improve Georgia schools, a military-style boot camp for first time drug offenders, and a repeal of the state sales tax on all food items. Taking 41 percent of the vote in the Democratic primary, Miller defeated several strong candidates —former Atlanta mayor Andrew Young (28 percent), state senator Roy Barnes (21 percent), state representative Lauren "Bubba" McDonald (6

Fig.88. Zell Miller

percent), and former governor Lester Maddox (3 percent). In the runoff on 20 August, Miller easily disposed of Young, garnering nearly 62 percent of the vote. In the general election Miller defeated a strong Republican candidate, state senator Johnny Isakson of Cobb County, amassing 766,662 votes, over 52 percent, to Isakson's total of 645,625 votes, 45 percent. The *Atlanta Journal*, which had endorsed Barnes, nevertheless praised Miller's independence and predicted that, because of his long experience in government and his detailed knowledge of the state's business and its people, he would become "one of Georgia's best governors."

Upon achieving his lifetime dream, Miller wasted no time in taking over the reins of government. He quickly assembled a first-rate staff and placed loyal appointees in key positions. He removed Curtis Earp as director of the state patrol and appointed Ronald Lee Bowman in his place. He made Joe Tanner director of the Department of Natural Resources and appointed Al Scott labor commissioner. He named DeKalb County District Attorney Bob Wilson to the new position of commissioner of public safety to coordinate the operations of the state patrol and the Georgia Bureau of Investigation. To find ways to eliminate waste in government, he appointed top-flight businessmen to the Commission on Effectiveness and Economy, headed by Stone Mountain businessman Virgil Williams, who also became Miller's chief of staff. Facing a severe fiscal crisis, the worst since the mid-1970s, he instructed department heads to operate within their budgets because there would be no tax increase. A forceful executive, eager to invigorate state government, Miller made all of these decisions before being inaugurated.

Pledged to serve only one term, Miller set the political agenda and, with the backing of Speaker Tom Murphy and Lieutenant Governor Pierre Howard, secured passage of most of his program. To cope with a sluggish economy, Miller, by necessity, adopted a policy of retrenchment during his first year, since the Harris administration already had spent all of the budget reserve. His first budget of $7.9 billion seemed to be frugal, but when revenues failed to meet projections, he had to call a special session of the legislature, which removed more than 2,000 employees from the state payroll and reduced expenditures by $415 million. After that difficult beginning, Miller enjoyed robust economic growth during the next three years and was able to provide increased funding for state projects and services. With substantially higher revenues pouring into the state treasury, the state budget increased to $9.8 billion in 1994.

The most important reform of the Miller administration was the adoption of the state lottery. Overcoming intense opposition from many sources, including his own Methodist church, Miller secured legislative approval of a constitutional amendment allowing the lottery, and the voters approved it in 1992. In its first year of operation the Georgia lottery set a record for success among all states by adding more than $362 million to state coffers. By law all lottery revenue had to be spent on education, and Miller directed the bulk of it to scholarships to students who had compiled at least a B average and to improved technology in the schools and colleges.

In addition to the lottery, Miller gained approval for an ethics bill that required lobbyists to report what they spend trying to influence legislation and set new limits on campaign financing, an anti-crime package, welfare reform, "boot camp" prisons for non-violent criminals, mountain protection legislation, and legislative and congressional reapportionment. Miller failed to remove the sales tax from food, as he had promised, and suffered a glaring setback when he attempted to change the state flag. Agreeing with blacks who saw the existing state flag as a symbol of segregation and the Confederacy, the governor put the prestige of his office behind the movement to adopt a new one, but the issue evoked such emotional and determined resistance from the public that he eventually abandoned it without success.

Violating his promise to serve only one term as governor, Miller decided to seek a second term in 1994. Although he had provided four years of solid executive leadership, his reelection, unlike that of his two immediate predecessors, was not automatic. Indeed, he had to campaign vigorously and spend $6.35 million to eke out a narrow 30,000-vote victory over Republican Guy Millner, an Atlanta businessman seeking office for the first time. Although Miller had achieved a noteworthy record of accomplishment, he also had many negatives besides breaking his promise to serve one term. Always combative and outspoken, he had made his share of enemies during his long career in public life, and his anti-crime bills, welfare reforms, state lottery, and efforts to revise the state flag also had alienated groups of voters. Moreover, in 1994 a tide of Republicanism swept the nation, giving that party control of both houses of Congress, including control of the Georgia delegation, plus significant gains in the Georgia legislature. That Miller, a lifetime Democrat, keynote speaker at the 1992 Democratic National Convention, and close friend of unpopular President Bill Clinton, survived the national renunciation of Democrats was a remarkable political feat.

During the election Miller acknowledged that the voters did not know his record, and Jim Wooten of the *Atlanta Journal* expressed amazement that Miller, after spending most of his adult life in the public arena, would have to define himself for voters. Pursuing an independent course throughout his lengthy political career, Miller is essentially a pragmatic politician who has often adjusted his policies to meet new circumstances. A unique individual, he fits no simple mold. A college professor, keen political analyst, and author of three books, he still speaks with a mountain twang, often wears cowboy boots, and fancies country music. Little wonder that he remains an enigma to many Georgians.

As controversial as Joseph E. Brown, another headstrong mountaineer governor, Miller, now affluent and powerful, has never forgotten his mountain roots and continues to maintain regular contact with the common people. Consistently supporting economic development of the north Georgia mountains, he also backs education with enthusiasm. Convinced that education must be the state's highest priority, he allocated almost $600 million in new state expenditures for education in his 1995 budget.

With a booming economy and the state lottery providing unprecedented revenue, Miller is poised at the beginning of his second term to achieve his goal of becoming "Georgia's education governor" and may become one of the most influential governors in the state's history.

Selected Bibliography

State Publications

Candler, Allen D., editor. *The Confederate Records of the State of Georgia*. 5 volumes. Atlanta: C. P. Byrd, State Printer, 1909–1911.

——. *The Revolutionary Records of the State of Georgia*. 3 volumes. Atlanta:Franklin-Turner Company, 1908.

——, and Lucian Lamar Knight, editors. *The Colonial Records of the State of Georgia*. 26 volumes. Atlanta: State Printers, 1904–1916.

Coleman, Kenneth. *Governor James Wright in Georgia, 1760–1782*. Atlanta: Georgia Department of Education, 1975.

——, and Jackie Erney, editors. *Famous Georgians*. Atlanta: Georgia Department of Archives and History, 1976.

Daniel, Frank, editor. *Addresses of James Earl Carter, Governor of Georgia 1971– 1975*. Atlanta: Georgia Department of Archives and History, 1975.

——. *Addresses of Lester Garfield Maddox, Governor of Georgia 1967–1971*. Atlanta: Georgia Department of Archives and History, 1971.

——. *Addresses and Public Papers of Carl Edward Sanders, Governor of Georgia 1963–1967*. Atlanta: Georgia Department of Archives and History, 1968.

Georgia. Department of Archives and History. *Georgia's Official Register*. Various compilers. Atlanta: State Printers, 1927–.

Georgia. General Assembly. *Acts and Resolutions of the General Assembly of the State of Georgia*. State Printers, 1811–.

——. *Journal of the House of Representatives of the State of Georgia*. Compiled and published by the state. Milledgeville, 1840–1866; Atlanta, 1870–.

——. *Journal of the Senate of the State of Georgia*. Compiled and published by the state. Milledgeville, 1808–1865; Atlanta, 1868–.

Books

Abbot, W. W. *The Royal Governors of Georgia, 1754–1775*. Chapel Hill: University of North Carolina Press, 1959.

Anderson, William. *The Wild Man from Sugar Creek: The Political Career of Eugene Talmadge*. Baton Rouge: Louisiana State University Press, 1975.

Arnall, Ellis Gibbs. *The Shore Dimly Seen*. New York and Philadelphia: J. B. Lippincott Company, 1946.

——. *What the People Want*. New York and Philadelphia: J. B. Lippincott, 1947.

Avery, I. W. *The History of the State of Georgia From 1850 to 1881*. New York: Brown & Derby, Publishers, 1881.

Bartley, Numan V. *The Creation of Modern Georgia*. Athens: University of Georgia Press, 1983.

Bernd, Joseph L. *Grass Roots Politics in Georgia*. Atlanta: Emory University Research Committee, 1960.

Biographical Directory of the American Congress 1774–1971. Washington: Government Printing Office, 1971.

Bonner, James C. *Milledgeville: Georgia's Antebellum Capital*. Athens: University of Georgia Press, 1985.

Candler, Allen D., and Clement A. Evans, editors. *Cyclopedia of Georgia*. 4 volumes. Atlanta: State Historical Association, 1906.

Carter, Jimmy. *Turning Point*. New York: Times Books, 1992.

____. *Why Not the Best?* Nashville: Broadman Press, 1975.

Cashin, Edward J. *Governor Henry Ellis and the Transformation of British North America*. Athens: University of Georgia Press, 1994.

Coleman, Kenneth. *The American Revolution in Georgia, 1763–1789*. Athens: University of Georgia Press, 1958.

____. *Colonial Georgia, A History*. New York: Charles Scribner's Sons, 1976.

____, editor. *A History of Georgia*. Athens: University of Georgia Press, 1977.

——, and Charles Stephen Gurr, editors. *Dictionary of Georgia Biography*. 2 volumes. Athens: University of Georgia Press, 1983.

——, and Milton Ready, editors. *The Colonial Records of Georgia*. Volumes 20, 27–32. Athens: University of Georgia Press, 1975–1989.

Conway, Alan. *The Reconstruction of Georgia*. Minneapolis: University of Minnesota Press, 1966.

Cook, James F. *Carl Sanders: Spokesman of the New South*. Macon: Mercer University Press, 1993.

Cooper, Walter G. *The Story of Georgia*. 4 volumes. New York: American Historical Society, 1938.

Coulter, E. Merton. *Georgia: A Short History*. Chapel Hill: University of North Carolina Press, 1960.

Davis, Harold E. *Henry Grady's New South*. Tuscaloosa: University of Alabama, 1990.

Duckett, Alvin Laroy. *John Forsyth, Political Tactician*. Athens: University of Georgia Press, 1962.

Duncan, Russell. *Entrepreneur for Equality: Governor Rufus Bullock, Commerce, and Race in Post–Civil War Georgia*. Athens: University of Georgia Press, 1994.

Eckert, Ralph Lowell. *John Brown Gordon, Soldier, Southerner, American*. Baton Rouge: Louisiana State University Press, 1989.

Felton, Mrs. William H. *My Memoirs of Georgia Politics*. Atlanta: Index Printing Company, 1911.

Fink, Gary M. *Prelude to the Presidency: The Political Character and Legislative Leadership Style of Governor Jimmy Carter*. Westport CT: Greenwood Press, 1980.

Fite, Gilbert C. *Richard B. Russell, Jr., Senator From Georgia*. Chapel Hill: University of North Carolina Press, 1991.

Flippin, Percy S. *Herschel V. Johnson of Georgia, State Rights Unionist*. Richmond: Press of Dietz Printing Co., 1931.

Foster, William Omer. *James Jackson, Duelist and Militant Statesman, 1757–1806*. Athens: University of Georgia Press, 1960.

Freehling, William W., and Craig M. Simpson, editors. *Secession Debated: Georgia's Showdown in 1860*. New York: Oxford University Press, 1992.

Galphin, Bruce. *The Riddle of Lester Maddox*. Atlanta: Camelot Publishing Company, 1968.

Gilmer, George R. *Sketches of the First Settlers of Upper Georgia*. Baltimore: Genealogical Publishing Co., 1965.

Glad, Betty. *Jimmy Carter: In Search of the Great White House*. New York: W. W. Norton, 1980.

Grantham, Dewey W., Jr. *Hoke Smith and the Politics of the New South*. Baton Rouge: Louisiana State University Press, 1958.

Hall, James W. *Lyman Hall, Georgia Patriot*. Savannah: Pigeonhole Press, 1959.

Harden, Edward Jenkins. *Life of George M. Troup*. Savannah: E. J. Purse, 1859.

Harris, Nathaniel E. *Autobiography*. Macon: J. W. Burke Co., 1925.

Henderson, Harold Paulk. *The Politics of Change in Georgia: A Political Biography of Ellis Arnall*. Athens: University of Georgia Press, 1991.

——, and Gary L. Roberts, editors. *Georgia Governors in an Age of Change*. Athens: University of Georgia Press, 1988.

Henson, Allen Lumpkin. *Red Galluses: A Story of Georgia Politics*. Boston: House of Edinboro, 1945.

Howell, Clark. *History of Georgia*. 4 volumes. Chicago and Atlanta: S. J. Clarke Publishing Co., 1926.

Jenkins, Charles Francis. *Button Gwinnett, Signer of the Declaration of Independence*. Garden City: Doubleday, Page and Co., 1926.

Johnson, Allen, and Dumas Malone, editors. *Dictionary of American Biography*. 21 volumes. New York: Charles Scribner's Sons, 1928–1937.

Johnson, Amanda. *Georgia as Colony and State*. Atlanta: Walter W. Brown Publishing Co., 1938.

Johnson, Michael P. *Toward a Patriarchal Republic: The Secession of Georgia*. Baton Rouge: Louisiana State University Press, 1977.

Johnston, Edith D. *The Houstouns of Georgia*. Athens: University of Georgia Press, 1950.

Jones, Charles C., Jr. *Biographical Sketches of the Delegates from Georgia to the Continental Congress*. Boston: Houghton, Mifflin & Co., 1881.

——. *The History of Georgia*. 2 volumes. Boston: Houghton, Mifflin & Co., 1883.

____. *The Life and Services of the Hon. Maj. Gen. Samuel Elbert of Georgia.* Cambridge: Riverside Press, 1887.

Kaufman, Burton I. *The Presidency of James Earl Carter, Jr.* Lawrence: University Press of Kansas, 1993.

Killion, Ronald G., and Charles T. Waller, editors. *Georgia and the Revolution.* Atlanta: Cherokee Publishing Company, 1975.

King, Spencer B., Jr. *Georgia Voices: A Documentary History to 1872.* Athens: University of Georgia Press, 1966.

Knight, Lucian Lamar. *A Standard History of Georgia and Georgians.* 6 volumes. Chicago and New York: Lewis Publishing Co., 1917.

Kucharsky, David. *The Man From Plains: The Mind and Spirit of Jimmy Carter.* New York: Harper & Row, 1976.

Lamplugh, George R. *Politics on the Periphery: Factions and Parties in Georgia, 1783–1806.* London and Toronto: Associated University Presses, 1986.

Lemmon, Sarah McCulloh. "Governor Eugene Talmadge and the New Deal." In *Studies in Southern History,* edited by J. Carlyle Sitterson, 152–68. Chapel Hill: University of North Carolina Press, 1957.

Lumpkin, Wilson. *The Removal of the Cherokee Indians from Georgia.* 2 volumes. New York: Dodd, Mead and Company, 1907.

Maddox, Lester Garfield. *Speaking Out: The Autobiography of Lester Garfield Maddox.* Garden City: Doubleday & Company, 1975.

Martin, Harold H. *Georgia, A Bicentennial History.* New York: W. W. Norton & Company, 1977.

McCall, Hugh. *The History of Georgia.* 2 volumes. Savannah: Seymour and Williams, 1811–1816.

Mellichamp, Josephine. *Senators From Georgia.* Huntsville AL: Strode Publishers, 1976.

Memoirs of Georgia. 2 volumes. Atlanta: Southern Historical Association, 1895.

Miller, Stephen F. *The Bench and Bar of Georgia: Memoirs and Sketches.* 2 volumes. Philadelphia: J. B. Lippincott Co., 1858.

Miller, Zell. *Great Georgians.* Franklin Springs GA: Advocate Press, 1983.

____. *The Mountains Within Me.* Toccoa GA: Commercial Printing Company, 1976.

Montgomery, Horace. *Cracker Parties.* Baton Rouge: Louisiana State University Press, 1950.

——, ed. *Georgians In Profile.* Athens: University of Georgia Press, 1958.

Murray, Paul. *The Whig Party in Georgia, 1825–1853.* Chapel Hill: University of North Carolina Press, 1948.

Nathans, Elizabeth Studley. *Losing the Peace: Georgia Republicans and Reconstruction, 1865–1871.* Baton Rouge: Louisiana State University Press, 1968.

Northen, William J. *Men of Mark in Georgia.* 7 volumes. Atlanta: A. B. Caldwell, 1907–1912.

Parks, Joseph H. *Joseph E. Brown of Georgia*. Baton Rouge: Louisiana State University Press, 1977.

Phillips, Ulrich B. *Georgia and State Rights*. Washington: Government Printing Office, 1902.

Roberts, Darrell C. *Joseph E. Brown and the Politics of Reconstruction*. Tuscaloosa: University of Alabama Press, 1973.

Saye, Albert. *A Constitutional History of Georgia, 1732–1968*. Athens: University of Georgia Press, 1970.

Schott, Thomas Edwin. *Alexander H. Stephens of Georgia: A Biography*. Baton Rouge: Louisiana State University Press, 1988.

Shaw, Barton C. *The Wool Hat Boys*. Baton Rouge: Louisiana State University Press, 1984.

Sherrill, Robert. *Gothic Politics in the Deep South*. New York: Grossman Publishers, 1968.

Shyrock, Richard Harrison. *Georgia and the Union in 1850*. Durham: Duke University Press, 1926.

Simpson, John Eddins. *Howell Cobb: The Politics of Ambition*. Chicago: Adams Press, 1973.

Steed, Hal. *Georgia: Unfinished State*. New York: Alfred A. Knopf, 1942.

Stephens, Alexander Hamilton. *A Constitutional View of the Late War Between the States*. 2 volumes. Philadelphia: National Publishing Company, 1868–1870.

Talmadge, Herman Eugene. *Talmadge: A Political Legacy, A Politician's Life*. Atlanta: Peachtree Publishers, Ltd., 1987.

____. *You and Segregation*. Birmingham: Vulcan Press, 1955.

Tankersley, Allen Pierce. *John B. Gordon: A Study in Gallantry*. Atlanta: Whitehall Press, 1955.

Thompson, C. Mildred. *Reconstruction in Georgia*. New York: Columbia University Press, 1915.

White, George. *Historical Collections of Georgia*. New York: Pudney & Russell, Publishers, 1855.

Articles

Belvin, William L., Jr. "The Georgia Gubernatorial Primary of 1946." *Georgia Historical Quarterly* 50 (1966): 37–53.

Brooks, Robert P. "Howell Cobb and the Crisis of 1850." *Mississippi Valley Historical Review* 4 (1917): 279–98.

Cook, James F. "Carl Sanders: Progress Amid Turmoil." *Georgia Journal* 13 (Winter 1993): 16–19.

____. "Ellis Arnall: Georgia's Great Progressive." *Georgia Journal* 12 (Fall 1992): 8–11.

____. "George Busbee: Builder of Consensus." *Georgia Journal* 14 (Fall 1994): 47–48.

____. "The Georgia Gubernatorial Election of 1942." *Atlanta Historical Bulletin* 18 (Summer 1973): 6–19.

____. "The One Conspicuous Failure: Gov. Carl Sanders and Constitutional Revision." *Atlanta History* 34 (Summer 1990): 17–27.

Coulter, E. Merton. "Edward Telfair." *Georgia Historical Quarterly* 20 (1936): 99–124.

Destler, Chester M., editor. "Correspondence of David Brydie Mitchell." *Georgia Historical Quarterly* 21 (1937): 382–92.

Elson, Charles Myer. "The Georgia Three–Governor Controversy of 1947." *Atlanta Historical Bulletin* 20 (1976): 72–95.

Flippin, Percy S. "The Royal Government in Georgia." *Georgia Historical Quarterly* 8–13 (1924–1929).

Grant, Philip A. "Editorial Reaction to the 1952 Presidential Candidacy of Richard B. Russell." *Georgia Historical Quarterly* 57 (1973): 167–78.

Griffin, Sam, Jr., and Roy Chalker, Sr. "Marvin Griffin: The Last of the Great Stump Speakers." *Georgia Journal* 13 (Summer 1993): 20–25.

Grimes, Millard B. "Gov. Ernest Vandiver's Hard Choice." *Georgia Journal* 13 (Fall 1993): 14–17.

Harden, William. "Sir James Wright, Governor of Georgia by Royal Commission 1760–1782." *Georgia Historical Quarterly* 2 (1918): 22–36.

Henderson, Harold Paulk. "M. E. Thompson: The Accidental Governor." *Georgia Journal* 12 (Winter 1992): 10–13, 75.

Herndon, Jane. "E. D. Rivers, New Deal Governor." *Georgia Journal* 12 (Summer 1992): 12–15, 60.

____. "Ed Rivers and Georgia's 'Little New Deal.' " *Atlanta Historical Journal* 30 (Spring 1986): 97–105.

Herndon, Melvin G. "George Mathews, Frontier Patriot." *Virginia Magazine of History and Biography* 77 (1969): 307–28.

Howell, Lee. "Herman Talmadge: Politics in His Blood." *Georgia Journal* 13 (Spring 1993): 10–13, 66.

Huhner, Leon. "The First Jew to Hold the Office of Governor of One of the United States." *American Jewish Historical Society* 17: 187–95.

Hyatt, Richard. "Jimmy Who?" *Georgia Journal* 14 (Summer 1994): 10–13, 48.

Jackson, Harvey H. "Consensus and Conflict: Factional Politics in Revolutionary Georgia, 1774–1777." *Georgia Historical Quarterly* 59 (1975): 388–401.

Jones, Alton D. "The Administration of Joseph M. Terrell Viewed in the Light of the Progressive Movement." *Georgia Historical Quarterly* 48 (1964): 271–90.

Lamplugh, George R. " 'To Check and Discourage the Wicked and Designing': John Wereat and the Revolution in Georgia." *Georgia Historical Quarterly* 61 (1977): 295–307.

Lee, David D. "The South and the American Mainstream: The Election of Jimmy Carter." *Georgia Historical Quarterly* 61 (1977): 7–12.

Lemmon, Sarah McCulloh. "The Ideology of Eugene Talmadge." *Georgia Historical Quarterly* 38 (1954): 226–48.

McCullar, Bernice, and Maj. J. L. Sibley Jennings. "The Men Who Governed Georgia." *Atlanta Journal and Constitution Magazine*, 17 April–19 June 1966.

Moseley, Clement Charlton. "The Political Influence of the Ku Klux Klan in Georgia, 1915–1925." *Georgia Historical Quarterly* 57 (Summer 1973): 235–55.

Parks, Joseph H. "States Rights in a Crisis: Governor Joseph E. Brown versus President Jefferson Davis." *Journal of Southern History* 32 (1966): 3–24.

Patton, Randall L. "A Southern Liberal and the Politics of Anti–Colonialism: The Governorship of Ellis Arnall." *Georgia Historical Quarterly* 74 (Winter 1990): 599–621.

Prout, Charles H. "Gubernatorial Patterns: A Statistical Profile of Georgia Governors." *Georgia Historical Quarterly* 78 (Spring 1994): 124–31.

Rabun, James Z. "Alexander H. Stephens and Jefferson Davis." *American Historical Review* 58 (1953): 290–321.

Reece, Chuck. "Zell Finally Gets His Chance." *Georgia Trend* 6 (January 1991): 28–32.

Rice, Bradley R. "Lester Maddox: The Unlikely Governor." *Georgia Journal* 14 (Spring 1994): 12–16, 53.

Sanders, Randy. " 'The Sad Duty of Politics': Jimmy Carter and the Issue of Race in His 1970 Gubernatorial Campaign." *Georgia Historical Quarterly* 76 (Fall 1992): 612–38.

Saye, Albert B. "Commission and Instructions of Governor John Reynolds, August 6, 1754." *Georgia Historical Quarterly* 30 (1946): 125–62.

Shadgett, Olive Hall. "James Johnson, Provisional Governor of Georgia." *Georgia Historical Quarterly* 36 (March 1952): 1–21.

Spalding, Phinizy. "Georgia and the Election of Jimmy Carter." *Georgia Historical Quarterly* 61 (1977): 13–22.

Thomason, Hugh M. "Governor Peter Early and the Indian Frontier, 1813–1815." *Georgia Historical Quarterly* 45 (1961): 223–37.

Waller, Tom. "Henry Ellis, Enlightenment Gentleman." *Georgia Historical Quarterly* 64 (1979): 364–76.

Ward, Judson C., Jr. "The Republican Party in Bourbon Georgia." *Journal of Southern History* 9 (1943): 196–209.

Theses and Dissertations

Bernd, Joseph L. "A Study of Primary Elections in Georgia, 1946–1954." Ph.D. dissertation, Duke University, 1957.

Bonner, James Calvin. "The Gubernatorial Career of W. J. Northen." Master's thesis, University of Georgia, 1936.

Bornet, Vaughn Davis. "The Struggle for Governmental Power in Georgia, 1754–1757." Master's thesis, Emory University, 1940.

Cannady, Robert Bruce. "The Public Life of George Mathews in Georgia." Master's thesis, University of Georgia, 1957.

Carageorge, Ted. "An Evaluation of Hoke Smith and Thomas E. Watson as Georgia Reformers." Ph.D. dissertation, University of Georgia, 1963.

Cleveland, Len Gibson. "George W. Crawford of Georgia, 1798–1872." Ph.D. dissertation, University of Georgia, 1974.

Coleman, Kenneth. "The Administration of Alfred H. Colquitt As Governor of Georgia." Master's thesis, University of Georgia, 1940.

Cook, James F. "Politics and Education in the Talmadge Era: The Controversy Over the University System of Georgia, 1941–42." Ph.D. dissertation, University of Georgia, 1972.

Culpepper, Grady Sylvester. "The Political Career of John Brown Gordon, 1868 to 1897." Ph.D. dissertation, Emory University, 1981.

Cummings, Josephine Newsom. "Thomas William Hardwick, A Study of a Strange and Eventful Career." Master's thesis, University of Georgia, 1961.

Doster, Helen O. "The Administration of Henry D. McDaniel As Governor of Georgia, 1883–1886." Master's thesis, University of Georgia, 1962.

Duncan, James Russell, Jr. "Rufus Brown Bullock, Reconstruction, and the 'New South,' 1834–1907: An Exploration into Race, Class, Party, and the Corruption of the American Creed." Ph.D. dissertation, University of Georgia, 1988.

Fortune, Peter L., Jr. "George M. Troup, Leading State Rights Advocate." Ph.D. dissertation, University of North Carolina, 1949.

Gabard, William Montgomery. "Joseph Mackey Brown: A Study in Conservatism." Ph.D. dissertation, Tulane University, 1963.

Hall, Joyce Ann. "The Public Life of John Milledge." Master's thesis, University of Georgia, 1958.

Henderson, Harold Paulk. "The 1946 Gubernatorial Election in Georgia." Master's thesis, Georgia Southern College, 1967.

_____. "The 1966 Gubernatorial Election in Georgia." Ph.D. dissertation, University of Southern Mississippi, 1982.

Herndon, Jane Walker. "Eurith Dickinson Rivers: A Political Biography." Ph.D. dissertation, University of Georgia, 1974.

Jones, George L. "William H. Felton and the Independent Democratic Movement in Georgia, 1870–1890." Ph.D. dissertation, University of Georgia, 1971.

Konter, Sherry. "The Public Career of John Marshall Slaton, 1896–1915." Master's thesis, University of Georgia, 1978.

Lemmon, Sarah McCulloh. "The Public Career of Eugene Talmadge, 1926–1936." Ph.D. dissertation, University of North Carolina, 1952.

Lyons, Margaret Spears. "A Comparison of Carl Sanders' Gubernatorial Campaigns: 1962 and 1970." Master's thesis, University of Georgia, 1971.

McFarland, Robert E. " 'The Union As It Was': George W. Towns and the Transformation of Antebellum Georgia." Master's thesis, University of Georgia, 1990.

Mann, Martha E. "The Public Career of James M. Smith." Master's thesis, Emory University, 1931.

Marshall, Elizabeth Hulsey. "Allen D. Candler, Governor and Collector of Records." Master's thesis, University of Georgia, 1959.

Miller, Zell Bryan. "The Administration of E. D. Rivers as Governor of Georgia." Master's thesis, University of Georgia, 1958.

Mixon, Val Gene. "The Growth of the Legislative Powers of the Governor of Georgia: A Survey of the Legislative Program of Governor Herman Talmadge (1949–54)." Master's thesis, Emory University, 1959.

Mobley, Annie Beth. "The Public Career of Nathaniel Harris." Master's thesis, University of Georgia, 1957.

Moseley, Clement Charlton. "Invisible Empire: A History of the Ku Klux Klan in Twentieth Century Georgia, 1915–1965." Ph.D. dissertation, University of Georgia, 1968.

Purcell, Clarice Eulone. "The Public Career of Samuel Elbert." Master's thesis, University of Georgia, 1951.

Pyles, Charles Boykin. "Race and Ruralism in Georgia Elections, 1948–1966." Ph.D. dissertation, University of Georgia, 1967.

Rabun, James Z. "Alexander H. Stephens, 1812–1861." Ph.D. dissertation, University of Chicago, 1949.

Rentz, Thomas Henry, Sr. "The Public Life of David B. Mitchell." Master's thesis, University of Georgia, 1955.

Roberts, Darrell C. "Joseph E. Brown and the New South." Ph.D. dissertation, University of Georgia, 1958.

Ross, Carl Augustus, Jr. "The Public Life and Accomplishments of John Clark." Master's thesis, University of Georgia, 1957.

Shipp, Mauriel. "The Public Life of William Yates Atkinson." Master's thesis, University of Georgia, 1955.

Simpson, John Eddins. "A Biography of Howell Cobb, 1815–1861." Ph.D. dissertation, University of Georgia, 1971.

Taylor, Thomas Elkin. "A Political Biography of Ellis Arnall." Master's thesis, Emory University, 1959.

Towery, James Gaston. "The Georgia Gubernatorial Campaign of 1886." Master's thesis, Emory University, 1945.

Vipperman, Carl Jackson. "Wilson Lumpkin and Cherokee Removal." Master's thesis, University of Georgia, 1961.

Ward, Judson C., Jr. "Georgia Under the Bourbon Democrats, 1872–1890." Ph.D. dissertation, University of North Carolina, 1947.

Index

STATE

HIGHWAY DEPARTMENT

OF

GEORGIA

OUTLINE MAP
SHOWING
COUNTIES